"If Hank's goal was to completely empower deer hunters and open up new perspectives on the possibilities of venison, then he has completely surpassed that with this book. It is a treasure, and—pardon the pun—a complete game-changer."

—**JESSE GRIFFITHS**, chef and author of the James Beard–nominated wild game cookbook *Afield*

"Hank Shaw has done it! He has written the definitive guide to everything venison. Whether you are the hunter who wants to learn what to do with the buck you just shot, or the cook who has been given venison from a friend, Hank will tell you everything you need to know. With recipes drawn from traditions around the world, Hank has elevated cooking venison to an art form. Steak, tacos, stew, short ribs, meatballs, pot roast, curry, kebabs, and more. It's all here."

—**ELISE BAUER**, founder of SimplyRecipes.com

"This book is not for everyone. If you are among those game cooks who insist on submerging your game in a slow cooker loaded with salty, canned goo, then save yourself some money on an incredible resource you'll never use. Hank Shaw demystifies antlered game preparation with simple techniques that can be applied to anything from a whitetail tenderloin to the bony neck roast of a bull moose."

—**SCOTT LEYSATH**, TV host, wild game cookbook author, food columnist

BUCK, BUCK, MOOSE

BUCK, BUCK, MOOSE

RECIPES AND TECHNIQUES FOR COOKING DEER, ELK,
ANTELOPE, MOOSE, AND OTHER ANTLERED THINGS

HANK SHAW

Photographs by **HOLLY A. HEYSER**

H|H

Copyright © 2016 by Hank Shaw
Photographs copyright © 2016 by Holly A. Heyser

ALL RIGHTS RESERVED
No part of this publication may be reproduced or transmitted in any form or by any means,
electronic or mechanical, including photocopying, recording, or any other information storage
and retrieval system, without the written permission of the publisher.

Published in the U. S. A. by
H&H BOOKS
www.honest-food.net
H&H books may be purchased for business or promotional use or for special sales. For information,
please write to: Special Markets Dept., H&H Books, P.O. Box 2984, Orangevale, CA 95662;
or email scrbblr@hotmail.com, attention Special Markets.

Designed, produced and edited at Laura Shaw Design, Inc., www.laurashawdesign.com
Food and prop styling by Hank Shaw and Holly A. Heyser
Photograph on page 8 © iStockphoto.com
Photographs on pages 21–23 © Matt Greene
Photographs on page 205 and page 279 © Hank Shaw

Hardcover ISBN : 978-0-99694-480-9

7 8 9 10 11 12
Printed in the U. S. A.

Library of Congress Cataloging-in-Publication Data
Shaw, Hank, 1970—
Buck, Buck, Moose : Recipes and Techniques for Cooking Deer, Elk,
Antelope, and Other Antlered Things / Hank Shaw
Pages cm   Includes index
Cooking (Venison) 2. Cooking (Elk) 3. Cooking (Game) I. Title.
2016908699

Dedicated to the many readers of *Hunter Angler Gardener Cook*.
Without you, this book would never have happened.

CONTENTS

INTRODUCTION 8

PART ONE: DEER BASICS 11

VENISON IN ALL ITS FORMS 12
A Deer is Not a Moose: Various Types of Venison 12
Venison: Nutritious, Lean, Sustainable 14
Venison and Food Safety 15
Buying Venison in the Store 18

WORKING A DEER:
FROM FIELD TO FREEZER 20
Skinning and Gutting 20
Hanging and Aging Deer 26
Butchering Your Own Deer 28
Storing Venison 46

INTERLUDE: THE WHITE COYOTE 54

PART TWO: DEER TO TABLE 57

MARINADES, STOCKS, AND BROTHS 58
Marinades: Why, How, and When 58
Stock, Broth, and *Glace de Viande* 62
   Basic Venison Broth 65
   Dark Venison Broth 66
   Venison Glace de Viande 67

PRIMAL CUTS 69
The Science of Carryover Heat 70
   Braised Shoulder of Venison 71
   Polish Pot Roast with a Venison Neck 73
   Whole Grilled Backstrap 74
   Roast Leg of Venison with Bavarian Dumplings 75

BACKSTRAPS, LOINS, AND TENDERLOINS 79
The Finger Test for Doneness 79
To Rest or Not? 80
Which One: Loins, Steaks, or Chops? 81
   Venison with Cumberland Sauce 83
   Steak Diane 84
   Jägerschnitzel 87
   Country Fried Venison Steak 88
   Thai Venison Satay Skewers 90
   Basic Venison Stir-Fry 93
   Chinese Tangerine Venison 94
   Venison with Morel Sauce 97
   Venison with Spring Vegetables 99
   Venison Steak with Cherry Tomatoes 101
   Icelandic Venison with Blueberry Sauce 103
   Venison with Caramelized Onions and Mushrooms 105
   Vietnamese Shaking Venison 107
   Souvlaki 109
   Ethiopian Tibs 112
   Venison Tartare 115
   Venison Stroganoff 117

ROASTS 119
   Basic Roast Venison 121
   Sauerbraten 123
   Italian Pot Roast 125
   Barbacoa 127
    Variation: Dzik de Venado (Yucatán Venison) 128
   Venison Confit 129
   Tri-Tip-Style Venison Roast with Chimichurri 133
   Marinated Venison Kebabs 135
   Kentucky Smoked Venison Barbecue 137
   Venison Pierogis 139

SOUPS AND STEWS 142
   Cajun Sauce Piquante 143
   Pozole Rojo 145
   Stifado 146
   Icelandic Venison Stew 147
   Minestra Maritata 149
   Ukrainian Borscht 151
   Carbonnade 152
   Kentucky Burgoo 154
   Massaman Curry 156
   Vindaloo 158

Scotch Broth   159
Chilindrón   161
Vietnamese Pho   162
Hungarian Pörkölt   164
Food Plot   167

MEATBALLS, BURGERS, AND OTHER GROUND MEAT DISHES   169
A Discourse on Venison Burgers   169
A Basic Venison Burger   173
Venison Smashburgers   175
Mushroom Burgers   177
Venison Chili   178
Venison Lasagna   180
Italian Venison Meatloaf   182
Venison Bolognese Sauce   185
Swedish Meatballs   186
Albóndigas al Chipotle   189
Japanese Teriyaki Meatballs   191
Indian Kofta Meatball Curry   192
Greek Dolmas   194
Cornish Pasties   195
Chinese Potstickers   197
Kefta Kebabs   201
South African Bobotie   203

FLANKS, SHANKS, AND RIBS   204
Tunisian Braised Venison Shanks   207
Portuguese-Style Shanks   208
Austrian Braised Venison Shanks   209
Braised Venison Shanks with Garlic   211
Osso Buco   213
Agnolotti with Tomatoes and Arugula   215
Grilled Venison Tacos   218
Venison Bulgogi   220
Italian Short Ribs   221
Smoked Ribs with Bourbon BBQ Sauce   223
Grilled Ribs, Korean Style   224

INTERLUDE: THE LEGEND OF SPORK   225

THE WOBBLY BITS   229
Grilled Deer Heart with Peppers   234
Peruvian Anticuchos de Corazón   237
Sichuan Spicy Heart Stir-Fry   238

Deer Camp Liver and Onions   239
Liver Dumplings   240
Faggots (British Meatballs)   241
Cajun Boudin Balls   243
Braised Venison Tongue   245
A Lovely Tongue Sandwich   246
Tacos de Lengua   248
Grilled Venison Kidneys   249
Deviled Kidneys   251
Venison Tripe Neapolitan Style   253
German Marrow Dumplings   255

CURING VENISON AND MAKING SAUSAGE   256
Sausages   256
Salami, Mettwurst, Saucisson   261
Corned Venison   263
Venison Pastrami   265
Jerky   264
Chipotle Jerky   267
Pemmican-Style Ground Meat Jerky   269
Venison Sausage with Sage and Juniper   270
British Bangers   272
Wisconsin Red Brats   274
Romanian Venison Sausage   277
Mexican-Style Chorizo   279
Kabanosy, The World's Greatest Meat Stick   281
Basic Venison Salami   283
Boerenmetworst   286
Spanish Chorizo   288
Icelandic Venison "Gravlax"   291
Potted Hough   293
Variation: Spicy Spanish-Style Rillettes   294
Deer Ham, Alpine Style   295

CODA: THE GAME AND THE FEAST   297

Acknowledgments   298
Selected Reading   299
Resources   300
Index   301

INTRODUCTION

DEER MAKE US HUMAN

Deer and humans have evolved together. We have hunted deer, and deer have escaped us, for so long that neither of us today are what we were when our intimate, eons-old relationship first began. Our dance with deer is eternal.

Many paleontologists believe that it was the ancient pursuit of deer-like animals that made us fully human, fundamentally changing our inner life, our identification with the world—even our cognitive powers—through the planning and execution of the hunt. Deer hunting is firmly embedded in our ancestral DNA, and deer, or the more general category of venison, is a staple food item recognized throughout the world. Tell most people you are deer hunting and they will barely shrug. Tell them you are swan hunting, or even bear hunting, and you'll likely get a very different reaction. Humans hunt and eat venison; it's just what we do.

The word "venison" derives from the Latin word *venari*, "to hunt." Evolving through Old French, the term came to refer to any hunted game, a reference that is still widely used today. Although venison can mean different things in different cultures, the word is most often used to refer collectively to all the deer-like animals: the cervids (especially deer, elk, and moose); and the non-cervid pronghorn and African antelopes. This is the definition that we'll use here.

Given our long history as eaters of venison, it is more than a little surprising to discover that, with the possible exception of waterfowl, there is no game animal more horribly treated in the kitchen by contemporary cooks than deer. Nasty, gloppy cream of mushroom soup. Bacon-wrapped everything. A disturbing use of processed cheeses. Venison loin cooked gray. Shoulders undercooked. And far too much waste. I am not sure why this should be, though I suspect it has to do with the fact that venison, even the easily cooked backstrap and tenderloins, requires some skill and practice in the kitchen in order to pull off properly. We're not talking about fancy preparations here; more often than not it is the simple, peasant dish that is the most deeply satisfying. But venison does have its quirks, and there are subtle but important differences between cooking venison and cooking beef or lamb, with which we are generally much more familiar—differences that we'll cover in great detail in the pages to come. But cooking a great piece of venison, no matter what piece you happen to have on hand, isn't rocket science. All you need is a good foundation of solid information, a fistful of tips, tricks, and techniques that work with venison, and, well, this book, and you'll be fine.

Ready to begin?

How to Use this Book

In these pages you will find pretty much everything you need to know to fully enjoy the deer, elk, moose, or antelope you bring home. Everything from how the different species act in the kitchen to techniques on butchering at home to tricks and tips on working with the fundamentally lean nature of venison. You'll also find recipes for all parts of the deer—I'll show you how to make wonderful dishes out of unloved parts like shanks, flanks, necks and the wobbly bits. And those recipes will come from all over the globe. No matter where you live on this planet, at least one thing binds us all: a tradition of hunting and eating venison.

The book you are holding takes you from the moment after you've recovered your animal all the way to the dinner table. While much of the book is dedicated to specific recipes, within those recipes you will, in many cases, learn the underlying techniques that govern them, allowing you to modify my recipe to suit your own tastes. I will walk you through the science of marinating, storing, curing, cooking and otherwise working a deer.

I hope these pages give you the tools you need to get the most out of your hard work in the field. Good luck out there, and enjoy!

PART ONE

DEER BASICS

This is, in many ways, the most important part of this book. Sure, I love the recipes, but the information you'll find in this section will ground you in all the best practices of field care, butchery, storage, and food safety. You'll learn about the different kinds of venison (an elk in the kitchen can be far different from an antelope in the kitchen), how to handle all part of the carcass (including the odd bits), and even which beer or wine goes best with venison.

VENISON IN ALL ITS FORMS

A DEER IS NOT A MOOSE:
VARIOUS TYPES OF VENISON

Any species of venison (deer, elk, moose, or ante-lope), can be used as the basis for any of the recipes in this book. However, there are some differences that you'll want to be aware of when working with each individual species in the kitchen.

Size Matters

Venison comes in an astonishing range of sizes, from giant moose in the Yukon to tiny Coues deer in the Sonoran desert. That's why I typically call for meat in weight rather than a specific cut; for example, a three-pound roast rather than a sirloin roast. In this way, you'll be able to use whatever sort of venison you have available. Having said that, there are a few size-related things you'll want to keep in mind as you explore the specific dishes later (don't worry—we'll review these again in Part Two).

For shank recipes with larger animals, use a cross-cut shank (the kind you'd buy for veal osso buco in the supermarket) rather than the whole shank.

To avoid overcooking, the backstraps of small deer should be cooked in long sections of a foot or so, and cut into medallions only after the meat has been cooked. The backstraps of elk or moose, on the other hand, can be cut into steaks one or two inches thick before cooking.

They Are What They Ate

Diet affects meat flavor. Deer can eat more than 1,000 different plants, and have been seen eating fish and eggs, and even baby birds. Elk tend to pre-fer grasses, while moose love to eat marshy plants and the new shoots of trees. Caribou are big fans of lichen. A mule deer that has gorged on a farm-er's grain will taste different from a mule deer that grazed on sagebrush.

To be sure, flavor differences aren't as dramatic in venison as they are in omnivores such as ducks, pigs, or bears, but perceptible differences do occur. I've had sage-y deer and even pond-y moose. Though not overpowering, it's definitely there.

The Culinary Variety of Venison

Most deer hunters will tell you that they prefer elk to whitetail or mule deer. Many say mule deer meat can be slightly drier than meat of a whitetail. White-tails in farm country tend to be better tasting than those in the deep woods of, say, the Adirondacks or the Appalachians.

Most people swear by moose meat as some of the finest venison in the world. Opinions on antelope vary wildly, though I suspect most negative experiences stem from poor handling.

The proghorn antelope (the so-called speed goat), is, in my opinion, the finest of all venison. However, it's worth noting that antelope must be gutted, skinned, and cooled quickly in the field. Let the meat heat up and it will be awful.

Among the exotic species, red deer is quite similar to elk in flavor, while axis deer will be almost sweet. These little Asiatic deer are, to many, the best tasting venison available in North America (though I rank them second behind a properly prepared antelope). Fallow deer are similar to whitetails and blacktails. Nilgai antelope and oryx can be found roaming around New Mexico and Texas; these are large cervids, and should be treated like elk or moose.

Age and Toughness

Older animals are tougher. It's just the way of the world. So if you're hunting for antlers, know that a big bruiser might be a little tough on the tooth when it comes down to the eating. Most deer hunters know this, but I've been surprised by how many elk and moose hunters forget this fact, only to be disappointed that their "hunt of a lifetime" resulted in 500-plus pounds of really tough venison. Hope they like burgers.

Of all the deer-like animals we chase in North America, the caribou is the earliest to mature. A good bull caribou may be only four years old; life's harsh in the Arctic. Whitetails and blacktail deer usually reach maturity between four and nine years, with blacktails tending to live longer. Mule deer can get even older, with average life spans between nine and eleven years in the wild.

A good bull elk is likely to be at least eight years old, and could be as old as fifteen. A nice buck antelope will probably be at least seven years old, and can

A Word about Bison

Although a good argument can be made to include bison among the venison, for the purposes of this book I chose not to do so. Bison meat is very similar to beef, and its flavor and texture are virtually identical to grass-fed beef. I love bison, don't get me wrong, but it's more of a beef substitute than a venison substitute. Having said that, absolutely don't hesitate to substitute bison for venison in any of the recipes in Part Two. Portion sizes will be different, of course, and a bison steak, being three times as large, will cook differently than a venison steak (though the tough cuts will cook the same). For stews, braises, and other slow-cooked recipes, bison will make a great venison substitute.

live to fifteen years in the wild. The longest-lived of all is the moose, which routinely lives longer than ten years; a twenty-five-year-old bull is not uncommon. And if you think the meat on a twenty-five-year-old moose will be tough, then you'd be right.

Boys Smell

Let's face it: Testosterone stinks. If you've ever been in a men's locker room after a game, you know what I mean. And while the body odor in male cervids isn't nearly as rank as it is in animals such as pigs or javelina, a buck in full rut will not make for the best eating. And there are other reasons beside odor that can adversely affect the meat of an animal in rut. A 1992 study in the *Journal of Animal Science* showed dramatic differences in tenderness and texture between those red deer of the same age and health that were slaughtered before the rut, and those that were slaughtered after. The pre-rut bucks were fatter, larger, and more tender than the post-rut bucks. The reason is obvious: During the rut, bucks spend all day running around chasing does; whatever time is left they spend fighting with each other. Now I'm not telling you not to shoot that giant, swollen-necked king of the forest who's been chasing all the ladies. Just know that it's the ladies who'll taste better at the table.

VENISON: NUTRITIOUS, LEAN, SUSTAINABLE

Venison is well-known as a lean alternative to beef. A typical venison roast or steak has about one-third the fat of a comparable piece of beef, and since deer and elk work for a living, they lack the lovely, intramuscular marbling we so prize in a ribeye. The composition of deer fat is significantly different from beef fat, too (see page 51).

But fat is only one part of the story. According to USDA data, a six-ounce venison steak has about 260 calories and only six grams of fat. It could be even less if you are scrupulous about trimming your venison. Compare that to a similar cut of beef, such as a trimmed top loin filet. This same portion of top loin will have roughly 410 calories and, depending on the grade (choice, prime, etc.), about twenty grams of fat. Real data on this sort of thing can be unreliable, however, as fat content can vary widely among individuals. Venison also tends to be far higher in niacin and iron than beef, and is a good source of vitamins B12, B6, and riboflavin, and minerals such as phosphorus, zinc, and selenium.

Not only is venison low in fat and nutritionally more dense, it's also about as organic as you can get without official certification. And speaking of official organic certification, it's worth noting that to meet USDA organic requirements, all feed must be certified organic, and must come with the paperwork to prove it; virtually no wild game can be officially certified as organic. For those of you who are concerned about organics, do be aware of deer herds

Lamb as Venison Stand-in

Where bison is close in flavor but not in size to venison, lamb is close in size but not in flavor. Lamb cuts are very similar to those in a typical whitetail or blacktail deer, but lamb's flavor is much more pronounced. Believe it or not, lamb is actually gamier than venison. But if you like lamb, it's a perfect substitute for venison, and, of course, it's readily available in stores.

One cooking note, though: Lamb, being a young animal, will cook far faster than most wild venison. A venison shank normally takes two to four hours to fall off the bone. A lamb shank can get there in ninety minutes. So if you're substituting lamb for the real deal, keep an eye on things.

that camp out in agricultural fields in which conventional or GMO crops make up most of the landscape. As I said, we are what we eat.

Free Range and Humane

Where venison really excels, though, is in the realms of humane animal husbandry and sustainability. You simply can't get more free-range, humanely harvested, or sustainable meat than wild game. Even farmed venison must be raised in a free-range way, because deer simply won't survive if confined like cows.

In terms of quality of life, every deer, antelope, elk, or moose we bring home to feed our families has led as free a life as nature allows: no confinement, no antibiotics, able to live as it was meant to live and to breed as it was meant to breed. As long as we hunters do our part to ensure a clean kill, the death of a deer is nearly as quick as in any slaughterhouse. When compared to death in the wild, a hunter's bullet or broadhead is a far cleaner way to go than by starvation or the claws and teeth of a predator. Because venison is a wild, renewable resource, it is among the most sustainable sources of meat available. Venison requires nothing more than healthy, natural habitat for their own health and survival, whether that habitat be in the Rocky Mountains or on your farm or backyard. And since venison forage for their supper, the resource load and environmental impact of commercial feed is avoided. The North American hunting system itself is entirely based on sustainable management practices, and hunters are allowed to take only as many deer as wildlife biologists say we can. Population census and hunting tallies are carefully tracked, and the numbers then used to determine how many deer can be harvested in any given year. If deer numbers are high, more licenses are issued and seasons are expanded. In this way, deer populations are kept in optimal balance with their associated ecosystems.

VENISON AND FOOD SAFETY

Deer meat is among the safest meats around, and the incidences of food-borne illnesses linked to venison are few and far between. But it's not impossible to get sick from eating venison, and there are some basic food safety issues that you should be aware of when butchering, processing, and eating venison.

SALMONELLA

Although salmonella is the most common food-borne illness in North America, infection from consumption of venison is extremely rare. The lone recorded case of a person getting salmonella from eating venison was in Hawaii in 2012, when a sixty-five-year-old man and his wife ate raw venison "sashimi" from a locally hunted deer. Deer feces can carry salmonella bacteria, but it's pretty rare, too; a 2006 study of Nebraska deer found salmonella in only 1 percent of deer feces tested. A 2005 study in Scandinavia found no salmonella in 611 tested deer.

E. COLI

The nasty strain of *Escherichia coli* bacteria, *E. coli* O157:H7, is even rarer than salmonella in deer. Another Nebraska study, this one in 2001, found *E. coli* in only four of 1,608 total samples of whitetail deer feces. That's one-quarter of 1 percent. Likewise, that Scandinavian study cited earlier found no *E. coli* O157:H7 in its samples. One Georgia study, however, did find that of seventy-seven deer tested, 3 percent carried this nasty strain of *E. coli*.

In a wide study of the medical literature, I could find only three cases of people getting sick from venison-borne *E. coli.*—two from blacktail deer, and one from a whitetail deer. In one case, the disease was caused by deer feces contaminating the tenderloin; the whitetail case involved a gut-shot deer that hung for a while, and whose gut cavity was not rinsed. Researchers suspected that the deer picked up *E. coli* O157:H7 from eating alongside cows, which are a far more common source of the bug. In another odd case in Minnesota in 2010, twenty-nine high school kids were poisoned by another strain of *E. coli* from whitetail deer. Most just got diarrhea, but two were hospitalized.

So can it happen? Sure. But it looks like you'd be more likely to get struck by lightning, live through it, and then be bitten by a shark. The take-away: Exercise some common sense when dealing with any part of any animal's digestive tract. Work clean and you should be fine.

TRICHINOSIS

According to the Centers for Disease Control and Prevention, only three cases of trichinosis could be traced to deer meat during the ten-year period from 2002 to 2012. Given the hundreds of thousands of tons of venison eaten in that timeframe, I'd say it's pretty rare indeed.

Given these statistics, I tend to be highly confident in the safety of venison, both rare and well-cooked. So why all the official warnings about the dangers of this or that, or the admonition to always cook venison to an internal minimum of 160°F? I really can't say. It seems to make little sense given the case history of food-borne illnesses in the Western world. But as always, you should make up your own mind about it and do only what you feel comfortable doing. Remember, the immune systems of the very young, they very old, and the chronically ill are not as strong as those of healthy adults. Keep that in mind when serving raw or very rare venison. As for me? I'll keep eating my venison medium rare, thank you very much.

CHRONIC WASTING DISEASE: WHAT YOU NEED TO KNOW

Chronic wasting disease (CWD) affects mule deer, whitetail deer, elk, moose, and some other cervids (note that antelope are not affected by this disease; they're not, biologically speaking, cervids). The disease makes them listless, emaciated, and generally sick. Ultimately, deer suffering from CWD die of general wasting, with pneumonia as the most likely proximate cause of death. Affected deer tend to be clumsy, too.

No one knows for sure what causes CWD, but many researchers point to either an odd bacterium that lacks a proper cell wall, or a "rogue protein" called a prion that can wreak havoc on an affected organism, producing scabies in sheep, Bovine spongiform encephalopathy ("mad cow disease") in cattle, and Creutzfeldt-Jakob disease in humans.

The epicenter of CWD is an area of northeast Colorado, southeast Wyoming, and the adjacent parts of Nebraska, Utah, and Kansas. The disease has also been detected in eight other regions in the US (New Mexico and far west Texas; North and South Dakota; Wisconsin and Illinois; West Virginia; Pennsylvania; Maryland; Oneida County, New York; Macon County, Missouri); and in the Canadian provinces of Alberta and Saskatchewan. Other states have detected CWD in the herds of deer farms.

For the most part, CWD is not a common affliction, although I saw one report of a herd in Wisconsin in which biologists estimated the rate of incidence at an alarming 30 percent. Whitetail populations in affected areas average around 2 percent infection, while the infection rate is less than 1 percent in elk, according to the Centers for Disease Control and Prevention.

Study after study has shown that CWD *is not transmittable to humans*; there appears to be a "species barrier" between us and the cervids. That said, chronic wasting disease does resemble mad cow disease, which has been shown to be able to jump the species barrier.

Bottom line: Every authority with whom I've consulted advises being safe rather than sorry. That means two things right off the bat: Deer brains are off the menu (I know, you're crushed); and if you live in a CWD state, don't cut your venison into bone-in chops—fillet the whole backstrap off the bone instead.

Some advise against ever using bones from any deer shot in CWD country. I think this is a bit much, but I'll meet the authorities halfway, and recommend that if you do live in areas where this disease exists, toss the spinal bones from the neck to the tail; if CWD is present, it will be primarily in the brain and spinal tissue, as well as the spleen and lymph nodes. So yeah, no Sicilian spleen sandwiches. (The spleen, by the way, is the pale, liver-like organ in the gut pile.) Again, I know you're crushed to hear this. My advice: Use only the leg bones for stock.

If you are worried about CWD, here are some extra precautions that you can take when you

"If you are hunting deer, ignore the hares."

—CHINESE PROVERB

are hunting in a state where the disease has been detected:

- First and foremost—and this is an iron-clad rule for all hunting—don't eat any animal that looks weird or sick, even if you just get a sense that something is wrong with it. Your instincts are generally good on this one.

- Wear latex, nitrile, or rubber gloves when gutting your deer or elk. I sometimes do this, and for a variety of food safety reasons, it's generally not a bad idea.

- Remove the bone from the meat. Don't saw through bone, and avoid cutting through the brain or spinal cord. I think this is wise in CWD areas, and it's not very different from how most people butcher their deer. The reason you don't want to saw through this stuff is that, in theory, the saw could become contaminated and affect the meat itself.

- Be extra clean. Wash your hands, knives, and saws thoroughly after field dressing. Use hot, soapy water, or a weak bleach solution.

- Don't eat the brain, spinal cord, eyes, spleen, tonsils, or lymph nodes of deer in CWD states.

- If you send your deer or elk to a butcher, tell him or her to process your animal individually, without adding any meat from other animals to the meat from your animal. Yeah, this happens a lot, especially with burger.

Note that some states forbid you from bringing home certain parts of deer and elk. California forbids all entry of heads and backbones, regardless of state of origin, but most states just forbid entry of such from those states known to have CWD.

If you're interested in finding out if your animal might have had chronic wasting disease, consider taking advantage of the free testing offered by many state wildlife agencies, often available at check-in stations. Testing takes only a few minutes, so if you do come across a testing station, it's well worth it. And if your deer comes back CWD positive? Well, that's your call. Some public health officials say you should toss the meat. If it were me, I would still eat the boneless meat, but toss everything else. But remember, that is my personal choice.

LEAD AND VENISON

This is a controversial one. Lead bans are a political *cause célèbre* with anti-hunting groups all over the country, and in my own home state of California they've succeeded in banning lead ammunition altogether. Let's get one thing straight right at the outset: Lead does indeed kill birds. Individual birds. But does the existence of lead shot or lead bullets endanger any populations of birds, other than perhaps the California condor? Absolutely not. I'm not here to talk about birds, though. It's your health that matters more to me here.

Back in 2009, the Centers for Disease Control and Prevention tested 736 North Dakotans and found that those who ate wild game had more lead in their blood than those who did not eat wild game. Lead levels were highest in those who ate not only venison but also other game. The study found that people who ate wild game had average lead levels of 1.27 micrograms per deciliter, compared with 0.84 in people who didn't eat game.

OK, that sounds bad. But the CDC's own health guideline is ten micrograms of lead per deciliter of blood, so we're talking about very low levels here for consumers of game. And, since the body can rid itself of lead, heavy, prolonged exposure would be needed to boost lead levels up toward that ten microgram level. Ultimately, it's your call. It's pretty much been proven that if you shoot lead ammo, you will ingest microfragments of lead in your venison. Whether this is harmful for most adults is unclear. What is more certain is that even tiny amounts of lead can damage development in a fetus or very young child, and most health agencies warn against pregnant women and young children eating lead-shot game. This is a warning I would heed.

Personally? I shoot copper.

Other Heavy Metals

In some cases, deer and other cervids can bioaccumulate heavy metals in their meat and organs. Cadmium and other metals, as well as selenium (a mineral salt), can occasionally accumulate to levels that are potentially dangerous. Such cases are usually traced to specific local and regional environmental issues, such as the site downstream of a chemical spill in Michigan in the early 2000s that caused the local deer to pick up so much cadmium that the state health department advised hunters to avoid eating the deers' livers. Similarly, the after-effect of acid rain during the 1960s and 1970s has led to deer and moose accumulating enough cadmium in their kidneys and livers to warrant a health advisory.

What to do? To be safe, check your state's public health department for its various health advisories; most will be for fish, but occasionally you'll see some for birds and mammals, too. Your body will rid itself of heavy metals over time, so a celebratory snack of your buck's kidneys, or a meal or two of its liver, isn't likely to give you problems. But if you live in areas that are troubled by heavy-metal contamination in likely deer habitat, and you shoot a lot of deer, you might want to limit your intake.

BUYING VENISON IN THE STORE

It has been illegal to sell truly wild venison in the United States for close to a century, thanks to a 1918 ban on market hunting. So how is it that you can buy venison in supermarkets?

The simple answer is that deer and elk can be farmed, and those farmed animals are legally considered livestock, not game. Although the number of deer and elk farms is growing in the U.S., most farmed venison sold in this country are red deer from New Zealand. Still, the US deer farming industry is an almost $1 billion-a-year enterprise, with close to 10,000 farms, mostly in Texas and Pennsylvania. Every state but Nevada and South Carolina has at least one farm. Unfortunately, most of the deer from these farms are shot by "hunters" seeking trophy bucks with minimal effort. Only about 20 percent are butchered and sold to the consumer market.

The quality of farmed deer varies wildly. While most cervids won't tolerate the tight, squalid conditions of a factory farm, even those farms that do offer acceptable accommodations for deer management and breeding are a far cry from natural, wild habitat. Meat from farmed deer tends to be lighter in color, softer, and less flavorful than that of a true wild deer. Deer from New Zealand is a step above most domestically-farmed deer since New Zealand deer tend to range wider than the deer on most American farms. And since most of the deer imported from New Zealand is red deer, a relative of our elk, the cuts are also larger and more beeflike.

Among the notable exceptions to this is the venison from Broken Arrow Ranch in Ingram, Texas. Broken Arrow Ranch is one of the few operations large enough to raise deer in a near-wild state, and is one of the only outfits able to harvest their deer via sharpshooters, who can haul the carcasses immediately to a mobile USDA truck for butchering. This "one shot, one kill" method of harvest results in higher meat quality than that from deer sent to the slaughterhouse, which are often heavily stressed. Consequently, of all the farmed deer I've eaten over the years, Broken Arrow's is the closest thing to actual wild venison on the market today.

If you've eaten venison in a restaurant, Broken Arrow is likely the source, although several other purveyors, such as D'Artagnan Foods, also sell nationally. Nicky USA is an excellent purveyor in the Pacific Northwest, and this company is also beginning to sell quasi-wild venison—axis deer harvested by sharpshooters in Hawaii.

If you want to buy venison, high-end supermarkets such as Whole Foods do sell it in the freezer section, but I've never seen it sold fresh. Broken Arrow and D'Artagnan sell online, as do several other outfits. But it'll cost you: Steaks can run up to $35 a pound, and even burger can be more than $10 a pound.

Better to find a hunter.

WORKING A DEER: FROM FIELD TO FREEZER

Well, we've come to the bloody section of the book. Here we'll cover skinning and gutting, field care, tips on getting the animal home, aging your meat, butchering your deer yourself, and storing it properly so you can enjoy it all year long.

SKINNING AND GUTTING

OK, you have a deer, elk, or moose on the ground. Now what?

First, get the animal out of the sun if you can. Obviously, moving a moose or elk in the field is not something one does casually. But keeping your animal out of the sun is especially important if, like me, you hunt in hot weather. If it's way below freezing, you can disregard this.

I really like a good fixed-blade knife with a gut hook to get things going. I like the way a gut hook unzips a paunch quickly. You'll also want some sort of compact saw for the pelvis, which you'll need to crack open to remove the gnarly bits near the rectum.

A good skinning knife is also a must. One good option is a trapper's pelting knife; these have been used for this purpose for several centuries. A better option, however, is a Havalon or some other scalpel knife with disposable blades. I've never used anything sharper. In fact, the only possible caveat to using a Havalon is precisely its sharpness. I've cut myself twice with a Havalon and barely knew it, once all the way to my knuckle. But I had allowed myself to get distracted when that happened. Keep your eye on the ball and your wits about you, and you'll be amazed how easily things go with a Havalon or any of its competitors.

I use gambrels to hoist a deer when I am in a forest, or if there are big trees around that I can use as attachment points. When I don't have gambrels, I typically skin one side of an animal, then flip it using the skin as a mat for the other side. This works fine, and is great in grasslands where trees are scarce.

You'll also want to carry a game bag made from real cheesecloth, not the cheap stuff that lets flies in. Regular sealable plastic bags are handy for the heart, liver, and kidneys, as long as you have a cooler in the truck. If you don't have a cooler, washable mesh bags are good, or you can make a pouch from some cheesecloth. Zip ties are a good idea for attaching your tag, although leftover twist ties from a loaf of bread work well, too. Some people like to wear nitrile or rubber gloves when they butcher animals, but I rarely do this when I am working with deer, elk, or antelope.

SKINNING

Skinning a deer is pretty easy. I will normally start at the animal's hind leg near the hoof. Pay attention to what you're doing and you'll only need the knife in those places where the skin sticks—you can literally peel the skin off most of the animal. Work both hind legs first, then the paunch, working all the way around to the backstrap.

Be careful around the paunch, as you don't want it open just yet. Face the blade away from the gut and you'll be fine. Run the blade up toward the genitals and then through the middle of the inside of the leg all the way to the last joint of the leg, if it hasn't already been skinned.

You'll need your knife to open up the skin on the front legs, which you skin like the back ones, which is to say all the way to the last joint. I will typically wait to cut off the feet until I'm all done skinning. You remove the feet with a good strong, stiff-bladed knife (a Havalon isn't the best thing here), working it between the joints, slicing tendons, and cracking the foot back against the way it ought to move. It's easy once you get the hang of it.

The hardest part is the neck, where the skin is tight to the meat. Just use short strokes with the blade to skin all the way up to the head. Now cut all the way to the bone at the base of the head. Here's the gruesome part: Yank the head in a circle, as though you were unscrewing the head from the neck, until it pops free. Slice the remaining bits with

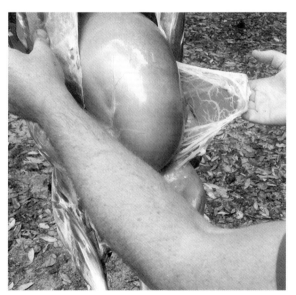

The stomach of a blacktail deer, full from his morning's meal. I'm pulling away the caul fat from it.

a knife, and set the head aside. You'll want to skin this later for either a skull mount or to eat.

GUTTING

Time to gut the animal. Again, starting at the sternum with the blade facing away from the guts, run the knife up to the genitals. Be aware that many states require that you preserve evidence of the sex of the deer, so don't toss them.

So you've opened the paunch and are staring at a bunch of stuff. Now what?

First, you'll notice a white, web-like membrane covering all the entrails. That is caul fat, and you want to save as much as possible. It's awesome stuff, made of clean-tasting fat latticing a thin but sturdy membrane. What do you do with it? Wrap things (typically meatballs—see British Meatballs, page 241). But caul fat also works wonders with lean cuts like backstrap or roasts. As they cook, the fat melts and bastes your meat, keeping it moist and lovely. Put it in a plastic bag, and into the cooler it goes.

Now you'll need to let the offal fall. First, look toward the pelvis of the deer for a bag of liquid. This will be the bladder, which may be full of urine. You need to remove this *carefully* or you'll get piss all over everything. I reach in to where it attaches to the urethra and twist it once to close it off. Then I pinch the twist tight with one hand, and cut off the bladder with the other. Toss it, unless you're in the mood to wash it out and use the bladder as a sausage casing, as they do in Italy with pigs; not such a crazy idea for the bladder of a big deer, elk, or moose.

What happens if the bladder breaks and you get pee all over everything? In most cases, you can wipe it off and move on, making sure to wash anything that the urine touched. If you're near a hose, this would be a good time to spray everything down.

On to the pelvis. Chances are that your deer will have some (ahem) bullets in the chamber. Mercifully, deer pellets aren't as toxic and stinky as pig shit, but you still don't want to be cavalier about it. You want to remove the rectum as cleanly as possible. A really easy way to do this is with heavy-duty shears to cut through the pelvis so you can crack it open and just lift the whole rectum out. This won't work on larger deer, though. For those you'll need that hand saw. Saw through enough of the pelvis without rupturing the rectum underneath to crack the pelvis and lift the plumbing out. Tie it off with a twist tie if you have one.

Now you can basically pull everything out. I go to the front of the gut cavity and grab the windpipe, yank or slice it off (depending on the size of the animal), and pull everything free of the carcass. It will be steamy and bloody, especially where the lungs were.

But this won't work if the animal is on gambrels. In such cases, grab the stuff in the paunch and turn it out of the cavity, then slice any piping that's holding it to the front of the cavity, where the lungs and heart are. Then deal with the heart and lungs.

Be careful when you're removing the heart. It's encased in a slippery membrane called the pericardium, within which it is firmly attached. You will need both hands: one on the knife, one to grab the stuff holding the heart in. Carefully slice that off to free the heart. This is where most people cut themselves, so have your wits about you during this procedure.

In this gut pile will be a large, burgundy organ. That's the liver. Take it and put it aside to cool. Once cooled, put the liver in a bag and into a cooler. Look at the inside of the carcass: You'll probably see the two little kidneys, which in deer look as you might imagine kidneys to look, only encased in heavy white fat. Save them, too.

If you are adventurous, you can save the stomach to make tripe. The stomach will probably be filled with green ick that must be cleaned out thoroughly. Cleaning tripe (see page 33) is something of

This is why they call it "offal." It's what "falls off" the carcass.

a process, but if tripe's your thing, deer tripe is perfectly usable.

You want to save the tongue, too. This can be tricky to remove, as it's a strong muscle, firmly attached to the base of the skull. The best way to remove the tongue is to come up underneath by slicing away the skin and tissue between the two mandibles of the lower jaw. Grab the tongue, pull it down through, and sever it as close to the base as possible, where there is a little bone. It's a bit grisly, and is, well, what they used to call a Colombian necktie in the drug wars. But it's an effective method.

Can you save other things? Well, yes. But I will admit I have not. That pale, liver-like organ in there is the spleen. Italians eat spleen sandwiches, which I hear are reasonably tasty. And of course, there are the intestines, which, if cleaned religiously, can be used for sausages or chitterlings. And finally, the lungs can be saved, rinsed free of blood, and ground into haggis.

If you're super dedicated, even the blood can be saved. There can be quite a lot in the cavity near the lungs. You'd need to pour it into a vessel somehow, and then stir in about a tablespoon of red wine vinegar for every pint or so to prevent the blood from coagulating. You could then make blood sausages if you wanted to. I have not done this, but it is possible.

Once you have all the wobbly bits that you want to keep, use paper towels to thoroughly wipe out and dry the cavity. Water is now your enemy until you can get the carcass chilled because bacteria like wet places above 40°F. If you are near a walk-in cooler, however, hose down the cavity and *then* dry it well.

Dealing with Gut-Shot Deer

It's every deer hunter's nightmare: a poor shot, a wounded animal, and a long search that either ends in anguish or a rapidly decaying carcass. It's on your honor to tag that animal anyway and deal with the meat as best you can. Hunt deer long enough and it is a near certainty that this will happen to you.

Deer are ruminants, and as such they host beneficial bacteria in their digestive tracts that break down twigs, leaves, grains, and anything else the deer decided to eat. Those bacteria aren't harmful in and of themselves (*Escherichia coli* bacteria may sometimes be present, though it's rarely the *E. coli* O157 strain that can make us seriously ill). But the digestive process is a stinky affair, no matter what animal you're dealing with, and if the gut cavity is pierced and those bacteria are allowed to run free and extend their activity outside the gut, the meat can become tainted.

Time and temperature are the critical factors that will determine what you can salvage from a gut-shot deer. One year, I killed a mule deer buck with the infamous "Texas heart shot." I'd been aiming for the animal's neck, but he moved at the last second and I put a bullet through the top of the buck's left hindquarter. It ripped through everything en route to a lung shot. Miraculously, the deer died of blood loss almost instantly, taking only a couple of steps before it dropped. My friend Randy and I were on this deer in a moment, and we gutted it as usual, using our bottled water to rinse any digestive ick off the meat. I ended up losing a little bit of that hindquarter and one tenderloin, but that was it. This was a best case scenario.

I've seen deer shot in the paunch and then felled with a follow-up shot. There was little or no meat loss in these cases. Other times, however, I've seen deer shot in the guts and not recovered for hours—sometimes as long as a day. This is where things get tricky. What you can salvage depends on temperature, and on how long the carcass has been exposed to its own gut contents. You're more likely to salvage more meat in freezing weather than in California's August A Zone hunt. But remember that deer hides are tremendous insulators, so even in sub-zero temperatures, the meat can spoil if it has lain too long.

Whatever happens, open up the deer as usual and clean out the cavity. It will stink. Some hunters put Vick's VapoRub under their noses to disguise the smell, which can get into your nostrils and not go away. For some people, this can be traumatic enough to put them off eating that deer even months later, even if by that time the meat had no smell at all. We create strong associations with smell, so beware of this effect.

I prefer to face the nasty business head-on. If I am close to civilization, I will use water bottles to clean out the carcass and then dry it with paper towels that I keep in my backpack. Then, when I get to the house or lodge, I'll forcefully hose out the cavity, dry it really well, and trim off any meat that appears to be contaminated.

But wait, you say: Isn't water bad for a carcass? Not really. What's bad for a carcass is long-term contact with water above 40°F, which invites bacterial growth. In that case, water can be truly harmful. That said, clean water—not stream or pond water—is your friend, *provided you can dry out the cavity well afterwards.*

Once I've cleaned the carcass and dried it, I will very carefully smell the inside. In paunch-shooting situations where delay has been minimal, as in the two cases I described above, the smell will normally be acceptable. If the carcass stinks, it will need further treatment. And if the deer has been on the ground for hours, those digestive juices can ruin the meat, especially the tenderloin, which is exposed to them directly. First, try wiping down the inside of the carcass with vinegar, then dry it again. Let the animal hang a bit to dissipate any vinegar smell, then take another sniff. If it still stinks, you'll need to sacrifice those parts of the hind legs that are touching the paunch. Ribs are likely done for, too. But most of the animal should be OK. It won't be prime, mind you, but it should be safe to eat.

The reason that I urge you to face the situation of a gut-shot deer head on and proactively should now be clear—a quick response, and careful, thorough assessment, are key to salvaging the most from your kill.

The Dreaded Bone Sour

Should you fail to cool off a carcass fast enough (and remember, the larger the carcass, the harder this is to do), another creeping disaster awaits you. No matter how well you shot an animal, if it lies un-gutted and warm, it can become what's called "bone sour."

You'll know it when it happens. The meat will stink horribly of rotten flesh, and there will be a green tinge near the bone, much like gangrene. Basically, what has happened is that the carcass did not cool fast enough, and bacteria have exploded within, rotting the meat from the bones outward. This is most common in larger animals like elk and moose, but it can happen in deer, too.

All cervids have body temperatures of at least 100°F, and mule deer can run as high as 104°F. You'll need to bring that temperature down to less than 80°F within the first hour, if at all possible. With a deer, this normally just means gutting it, unless it's hot out, in which case you'll need to skin the animal quickly, too. But with elk, moose, and even caribou, you must not only gut and skin the animal, but also quarter it—unless it's really cold out.

Why? Airflow. A big elk hindquarter can be two feet thick, and without enough airflow around it to cool the ham, it can start to spoil right where the femur attaches to the pelvis, the most common origin for bone sour. An exception is cold-weather hunting. If you're in bitterly cold weather, quartering an elk, moose, or caribou is still a good idea, but leave the hide on as protection against freezing.

On the other hand, if you're elk hunting and it's very hot out, say 80°F or warmer, you might want to go one step further and use a knife to separate some of the large hind leg muscles from each other, cutting down to the bone, but not removing the meat from the femur. Prop the two muscles apart with a stick or something similar to cool down the meat even faster.

If you can't hang the quarters, prop them up off the ground or the truck bed with logs or PVC pipe—anything that will allow air to flow underneath those giant hindquarters. Do this for the front legs, too, once you have your hind legs squared away.

HANGING AND AGING DEER

Hanging and aging deer and other cervids is one of the more controversial topics of deer hunting. Some swear by it, while others never age their deer, and swear by that. I've eaten deer aged a month and deer aged a couple of days. Both were fine. So what's the real deal? What happens when you age meat, and what should you do once you have your deer up on the gambrels?

The short answer is that by aging meat, you are removing moisture and allowing enzymes present in the meat to break down connective tissue. The longer this goes, the more flavorful the amino acids that are created by this process—up to a point. Really old meat, even when perfectly aged, will begin to smell and taste like blue cheese. It's not bad for you, but it can be more than a little off-putting.

Before we get into aging and hanging deer, you need to know this: Remove the tenderloins! They don't need aging, and if you leave them on the carcass while aging, the rind that forms on them will need to be trimmed, and there will be nothing left. Maybe, just maybe, you could leave moose tenderloins in, but that's about it.

The perfect deer aging scenario would look something like this: You'd shoot your deer in weather somewhere below freezing, say around 20°F. You'd have gutted it close to the truck (and saved the offal), and got it to your locker. Yes, to properly age a whole carcass you need a walk-in cooler or locker. If you had access to such an enviable appliance, you'd hang your deer, still in its skin, for up to three weeks between 33°F and 37°F, with the humidity in the cooler somewhere between 60 percent and 70 percent. Then you'd skin the deer and butcher as normal.

Why is this perfect?

- The deer cooled down very fast after the shot.

- The deer was hung in a perfect environment: humid enough to prevent the carcass from desiccating, and cold enough to inhibit bacterial growth. Aging, remember, is enzymatic, not bacterial.

- You kept the skin on, which prevented that rind from forming on the outside of the meat. That rind needs to be cut away in dry aging, which results in significant meat loss.

- The deer aged for three weeks, a duration that has been shown in a number of studies to yield the best combination of tenderness and "dry age-y" flavors that most of us love.

Sadly, this just ain't happening for most of us, including me.

Our primary limitation is lack of a locker. This can be solved with a friendly butcher, and I've seen many, many places in this country with rural meat lockers that the butcher will let you use for a small fee. I know a couple of zealots who have built home walk-ins, and to them I say rage on! But there are a few other solutions, too.

Got a spare fridge in the garage? You know, the one with all the beer in it? Drink the beer, clean out the fridge really well with a diluted bleach solution or other anti-bacterial cleanser, and remove all but the top rack. Quarter your deer, and age the pieces in that fridge by suspending them from the top rack with hooks and twine. I recommend hanging the back legs, and resting the backstrap on that top rack. Unless the deer is huge or you have an elk, save the front shoulders for grinding; trimming rind off shoulders is a pain.

Another option (and this is what I do) is to skin the animal, break it down into big pieces (legs plus body), and keep it over ice in a cooler for at least twenty-four hours (forty-eight hours is standard). Then break the animal down and age the pieces in the fridge in plastic containers for another few days. Only then do I vacuum seal them.

Let me walk you through my reasoning. I live in California, where our A Zone deer season starts in August, when daytime temperatures can routinely top 100°F—not ideal deer-hanging weather. Even our late-season temps are rarely cooler than 35°F. So the need to cool the carcass is serious. Gut and skin quickly.

Melting ice water on meat is to be avoided. The water will likely be about 40°F or even warmer, and it will encourage any bacteria already on the meat to start growing. Water will also wash out the meat itself, making it pale and tasteless. So you need to keep the meat off the melt water if at all possible. It won't be ruined if it gets a little wet, but it's not ideal. Initially, I use burlap sacks to shield the meat. Then, when I am doing the preliminary aging of the primals (legs, shoulders, etc.), I set them in a large, open plastic container inside the cooler. If you have a big deer, you'll need several coolers going at once.

Why not butcher right away then? *Because you never, ever want to butcher an animal while it is still stiff with rigor mortis.* Doing so will cause what's called "shortening," a process that results in tough meat, especially if you freeze the meat after butchering. The most important thing to remember is that you just need to let rigor take its course. Patience.

After the meat has relaxed for a day or two, you can butcher without problems. You can then move on.

You may have heard of wet aging. Wet aging is what the supermarket industry does to the meat it sells you. The animal is aged a few days, then butchered, then vacuum sealed and kept refrigerated for up to a couple of weeks, but no longer. After a couple of weeks, the meat will get weirdly sour, and not in a good way. Over this period, wet aged meat may become more tender than meat that's absolutely fresh, but it will never develop the flavor complexity or melt-in-your-mouth tenderness of dry aging.

My method—keeping larger roasts, whole backstraps, etc., in the fridge for up to a week before vacuum sealing—gives you a hybrid dry age. It's not as long as a real dry age, but nor is it as difficult. The venison loses some moisture, but you don't get a rind, so you need not trim before vacuum sealing. I am very happy with the meat quality resulting from this process, and I think you will be, too.

DRY AGING

Let me start by saying that there is very little reason to dry age a whole carcass for weeks. Not that it hurts the meat, but the changes that meat goes through during the dry aging process are most noticeable in those cuts that are best when served rare to medium-rare—not shanks, neck roast, ribs, or, in most cases, the shoulder. Put it this way: If it's a cut you want to eat rare, it's a candidate for dry aging.

I dry age at least a few choice roasts and the backstrap on every old or large animal I bring home. But be forewarned: If you want to do this too, you will need to commit to aging *at least* ten days because the flavors you are seeking just don't develop before one week.

If you want to age venison the way they age steak in the finest steakhouses, cut the carcass into sub-primals—for example, a whole backstrap (or one sliced in two when it's from an elk or a moose), a long length of chops, or a big roast. Why? Because you get better yield, and more evenly distributed moisture loss this way, leading to better flavors in the long run. *And you must leave any fat cap on.* This is vital. The fat protects the meat. You will trim much of it off later, but you need it now.

OK, go back to your fridge. (Ideally, you're using the spare beer fridge in the garage, because aging meat smells funky, and because the meat can pick up odors from all the other food in the refrigerator, and vice versa.) Set the fridge to between 33°F and 35°F. This is colder than normal, but still possible for most standard fridges. Set the large pieces of venison on a rack. They *must* be elevated for good airflow.

Set a pan of salty water somewhere in the fridge to promote decent humidity. If it evaporates, refill it.

The hard part: You need a fan in the fridge. I've tried battery-operated fans, but have found them to be frustrating. The batteries seem to run out every other day or so, and yes, you can recharge them, but it's a pain. Better to have a little fan with a power cord that you can snake out the side of the fridge and into an outlet. You might need to cut a small notch in the rubber seal on the side of the fridge door to do this.

Now you wait. How long? At least ten days, but honestly, real dry-aged flavor doesn't happen until two weeks; three weeks is even better. If you *really* like that funky-cheesy flavor of old meat, you can go to sixty days or more, but that's pushing it.

When the meat is ready, trim off the gnarly, often moldy outside of the venison. Don't worry; mold is normal. Usually, you will need to slice off about a quarter-inch or so. See why you don't want to do this with small deer? Too much meat loss.

A few final tips:

- The older the animal, the longer the hang time and the longer the aging process. This goes for both does and bucks. Shoot a matron cow elk and you will want to hang and age it as long as a bull.

- Artificial tenderizers like pineapple or papaya juice don't really work. All they do is attack the surface of meat, making it mushy. Aging works from within.

- The so-called "dry aging bags" are also useless for true dry aging. Don't buy them.

- Keep your meat in darkness. Sunlight oxidizes fat, especially venison fat, which is much higher in omega-3 fatty acids; these oxidize faster than typical beef fat.

Oh, and you can age pre-frozen meat, since freezing simply puts the enzymes that make the magic happen into suspended animation. But keep in mind that aging improves the water-holding properties of the meat, and, since you lose moisture when you freeze meat (the water in the cells turns to ice, breaks the cell walls, and then, when you defrost, those cells leak fluid), aging it before you freeze will keep your venison juicier when you cook it. Nevertheless, butchers age meat that's been frozen first all the time. Just don't age on both ends of the spectrum (don't age, then freeze, then age again). Butcher and age then freeze, or butcher then freeze, then age. Don't age twice.

BUTCHERING YOUR OWN DEER

For many of us, the time spent butchering our own animals is a vital period of transition; in the act of butchering, we make the shift from hunter to cook. It's a quiet time during which to focus on the animal, sharp knife in hand, and to think about your plans for this creature you've just laid low for your nourishment. For butchery is an intensely personal business—you cut up an animal in exactly the sort of pieces that you intend to cook in the days, weeks, and months ahead.

Chops are my favorite example. On most whitetail deer, the chops are so small and thin as to be worse than useless; they get you all excited when you break them out of the freezer, only to dash your

hopes as you watch them go from lovely to leathery in seconds in the pan. In these cases, the answer is to cut long rib roasts, the way they do with lamb, so that you have many chops, all attached, which you can then cook as a whole, slicing them into pretty, individual chops just before you serve. Oddly, I have yet to see a professional butcher do this for a deer, for reasons known only to them.

A while back, I asked readers of *Hunter Angler Gardener Cook* whether they butcher their own deer (or elk, antelope, or moose), or take them to a processor or butcher. Of the more than 300 answers I received, only nine people said they use a butcher exclusively, and several of those nine knew the butcher personally. A few more noted that using a professional butcher is a convenience when they are

hunting outside their home state or province, and a few more said they'd take a few deer to a processor, especially when the plan was to give the meat to others, but that they'd always butcher the "important" deer themselves.

This was wonderful to hear. I've always likened the process of butchering to opening up a present. This might sound odd to those who've never done it. But the practiced dismantling of a deer, elk, or antelope is strangely calming and exciting at the same time. It's lovely to move your knife in just such a way that a perfect holiday roast comes off the hind leg, a single muscle ready for roasting. And yet there are always surprises. Maybe you've shot an elk, an animal large enough to collect the hanger steak from; I know this was downright thrilling for me, after so many little deer that had come before. I love hanger steak in beef, that slab of meat that hangs between the upper and lower body cavity (basically the diaphragm). But you need a big beast to get a usable hanger steak, and an elk is just about big enough.

There is also the warm sense of satisfaction that comes from knowing that you know how to break down a deer, and that you did it well. What's more, you know that you alone touched the meat that you plan to feed yourself, your friends, and your family. If there are any food safety issues, you have only yourself to blame. This is a responsibility many people are more than willing to accept.

Now, to be sure, I have nothing against professional butchers. Many are true artisans who work magic on a carcass. But the most common complaint I heard from readers when I asked about outsourcing the processing of their game was the instances of bad butchery they'd encountered—sloppy, callous, and careless. Bone fragments in steaks. Burger ground with no extra fat, or with a type of fat the hunter specifically asked not to have included. Missing tenderloins (this happens a lot, apparently). The aforementioned micro-chops. Not getting your own deer back (borderline criminal, in my opinion). And most of all, stupid cuts, the infamous leg steak chief among them.

What the hell is a "leg steak," anyway? You may know what I mean: that horrid "steak" that's been cut with a bandsaw right through a deer's hind leg? I'll tell you what it is: A "leg steak" is an abomination. It's three to five separate muscles (depending on where it's been cut), barely attached to each other by membrane, with a disk of sliced femur in the center. Surrounding each of those muscles is a skein of silverskin that, in most cases, is so strong you could lash up your snowshoes with it. When you cook this thing, the silverskin contracts, making the whole piece of meat curl. The separate muscles try

to fall away from each other—and sometimes do— and there is so much surface area relative to mass on the thing that it's virtually impossible to cook medium-rare, as a decent steak ought to be. And even if you manage to succeed in this feat, that silverskin will not have broken down, and it will resist all but the sharpest knives; your teeth will be no match for it. Revolting.

And yet I've seen this cut of meat all across the country. Even weirder, I've seen "chops" of backstrap, with both sides of the loin and tenderloin still attached to a sliver of vertebrae. Bizarre.

All of this leads a great many people to home butchery. But how to go about it? How even to get started?

First, you need some tools, both physical and mental. Learning how to butcher a deer from a book isn't ideal, though indeed, there are whole books devoted to the task. And while I will give you instructions on how I butcher, you could do worse than pick up copies of Al Cambronne's *Gut It, Cut It, Cook It*, as well as John J. Mettler, Jr.'s classic *Basic Butchering of Livestock & Game*. Philip Hasheider's *The Complete Book of Butchering, Smoking, Cooking and Sausage Making* and Steven Rinella's *The Complete Guide to Hunting, Butchering and Cooking Wild Game, Vol. I*, are worth reading, too. If you are looking for good information about gutting a deer in the field, Cambronne's book, as well as Jackson Landers's *Hunting Deer for Food* are great sources. None of these guys butcher large animals the way I do, but they are all skilled at the task.

Now you need some implements of deconstruction. I am hesitant to suggest too many brand names here, as models change over time and often become obsolete. But a few companies do have innovative products that might become standard down the road; those I'll mention by name.

AT HOME

Once you get home, you need an area in which to work. I use my little galley kitchen—sixty-seven square feet, including the counters. Turning the family kitchen over to butchering may not be possible for everyone; admittedly, I have a distinct advantage here, since my partner, Holly, is also a hunter, and butchery in our little kitchen is just a regular family affair. I know many people who set up stations in their garages, complete with stainless steel tables and special sinks. That'd be awesome, but during our deer seasons here in California, my garage can often be 95°F, which is not ideal for game processing. So for me, the kitchen works best.

You'll want lots of cheap kitchen towels and large plastic tubs, both of which are available at your local supermarket. Have several rolls of paper towels around, too.

If you haven't done so already, you'll need to quarter your deer. I use a pair of boning knives for most of this work as well as for the fine work that follows. My go-to tool is an ancient, stiff-bladed boning knife that I, well, borrowed from my friend Elise. I like a stiff blade for most uses because it feels more substantial somehow. That said, I switch to a flexible boning knife when I remove the backstraps and slice off silverskin because the bend in the blade really helps me extract as much meat—or in the case of silverskin removal, to save as much—as possible. Flexible blades tend to be thinner, too, which helps a lot.

I can do almost all my butchery with just those two knives, plus my regular chef's knife. The only other tool I need is a saw of some sort. I used to use a regular hacksaw, but I've graduated to a proper cordless Sawzall. I use the saw only for ribs and shanks. Everything else I can do with a knife. Keep in mind that I don't cut chops, so I don't need the saw for that.

Keeping your knives sharp is a must. Invest in a good sharpener, or, if you are really serious, a set of Japanese water stones in various grits (one 1000 grit stone and one 6000 grit makes a good, all-purpose set). A sharpening steel is essential, too, for honing the blade and realigning the micro-serrations at the edge. That's what I use to keep my blades lightning sharp.

GETTING TO IT

I am going to assume you have a dead, gutted, skinned deer in your kitchen or work area. Once again, this is how *I* butcher a deer. It's a method that works for me, and is very similar to what the French call "seam butchery," which respects the natural seams between muscle groups. American butchers tend to ignore these seams and just cut things seemingly willy-nilly (thus the "leg steak.") Ready? Here we go.

Offal

Start with the offal, the wobbly bits. These are probably sitting in a plastic bag in your fridge or cooler. Mostly, I am talking about the heart, liver, kidneys, and tongue. Although there are those who keep the spleen (Sicilians, mostly, who make spleen sandwiches with it), and the lungs (the Scots, for haggis), I myself don't tend to use these parts, and we won't be covering them here. Tripe (stomach) is a special case that we'll deal with separately (see the sidebar on the next page).

Wash all the various bits under cold water and pat them dry. Slice the top off the heart, above the ring of fat; this is mostly vein-y and arterial stuff, anyway. Rinse out any blood clots, and you're done for now. If you want to make heart cutlets, see page 232.

Pull the fat off the outside of the kidneys and wash it well. Use this kidney fat for Suet Boots (see page 53). Find the gossamer membrane surrounding

The wobbly bits. Clockwise from upper left: liver, tongue, kidneys, tripe, caul fat, and heart.

the kidney and pull it off (it's like the finest cellophane). You're good for now.

I like to soak the liver in milk for a day before storing it. This pulls a lot of the musky, gamey flavor from it. And mind you, I am no wuss when it comes to gamey flavors, but deer liver can get a stink on it something fierce. When you are ready to store it, rinse off the milk and pat it dry. Cut out any weird connective tissue and cut the liver into portions that you might eat in one sitting; I like one-pound pieces.

The tongue is easy. Just rinse and dry and you're ready to store.

Cleaning Deer Tripe

OK, this one is for the gastronauts among you. If you like beef or lamb tripe, you will like deer tripe, which is thinner and more tender than either. First, cut the big stomach away from the other ones; deer have multiple stomachs, as do all ruminants. Unless you are dealing with an elk or moose, the other stomachs are too small to bother with.

Now slice open the stomach and stand back. A tsunami of stinky green ick will flow out like vegetal lava. Yay. Now hose off the stomach as best you can. A good spray jet works well for this.

You'll notice that the inside looks disturbingly like brownish-grayish-green terrycloth. Hose this *thoroughly* and set it aside until you are ready to work on it.

When you are ready to continue preparing the tripe, cut the stomach into large pieces that will lay flat. Sprinkle coarse salt on one side and scrub vigorously with a scrub brush to make sure you get every last bit of stray greenery out. Do the same for the other side. Rinse off the pieces.

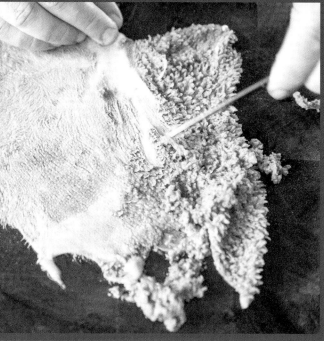

Now put the pieces in a non-reactive (for example, *not* aluminum or copper), lidded container and cover with water. Add two tablespoons of hydrogen peroxide and mix well. It will fizz alarmingly. Why do this? Hydrogen peroxide will both kill bacteria and slightly bleach the tripe. Soak the pieces in this solution in the fridge for one hour.

Now rinse again. Finally, use a paring knife to scrape away the terrycloth-looking stuff. It will zip off easily in some places and stick in others. Slice off any ugly looking bits.

You now have tripe ready for cooking (Venison Tripe Neopolitan Style, page 253), or for freezing.

PRIMAL CUTS

Legs

Put the deer on its back, and with your off hand push one front leg away from the ribs. Using a stiff boning knife, slice into this gap to free the leg. You will see a cobwebby substance between the leg and the body—this is the connective-tissue membrane that separates things. It's what you always want to keep in view during this whole process, as these membranes will demarcate the seams between muscle groups. Keep slicing upward until you find the white cartilage of the animal's shoulder. Try not to slice right through this (as can so often happen) so that you can keep the shoulder whole. Slip the knife under

Removing the front leg.

the cartilage, leaving a fair bit of meat on the body attached to the ribs; you'll get to this in a bit. Free the front leg. You'll notice that the front legs of deer, elk, moose, and antelope aren't actually attached to the body by a bone. Our own front "legs" (our arms) are attached by our collarbone (the only game animal I know of with a collarbone is a squirrel. Neat, eh?). Now do the other front leg the same way.

I like to have a giant cooler with ice close at hand when I do this. I'll put the various primal parts into plastic tubs set in the cooler to keep them cold while I work. A fridge would work just as well, but I rarely have room in mine for this.

With the front legs removed, I move to the back legs. All game animals (and birds) have their back legs attached by a ball-and-socket joint. Again, with the deer on its back, feel around for where the ball-and-socket joint ought to be—in the middle of the pelvic bone you probably sawed through in the field.

Use your knife to slice downward along the pelvic bone until you find the joint (1). When you do, give a good strong yank downward on the leg with one hand while anchoring the pelvis with the other. Your goal is to pop the ball out of the socket (2). When you do, stop and look at the back end of the ham. You'll notice that it comes up, over, and around the pelvis. This is the rump. Use your knife to free the leg from the pelvis, keeping in mind that it's not one straight cut. If you've ever seen a nice country ham or a whole prosciutto, you may remember that the meat on the outer side of the ball joint (the joint's exposed in a ham) is higher than the inner side. Aim to replicate this. It takes a bit of practice, but all is not lost if you are sloppy here; the meat in this area is excellent for stew or for sausage if for some reason the larger cuts couldn't be kept whole.

Do this for both legs. Move each one to the cooler or fridge.

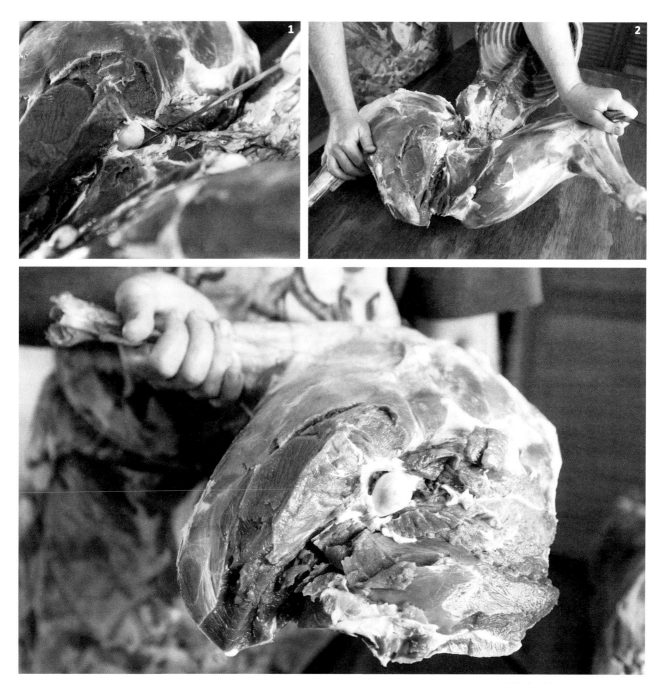

The hind leg, properly removed.

Backstraps and Tenderloins

Now you're left with a (probably) headless torso. If you have the head still attached, sever it where it meets the neck by cutting with a knife all the way around until you can see bone. Now twist forcefully until the head comes free. You can also saw it off. I save doe heads to make Mexican Barbacoa (page 127).

At this point, you have several options for how to proceed, but I like to move on to the backstraps from here.

The backstraps are the loins of the deer, akin to the ribeye in beef. They run along the outside of the entire spine in two thick bands of muscle. You will want to slice them off whole so that you get two pieces, one for each side of the spine. Use a flexible knife for this so you can slide it along the bumpy road of the vertebrae. I move the carcass so the animal is on its side, with its back facing me. Using the knife, start slicing right behind the neck, then cut along the backbone back toward the pelvis. You want to press the blade against the backbone as you cut so you don't miss any meat. As you slice, tap the point of the blade on the lateral flange of the vertebrae that anchors the rest of the backstrap meat. Doing this ensures that you are cutting all the way down. Slice all the way down to the pelvis.

Now, using the ribs as your guide, free the backstrap from the spine. As you slice, keep the blade anchored on the ribs so you don't miss any meat, and tap the point of the blade on the vertical flange of the backbone. The backstrap should pull away nicely. Do this for both sides (*photos, left*).

Underneath the backstraps are the tenderloins, little torpedoes of meat that are the most tender parts of the animal. You can just pull them off, or you can slice them off the same way you did the backstraps.

Use a flexible boning knife, and take your time so you don't miss any meat along the backstrap. The precious tenderloins are underneath the backstrap, just in front of the pelvis. When removed, they form twin torpedoes of tastiness (*above*).

Neck

For the neck, you can do one of three things: You can hack off as much meat as possible and use it in the grinder; you can saw it off whole and use it as a bone-in pot roast, a nice option with small deer; or you can bone the whole neck and use that as a pot roast (this is what I do most often—see Polish Pot Roast with a Venison Neck, page 73). I'm sorry to say that there is no magical shortcut method for boning a neck. With all those weird angles from the vertebrae, you just have to work at it with a small knife in short strokes (I use a paring knife for this). I love how Mettler puts it in his *Basic Butchering of Livestock & Game*: "using your ingenuity . . ." Yeah, that's about it. Figure this one out. There is just no easy way.

That said, it's no biggie if things are a little ragged. If you use the neck as a pot roast, you'll want to roll it and truss it anyway, or just braise it long enough that it falls apart, and then shred the meat.

On a very large deer, elk, or moose, you can get two funny little steaks (called whistlers) off the twin muscles guarding the windpipe and esophagus. They look like a tenderloin, but are not as tender. Nevertheless, cooked whole and sliced into medallions, they are very nice. On smaller deer, I use these pieces of meat for stew or stir-fry.

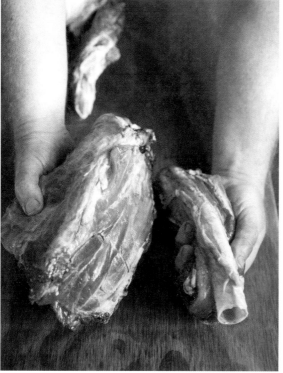

Removing the windpipe and "whistler" steaks alongside it. On a small deer like this one, these steaks are best for stew meat, but on a large animal they make nice medallions.

Brisket or Breast

I happen to love the old recipes that call for "breast of venison," a good description for what is essentially the brisket. To keep the "breast" whole, I never split the sternum when I gut a deer; I just reach up under the ribs to grab the heart, lungs, and windpipe. Once the carcass is ready for butchering, you'll see the brisket cupping either side of the front of the sternum. It's a flat piece of meat we call the brisket in beef, but alas, unlike beef brisket, the brisket from venison is usually not fatty. It makes a fantastic pot roast or braise, though, so I like to keep it in one piece. It is easily removed from the ribs with a short, sharp knife.

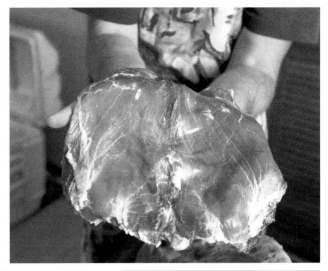

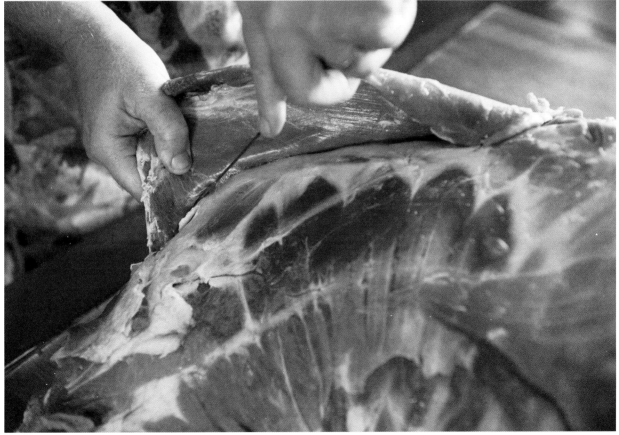

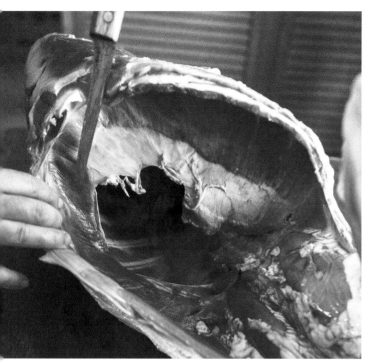

Flanks and Ribs

By now, the carcass is looking a little worn. Most of the goodies are gone, except for the flanks and ribs. The flanks can be great eating in larger animals, where you can separate the various layers of meat from the fat and connective tissue. Flank steak, anyone? And if you have an elk or a moose, you can nab a strip of flank-like meat on the *inside* of the ribs—that's the skirt steak, the best piece of meat on the animal, in my opinion (*photo, top left*). But it's really only available as a steak on the bigger species. On smaller deer and all antelope, your best bet is to slice it off in as big a piece as you can manage and grind it.

If you plan to cut ribs to eat, you'll want to leave all the meat from the flank that sits above the ribs. if you don't have this in mind, you can easily slice this off, resulting in ribs without much meat on them.

If you do want to cut ribs, use a saw to cut them off right where you sliced off the backstrap. Now you'll want to cut off, at the very least, the ridge of bone on the bottom of the ribs. If you don't do this, the ribs get unwieldy. I prefer to cut short ribs about five or six inches wide—deer ribs are best treated like beef short ribs rather than pork spare ribs. That leaves a few inches of waste underneath, where that ridge of bone is. I just use a knife to cut out any usable meat from that part; that goes in the grinder.

If you don't feel like making ribs, just use a knife to cut out all the usable meat from between and over the ribs. This meat is only good for the grinder.

There, you've finished the rough cut! Time to clean up and have a beer and some lunch before you get set for the fine work.

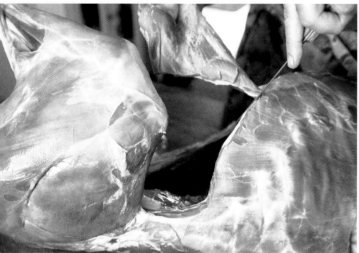

Above   Removing skirt steak.
Below   Removing the flank meat from a blacktail deer.

FINE WORK

You now have a deer (or elk, or moose, or other venison) broken down into some primal cuts. You can, of course, cook some of these as-is, especially if you have small animals like whitetail does, axis or roe deer, or an antelope. But for the most part, you will want to do some extra trimming and slicing to get your animal into more useful pieces.

Much of the work has already been done. The ribs need no more treatment after you've sawed them off to the length and width you want. The neck roast is done, too. Flank steaks just need to be separated from the various layers of connective tissue and fat. The tenderloins are also ready to eat. Everything else needs some tending.

Shanks

Let's start with the shanks, the last bits of meat on the legs, akin to your calf. To remove the shanks, you'll need your saw. Whether you keep your shanks whole or cut them in cross sections depends on size. Most deer have small enough shanks to cook whole; the size of your Dutch oven or other heavy pot will determine this, as shanks need to be braised. Sometimes, shanks are just a little too long for the pot. In such cases, saw them to fit, taking off the narrow end, not the top where it attaches to the leg. Elk, moose, and really big deer have shanks that are much too large for the pot. Saw these into thick (two- to four-inch) cross sections for braises, and for Italian Osso Buco (page 213).

To saw off a shank, find where it bends, then use your knife to cut the meat down to that level; you don't want to saw meat. Saw through the bone and you're good to go. It helps if you have another person hold the shank steady while you saw, but I do it solo all the time.

To saw your cross sections, do the same thing: Use your knife to slice down to the bone, then saw.

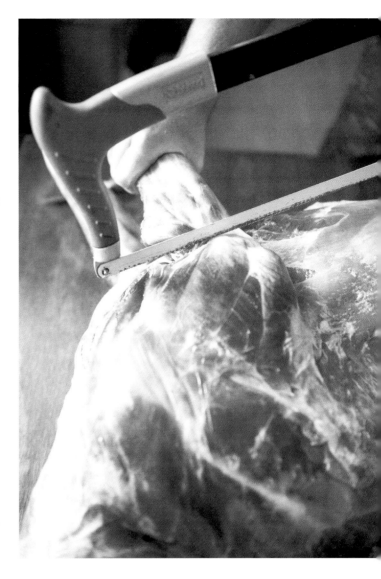

Front Legs

Front legs are something of a quandary. Unless you are dealing with an elk, moose, or really big deer, there's no real point breaking down the front leg into its constituent muscle groups—there's just too much connective tissue in the front legs to make the effort worthwhile. My advice: Just slice off all the meat you can, and use the good bits for stew, and the gnarly bits for the grinder. Front legs are the main source of my sausage and burger meat.

Now, if the deer is small, or you have a doe antelope or some such, you can actually braise the front leg whole (minus the shank) until all that connective tissue melts. To my mind, this is the best thing to do with this part of the animal. When contemplating this, keep in mind the dimensions of your cookware: If a shoulder can fit into something with a lid, or something you can cover with foil, you can braise it whole. Whole braised shoulder is one of my favorites (Braised Shoulder of Venison, page 71).

If you're dealing with an elk or moose, however, the front legs will indeed be large enough to portion out into whole muscle cuts. In general, the front shoulder and leg will be the chuck on a beef, and you can wrangle a few nice roasts from it in moose and elk.

The primo cut from the front leg is the flatiron steak (called the "butler's steak" in Britain, and the "oyster" steak in Australia). This is the blade roast, sliced in half horizontally to remove a thick, nasty band of connective tissue that runs down the middle. You get four flatirons per animal, two from each blade. And of course you can then portion these smaller if you want. You find the blade roast nestled on the outside part of, well, the shoulder blade. You'll notice that the shoulder blades have a strong ridge of bone in the middle of them. The blade roast is the triangular muscle tucked into the wider half of the shoulder blade. You can get a similar steak from the narrower side of the shoulder blade, too.

Remember that these steaks are quite small in deer, although if you brought home a big bruiser, it would be worth it.

Keep the bones in the front leg for stock and broth.

Backstraps

A common misconception is that backstraps are all one lovely piece of meat. The fact is that there are several muscles running through the backstrap, each separated by connective tissue strong enough to mess things up when you cook it. You need to separate those muscles to get to the good stuff.

Start with the fat cap. Honestly, as much as I love to work with venison fat, I usually pull this off. Why? Because there's a thick layer of silverskin between the fat and the meat. In a boneless steak or roast, this tends to fall partly away from the meat during cooking, making it tough to properly cook that side of the meat. It's a different story if you've cut chops; the fat cap stays on better when you have the bone on the chop. Think about doing this with big, fat deer like a nice muley buck, and definitely with elk and moose. You could also take this route with smaller deer if you cut longer sections of chops, like the lamb racks you see in the store.

Most often, I break the backstrap down into boneless lengths of loin. To start, you need to remove the "chain" from the loin (1). This is a strip of meat that runs alongside the main loin, separated by connective tissue. It's shaped like a very long, skinny triangle, and is widest at the end of the backstrap that was closest to the shoulder. You should be able to just pull this off if you follow the natural seam of the meat. Use the chain for sausage or burger.

Now the only thing you need to do is carefully slice the silverskin off the loin (2,3). For this I use my sharpest, thinnest blade which is either a flexible blade boning knife or a fish fillet knife, depending on which is sharpest at the moment.

Why not medallions? Fair question. Here's why: Unless you have a very thick and wide steak, the mass-to-surface-area ratio is all wrong. Think about a typical backstrap steak, which is about four inches across. Most butchers cut these less than an inch thick. Sear that in a pan and you've seared the two largest halves of the piece of meat. Yes, you get a nice area of crust, but cooking it this way makes it a lot tougher to control the doneness. You go from just right to overcooked in the time it takes to get your sear on. Many a backstrap steak has been ruined because of this.

Better to cut lengths of backstrap (4) and sear the outside, cooking the whole thing until it's done to your liking, and *then* slice them into steaks when serving. Doing it this way makes it easier to control the internal temperature. See page 81 for a further discussion of medallions vs. lengths of loin.

Hind Legs

This is where seam butchery really comes into play. On small deer, I find it's best to just roast the whole haunch—this makes one helluva party dinner. But more often, I take the leg apart the way it was put together: muscle group by muscle group.

The first thing you do is remove as many layers of silverskin as you can from the outside of the leg (1). These just get in the way. You can pull a lot of it off, slicing where it sticks to the meat. Try to get most of it off, but you need not be too worried about it at this point.

Now you're ready to rock. Just so you know, the top of the hind leg, the rump, is the toughest part to separate into a cohesive roast, unless you're dealing with a large animal, and even then you are basically just slicing off a big ole' hunk at the top of the leg. This is where I most often get my best stew meat.

Starting the process is the hardest part, and the only part during which you're cutting *through* muscle instead of *alongside* it. Turn the hind leg to the ball joint that is facing up; this is the inner side of the leg. Now trace where the femur goes from that ball joint down to the "knee." That's your line. Slice down along this line, tapping the point of your knife on the femur the whole way down toward the "knee" (2).

From here, you are deboning the leg exactly as you'd do with a leg of lamb. You have the bone slightly exposed from your first cut. Now use the last inch or so of your knife blade to carefully free the bone from the muscles (3). Use short strokes, and think about "freeing the meat" rather than cutting or slicing. Work your way around the bone until it's attached only at the "knee." Free the femur by cutting through the soft cartilage where it meets the knee.

Save the femur for soup or for marrow (more on marrow on page 231).

Now you have a big lump of meat. How to separate it? Take a look: You will see seams of connective tissue here and there. Put your knife down for a moment and start working your fingers into those seams (4). You'll see that they pull apart fairly easily. They stay together with that same cobwebby substance that holds the front leg onto the body (5). You'll see that in some places the connections are too tough for you to just pull them apart without ripping the muscle. That's where you use your sharp boning knife. Again, always think about "freeing" the various muscle groups from each other (rather than "cutting them apart"), and you'll get most of the leg separated into nice, big roasts, plus a few oddly shaped smaller muscles that are great as stew meat.

As you proceed in this way, three main roasts will begin to appear: One is the sirloin tip, which I call the "football roast" (because, well, it looks like a football); and two other rectangular roasts with a strong grain to them that will guide you (6).

Attached to one of the rectangular roasts is a nifty little cylinder of meat that looks an awful lot like a tenderloin. This is the eye round, or "hidden tenderloin." It's not actually as tender as the real tenderloin, but it's definitely steak-worthy. Removing it is the one hard part of separating the leg: The connective tissue that attaches the eye round to the larger roasts is tight. Just take your time and work that edge and you'll be fine.

Never Refreeze Uncooked Meat

Why? Primarily because of meat quality, but there is also a potential health risk.

The most important reason for the taboo on refreezing uncooked meat is best explained by the renowned food scientist Harold McGee, who wrote in his *On Food and Cooking*:

> The intercellular spaces [in meat], which are often large and which contain some water but very little else, freeze first, and then draw water out of the cells by osmosis. This in turn increases the concentration of dissolved substances within the cell, which further lowers the freezing point. Parts of the cell interior do not freeze at all.

Put simply, freezing damages meat. And when you thaw it, that damage manifests itself as the blood-like fluid that seeps out of the meat. It's not actually blood, but rather cell fluid weeping from the damaged cells. The meat's still fine, just not as good as fresh.

Now, if you put that same piece of meat through the whole freezing and thawing process again, well, let's just say you'll notice it. The meat will be even dryer and mushier than once-thawed meat.

This will be especially noticeable if all you have is a regular stand-up freezer and not a deep freeze. This is because the longer it takes to freeze meat, the larger the ice crystals that will form within its cell walls. The larger the ice crystals, the more damage done. This is why commercial processors use blast freezers, which can achieve temperatures as low as -100°F, freezing the meat so fast that the ice crystals formed are tiny, and meat damage minimal. Your home freezer won't get much colder than about 0°F, and even a top-of-the-line home box freezer won't get colder than -25°F; most only hit -10°F.

Depending on how you thawed the meat in the first place, you might also be exposing yourself to some nasty bugs. If you've thawed the meat from freezer to refrigerator, you're good. Everything's stayed cold enough. But if you thawed that backstrap on the counter, which you should never do anyway, there's a distinct chance that the exterior will be covered in bacterial nasties. If you then refreeze that meat, and then thaw it one more time, as soon as the temperature of that meat rises to about 45°F, the bacteria will become active again, and will now have even more cell wall fluid to feast on. This is not good.

Cooking meat alters its cell structure, so it's OK to refreeze meat once you cook it. I often make venison sausages from frozen meat, but I will then hot smoke or poach them so they're fully cooked before I refreeze them.

"The caribou and the wolf are one; for the caribou feeds the wolf, but it is the wolf who keeps the caribou strong."

—INUIT PROVERB

pressure canner, tighten the lid, and vent for ten minutes before putting on the weight to build pressure. Once you get to 10 psi (15 psi if you live at elevations at or above 1000 feet), pressure can your venison for ninety minutes. Bottom line: Be sure to follow the directions with your pressure canner; each one works a little differently, and details for safe, correct use will vary.

TOP FACTORS AFFECTING MEAT QUALITY

I've talked with many, many butchers, deer hunters, meat experts, and cooks over the years about what they consider to be the most important factors affecting the flavor of your venison. Here's the consensus:

1. **FIELD CARE** By far the number-one cause of nasty-tasting venison is poor meat care. If you think strapping a buck to your truck and driving around with it is a good idea, I'm talking to you. Take your photos, then get to work. And I don't mean back in camp after a cup of coffee—I mean right out there in the field (unless it is beastly cold out). Cooling down the carcass quickly is the single most important factor in assuring good meat quality. This is most important in warmer climates.

2. **SHOT PLACEMENT** A good hunter is something of an assassin, killing silently, swiftly, and cleanly. Your animal should have no idea it's being hunted, and, when shot, die quickly. A clean heart-lung shot on an unsuspecting deer will go a long way toward tasty venison. A liver shot (or worse), or a shot on a fleeing deer, will flood the animal with adrenaline, which can make the meat nearly inedible.

3. **HANGING TEMPERATURE** If you are hanging your deer, you need the temperature to be no higher than about 40°F; just above freezing is better. One of the reasons people get nasty venison back from meat

processors is that in deer season, the door of their meat locker is opened and shut all day, letting warm are sneak in, and allowing temperatures to creep up past 40°F. Processors don't like to talk about this, but it happens.

4. **THE RUT** Note that this is the first time the animal itself comes into play as a factor in meat quality. Rutting and post-rut bucks and bulls are in ragged shape. They've been running around and fighting for weeks, and have a lot of hormones racing through them. They'll be leaner and tougher than before the rut, let alone when they are well out of their rutting season.

5. **AGE AND SEX** All things being equal, a young doe or cow will be more tender than an old male. But keep in mind that a young male might be more tender than an old doe. You *can* get good venison from an old, rutting buck, provided that the first three factors are all done right.

6. **DIET** Grain-fed whitetails and mule deer will be fatter and nicer tasting than those deer subsisting on sagebrush or pine needles. That doesn't mean a muley that's shot in the sage won't be good, it's just that you might find yourself preferring the whitetail doe that you shot in the alfalfa field. That said, venison from all sorts of animals, with all sorts of diets, can be wonderful; these observations are just the fine distinctions that can elevate your culinary awareness and enjoyment.

7. **BUTCHERY** Bad butchery, whether in the form of sloppy knife and saw cuts, meat ground with loads of sinew and no added fat, or failure to remove enough silverskin from roasts and stew meat, can seriously damage meat. This is why many of us chose to butcher our own deer and elk. Good butchers are like good mechanics: Hold onto them, and treat them well.

DEMYSTIFYING DEER FAT

I've long been a proponent of using deer fat in cooking. In fact, the widely accepted injunction against using deer fat is one of the hunting myths I most like to puncture when I talk to other hunters about game cookery. After all, it just makes sense that the fat on venison would taste good, especially if you are hunting either in the Grain Belt, or wherever there are a lot of acorns: Most of us like the taste of grain-fed beef, and acorn-fed pork is some of the finest in the world. The same holds true for venison.

Still, the majority of sources on the subject will tell you to remove any and all fat from your deer, calling it gamy, "strong," or otherwise unpleasant. Even the normally sporty *The L.L. Bean Game and Fish Cookbook*, which I have great respect for, says venison fat is nasty (but, oddly, that moose and caribou fat isn't). Some critics skip the flavor aspect altogether, and stress how quickly venison fat goes rancid, even in the freezer. There has to be something to this, right?

Turns out, there is—to both sides of the deer fat debate. Let me start with the obvious: Deer, elk, antelope, caribou, and moose are all separate critters, with different diets among the different species, compounded by regional differences within the same species, and individual differences within the herd. The menu for an Arizona coues deer is nothing like that of an Iowa whitetail deer, for example. And one buck may love acorns, while the one eating next to him prefers your azaleas. Given this enormous range of factors, any hard-and-fast universal ideas about the flavor or composition of deer fat should be taken with a grain of salt. Being wild, variability is the name of the game.

Nevertheless, all our "deer" are ruminant cousins of sheep, goats, and cattle. And ruminants tend to have a narrower range of flavor differences than do animals with a less intense digestive system and/or

a wider diet. Ruminants all eat grasses, plants, and nuts; despite the oft-quoted story about deer eating baby birds or eggs, only rarely do they eat animal protein. Contrast that with ducks, bears, and wild pigs, which can all run the flavor gamut from abominable to sublime depending on what they last ate. A salmon-eating bear is foul-tasting; a berry-eating one fantastic. Deer taste like deer, with real, but far subtler, differences in flavor.

Not all fat is created equal. Muscle fat is different from body cavity fat. You will often see a lot of fat around the kidneys, as well as some stuck here and there within the gut cavity. This latter is suet. I tend to toss it, or use it as waterproofing material (see page 53). Why? Body cavity fat (suet) is *always* harder than fat on working muscles. If you are a soap or candle maker, this stuff is golden. But the very qualities that make suet so good for the candle maker, particularly its high melting point (around 120°F), make eating it less than ideal. It just tends to be really waxy. (By comparison, rendered wild duck fat melts at around 68°F.) Some people like beef and lamb suet; I don't. Birds really love it, though, especially in winter. So if you live in a place with cold winters, save your deer suet for them.

Are you hanging your deer or not? This is a big one. If you intend to hang your deer *in the hide*, you can still use the fat. Not many people do this because it requires very cold temperatures. If, like most people, you hang your deer after it's been skinned, you probably want to trim off at least the top layer of fat when you are ready to butcher. The reason why gets us into what venison fat is made of.

Good data is hard to find on this subject, but it does exist, mostly from New Zealand, Scandinavia, and Great Britain, although there are a few studies from the United States, too. They all come to the same conclusion about deer fat:

- It is high in omega-3 fatty acids, due mostly to a diet of grasses.
- It has some of the highest levels of stearic acid in any food animal, for reasons not entirely clear.
- Deer fat is more saturated than fat from beef, lamb, or pork.

Saturated fat is bad, right? Actually, no, but that's another story. Most saturated animal fats are composed of palmitic and myristic acid, which are present in all ruminants, including deer. As it happens, stearic acid, a third saturated fatty acid, is an anomaly. Diets high in stearic acid actually decrease the levels of "bad" cholesterol in people, and may even increase the "good" cholesterol, too. At the very least, it is cholesterol neutral. Beef has some stearic acid, lamb more. But you know what has even higher levels of it? Chocolate. Crazy, eh? Well, maybe not so; it's just this fact that will soon help explain something critical about eating venison fat.

So, back to the question of hanging your deer. If you hang your deer with the fat exposed, the fat will begin to go rancid. The reason has to do with temperatures above freezing, exposure to the air (which causes oxidation), and because fats high in omega-3 fatty acids tend to go rancid more readily. This is why people contend that venison fat goes rancid quickly. The quicker you can cool the deer carcass, and the faster you can get the meat away from oxygen and into refrigeration, the better tasting the fat will be, and the longer it will keep in storage.

A word on taste. Flavor in deer fat is all about meat care (which we just discussed) and diet. A deer that had been pillaging an alfalfa field or a cornfield will have fat that tastes a lot like beef or lamb fat. A deer eking out a living in the Great Basin or in the desert might not have any fat at all, and what fat there is may well taste unpleasant. How can you tell?

Render some in a pan with a little water, and if it smells good, it *is* good. Your nose won't lie.

That said, the primary carrier of individual flavor in animals is the fat, not the lean meat. If you like the flavor of lamb or beef fat, you'll like venison fat. Others might find it too strong. And that's fair, but I am betting it isn't the flavor of the fat that's got them— it's the mouth-feel.

And this brings us to the final issue with deer fat: It can coat your mouth. Blame the stearic acid. You know why you love chocolate so much? One big reason is because that lovely flavor coats your palate. But when that coating is deer fat rather than chocolate, the experience is something else entirely— and not altogether pleasant. A little is fine, largely because it carries that nice venison flavor. But when I eat sausages I've made from venison alone, without other meats, they do taste fantastic, but I find that I need to drink something acidic, like red wine, to cut that very perceptible coating. Is it a deal-breaker? No. But it's something to be aware of.

So. Bottom line. If you want to eat your deer fat, I'd follow these guidelines:

- Save the fat when it's from deer that had been eating nice grasses, grains, or acorns. Remove the fat from deer inhabiting sagebrush or sketchy areas.

- Toss the suet (unless you want to make waterproofing material, candles, or soap, or want to use it to feed the birds).

- Slice off any fat that was exposed to air after you've hung the carcass.

- Never use deer fat in dry-cured salami. Uncooked deer fat is nasty and chalky.

- Use deer fat sparingly in sausages and burger. A little adds a lot of flavor; a lot can give you that "coated mouth" thing.

- Eat cuts with a lot of venison fat, or burger or sausages made with venison fat, within three to six months, as the fat will eventually go rancid, even in the freezer; it's a little like salmon fat, which, when thawed, gets that nasty smell we all find so offensive.

- Venison fat crisped on a roast or steak is awesome when eaten piping hot. You're welcome.

Suet Boots

I like venison fat. A lot. But on a fat deer there is often more than even I want to use for sausages or ground meat. Don't waste the excess! An old-timer's trick is to render down the fat into suet, and use it to waterproof things, notably your hunting boots.

To render venison fat, cut it into little pieces about one inch across or smaller—the coarse die on your grinder is great for this—then put the pieces into a large, heavy pot. Cover with water and bring to a boil. Lower the heat to a simmer and cook the fat down until all the water has boiled away, which should take an hour or two, depending on how much fat you have.

When all the water has boiled away, most of the fat should have liquefied. Turn the heat down to low and keep cooking until the fat turns clear. Strain the fat through a paper towel into a wide-mouthed jar or can; I like to use a wide-mouthed pint or half-pint Mason jar. Let the fat solidify, and you now have a jar of some of the best waterproofing material there is.

What's more, legend has it that with this stuff on your boots, you won't scare deer with your scent. Whether or not this is actually true I have no idea, but I'd like to think it works.

INTERLUDE: THE WHITE COYOTE

Chest heaving, my pulse thumped in my ears as I crested the ridge. For several seconds I could do nothing but stand, hands on my thighs, breathing like a bellows. Slowly, things began to focus. I stood on a great slab of weathered granite, a chunk of mountain rock exposed to the Sierra Nevada's harsh elements for eons. Great fissures ran through it, cracks from a hundred thousand winters' worth of heaving and thawing and freezing. In front of me yawned a gigantic gap between ridges, Devil's Peak on the mountain beyond looking like a Roman nose stuck atop a forested face.

Soft rain coated the world. My breath sent out smoke signals, my lungs calling for more oxygen. The birds, of course, took no notice of me, and continued about the business of being birds. Flocks of tiny juncos flitted about like gray butterflies. Nuthatches, high in the pines, droned on and on— yank yank yank yank. Northern flickers did their best impression of hawks, while Steller's jays chattered in that scratchy, metallic voice they're so known for. Beneath it all, a low, constant roar—the sound of traffic on Interstate 80, which split the gap more than 1,500 feet below me. The twin white ribbons of roadway seemed so alien up here, an intrusion on the wild world.

This was where Joe Navari and I had decided to hunt deer.

Joe and I hunt, fish, and forage a lot together. Joe's short but powerfully built—"mountain stock" is how he puts it—with the vise-grip fingers of a professional deckhand, although he is an archaeologist by training. He has a shock of dark, curly hair, and a full beard that has a tendency to run wild across his face. In his more feral moments, Joe can bear a striking resemblance to Grog from the old comic strip B.C., but mostly he looks like Dionysus, or Pan. And like Pan, Joe is relentlessly amiable, so slow to anger that I'd hate to see what it would take to get him there.

Joe had hunted this spot before. In fact, he shot the biggest buck of his life just below where we stood, a gigantic mule deer with six tines on one side of its antlers, four on the other—a buck that would be right at home on one of those slick hunting shows. We were headed to Clark's Rock, where our host, Clark Blanchard, had shot an equally impressive muley that same year. It was Opening Day for California's dreaded D Zone, a hunting area stretching from Mount Lassen in the north to Mount Whitney in the south that happens to be one of the hardest places in America in which to kill a deer. So far, on this day, it was proving itself to be so.

Habit has a way of gripping us. We succeed at a thing, and, when called upon to do that thing again, we repeat the steps that brought us success in the past. This is why Joe and I were atop a mountain in the rain and unseasonable cold, looking for the Phantoms of the Sierra. But Joe knows full well that the deer up here cannot be patterned. This is not Midwestern farm country, and these are not whitetail deer. Food is scarce at 7,000 feet, and predators plentiful: I saw the tracks of coyotes, bobcats, and bears that day. These deer, living near the crest of the Sierra Nevada, can number fewer than ten per square mile. Compare that to the East, where deer densities of 100 per square mile are not unheard of. Here, you find a deer—any legal deer—and you shoot it. Even a young buck can be a trophy in this country.

Joe and I would have paid a fair dollar to get a chance at even a young buck at this point. We'd hunted hard since dawn, and here it was close to 5 p.m. We'd seen exactly five deer so far: A tiny buck with a fork on one antler and a spike on the other that never really gave us a shot; and a group of four as we were driving out for lunch. One of those four was a forked horn, but it never presented a shot. Our hunting companions, Oggie and Stu, who had been hunting at the base of the mountain all day, had had similar luck.

Now, Clark, Joe, and I had climbed the mountain again, to see if we might get lucky that evening. The hunt had started well. Just as we neared the top of the ridge, Joe and Clark spotted two adult deer just ahead of us; we had no idea whether they were bucks or does. The deer had heard us coming and sauntered through a grove of Jeffrey pines and down the side of the ridge, out of sight. Joe decided to track them and went off down to the next bench below us. Clark went up to his rock to see if he could spot something. I decided to creep around this mountaintop, hoping to either spot a buck before the buck saw me, or, more likely, to bother the deer just enough so that he'd get up and walk a few paces to see what I was.

Creeping about in the rain is a helluva lot easier than the hunting I'd done earlier this season in the dry forests of California's Coastal Range. Yet it still wasn't a walk on pillows. Sierra winters are legendary, and we were not far from where the Donner Party ended up munching on each other back in 1847. Trees that survive grow arthritic, stunted, and wind-chiseled. For many trees, winter is dying time. Their skeletons litter the ground, some as wide as I am tall, others just bunches of kindling, ready to snap when found by a misplaced foot fall. Someone once said that when a leaf falls in a forest, the bear smells it, the eagle sees it, and the deer hears it. Every time I took a wrong step and heard that crunch, I heard my chances of seeing a buck diminish.

Finally, I found a spot to wait out the dusk. I sat underneath a red pine with an open view of a brush-choked ravine before me. Spruces and pines dotted the area, but it was largely open. Perhaps an avalanche had cleared it some years before. We'd checked this spot earlier in the day, and saw deer trails latticed through the manzanita and buckbrush. Joe said he'd seen the telltale oval of flattened grass—deer beds—there the year before. Seemed as likely a spot for a buck as any. So I sat.

Always the roar of the Interstate. Its omnipresence offered protection to us all, hunter and hunted alike. It muffled some of my missteps and certainly prevented my imperfect ears from hearing any deer I'd failed to spot earlier that day. But now, sitting still, I began to hear, actually hear, for the first time. The roar faded and the birdsong returned. I could finally hear the subtle chipping of the juncos. What did they say to each other? I realized that a particular snapping sound we'd heard all day was not in fact an animal—it was the sound of pine cones hitting the forest floor. I learned that pine squirrels make a certain set of noises that are different from the frenetic rustlings of the smaller lodgepole chipmunks.

And then I heard something else entirely. Not a pine cone. Not a rodent, not Joe or Clark or any other human being. I heard the sound of an animal walking up the draw towards me. I adjusted my grip on my Remington 700, my old Dodge Dart of a rifle that suits me just fine. If this creature should be a legal buck, and should it make a mistake and show itself, I was confident I could make this shot.

A glimpse of white. A deer? No, a fox. No. Too large, ears too long. Coyote. Then it walked into the open, ambling as carefree as you might be walking down a city street looking for an ice cream shop. He wasn't an icy white like an Arctic fox or an albino, more ivory-silver-gray. I'd never seen a white coyote before. Shooting it was out of the question, even though it would have been legal and this coyote was well within range. It seemed wrong.

About fifty yards away the coyote stopped. Maybe he saw my blaze orange hat. Maybe he caught my wind. Regardless, he (she?) looked right at me and cocked his head. Silently, I wondered how he was doing, where he was going. He must have wondered the same. We stood there, two fellow predators, for a long moment. Then he ambled along on his way. I watched him go.

The sun fell soon after. No deer appeared. But sitting there, absorbing the wild world for a few hours, reminded me that deer hunting is not just about putting meat in the freezer, and it's certainly not about the size of the buck's antlers. It's about shedding your synthetic self just long enough to see the world as the deer, and the coyote, and the pine squirrel, and the jay see it. To be accepted back into the company of your fellow animals, to take your role as one among equals. If only for a while. Killing a buck may be the goal of deer hunting, but it's not the point.

PART TWO

DEER TO TABLE

The first thing you need to know when you have some venison to cook is that *the whole world cooks it*. That means that you can use venison as a substitute for beef, lamb, or goat in pretty much any recipe. In fact, many of the most common meat-based preparations, including curries, stir-fry, soups, stews, braises, meat pies, pasta sauces, and Mexican moles and salsas, originated with venison of some sort, and only later evolved to include domesticated meat. No matter where you live on this planet, at least one thing binds us all: a storied tradition of hunting and eating venison.

MARINADES, STOCKS, AND BROTH

MARINADES: WHY, HOW, AND WHEN

"What marinade do you use?" is perhaps the most common question I get when people ask me about cooking venison. Truth is, I don't always use a marinade—a really fine piece of backstrap needs little more than fire, salt, and maybe some black pepper. But marinades most definitely have a place in venison cookery. You'll just want to develop a good sense of when it's better to break out your favorite marinade, and when it's better just to make it a sauce you serve at the end.

WHY MARINATE?

Marinades are acid-based (or occasionally enzyme-based) liquids or loose pastes that are used to infuse meat (or veggies) with flavor, while at the same time tenderizing them. At least that's the theory.

Bathing venison, or any other meat, in an acidic sauce (or with certain fruit juices like those from papaya or pineapple) will indeed break down some of the muscle tissue on the outer surface of the meat. The acid or fruit enzymes denature the proteins (essentially modifying their molecular structure), making them actually a bit mushy, but which

we register as tenderness when we eat it. What's more, you should know that marinades cannot penetrate meats the same way that salt-based brines do. According to most food scientists, a marinade penetrates a piece of meat no deeper than an eighth of an inch, even after several days.

The bottom line: Not only don't acidic marinades truly tenderize meat, those with pineapple or papaya juices actually make the meat mushy. I can hear you saying, "But when I marinate venison roasts, they are absolutely more tender than when I don't!" And you are right—but not for the reason you may think.

According to the great French food scientist Hervé This, long marinades do have an effect: "The meat *is* more tender," This told the Washington Post. "But it is not the marinade that makes it tender: It is time. If you use an acidic marinade, it will protect the surface from spoilage while the rest of the meat matures. And you know when meat matures, it becomes tender." This is the secret behind the long marinades in German sauerbraten, which can marinate for a week in the fridge.

And marinades *do* impart flavor onto the meat's surface. Even a few minutes' worth of marinating time will give you some added flavor in the finished dish because the flavorful liquid soaks into any crevices and cuts in a piece of meat.

Most importantly, marinating meat in an acidic sauce for at least forty minutes has been shown by the American Cancer Society to reduce by up to 90 percent the amount of cancer-causing heterocyclic amines, chemical compounds created when meat is cooked by a direct, open flame, for example, by grilling. This means that a marinade not only improves flavor, but can also make that char-grilled piece of venison healthier.

Which cuts?

Because marinades can only penetrate a few millimeters into a piece of meat (at best), you'll want to use cuts of venison that aren't too thick. This means backstrap medallions from large deer, elk, or moose, all leg steaks, flank steak, cubes for kebabs, and so on.

Or, go the sauerbraten route and marinate a large roast for a week or more. Just remember that the acid in the marinade (don't do this with the enzyme-based marinades!), usually red wine, is just there to protect the meat from spoilage, not actually to tenderize it. It's the wet-aging of the meat for a week that does the trick.

One thing a marinade will *not* do? Tenderize silverskin and connective tissue. You absolutely must trim all this off before marinating, because not only will it not tenderize, the silverskin will actually block the penetration of a marinade.

HOW TO MARINATE

You will want to marinate your venison in a sealable plastic bag, or in a covered, non-reactive container such as glass, stainless steel, enamel, or plastic; aluminum reacts to acidic ingredients and can produce off flavors. Do this in the fridge to slow the growth of any bacteria.

Here's a tip: If you like stir-fries and fajitas, marinate the venison slices before you stir-fry them. You'll get more flavor that way.

When you're ready to cook, take the meat out of the marinade and pat the meat dry with paper towels. Wet meat won't brown.

If you want to use your marinade as a sauce, you can do one of two things: Boil your marinade for five minutes before using it; or, if boiling would destroy your marinade (as it would in chimichurri, which relies on raw, fresh herbs), make more than you need, and use the extra for the sauce. Do not just reuse the marinade in which you soaked the raw venison—there is a chance, albeit small, that you might get food poisoning.

Deer Camp Essentials: When Your Table is under the Stars

I am often asked for recipes that can be done in a rough kitchen, either in the field or at deer camp. My advice is always the same: So long as you have a few staples on hand, you can always make a great meal after a long day in the field. Here's what I'd want to see in the cupboards of every deer camp:

- **Salt and pepper** Sounds like a no-brainer, but you'd be surprised how many times I've seen people forget these most basic ingredients. And while you're at it, get kosher salt and one of those built-in pepper grinders in the supermarket spice rack so you can get freshly ground pepper easily.

- **Onions and garlic** These staples keep for a long time in the pantry, and form the basis for almost every recipe in this book.

- **Stocks** Yes, homemade stock is better, and you can make shelf-stable stock if you pressure-can it (page 48). But having a few boxes of store-bought chicken and beef broth around will greatly improve your camp cooking.

- **Wine, port, and brandy** For obvious reasons, but also to add flavor to sauces and stews.

- **Jelly, honey, syrup, or molasses** Venison often benefits from some sweetness.

- **A few packages of dried chiles and dried mushrooms** Every decent supermarket sells them, they are lightweight, and last for years. A few in a stew make everything better.

- **Vinegar** Any kind but distilled. A splash brightens any dish.

Backcountry Essentials

Going even farther into the field? Cooking from an open fire instead of a cabin? Here's a stripped-down set of essentials to tuck into your pack. With the exception of the brandy in a flask, everything can be carried in resealable plastic baggies.

- **Salt and pepper** Even a little salt makes food taste so much better in the wild places of this world. My advice? Nice salt, like good sea salt or smoked salt. It will make things all the more wonderful when all around it is cold or dreary.

- **Garlic powder** I normally don't love this stuff, but it has a lot of flavor.

- **Bouillon cubes** Not great, and really salty, but compact and easy to carry.

- **Brandy in a flask** It gets cold out there!

- **A bit of white or brown sugar** You'll be craving sweetness after a few days in the open.

- **Dried chiles and dried mushrooms** See Deer Camp Essentials, left. They are lightweight flavor bombs.

- **A bit of citric acid powder** I know, this may sound odd. But you'll want something acidic to brighten the flavors of your camp food, and this stuff will do it. Lighter than vinegar and less perishable than citrus, you can find this stuff sold as "fruit fresh" in the canning section of your local supermarket.

"Sometimes dreams are wiser than waking."

—BLACK ELK, LAKOTA HOLY MAN

Beer and Wine with Venison

Talking about pairing wines with food always seems to conjure up images of snooty sommeliers in tuxedos telling me what I can and cannot drink with my dinner. Too often there's a holier-than-thou element to discussions of wine pairings—and even beer pairings—when you broach the topic with food professionals. It need not be so.

Remember, the Prime Directive in all pairings is to *drink what you like*. Period. End of story. If you love drinking Pabst with your backstrap, go for it. Don't let anyone tell you otherwise. That said, certain pairings really can make both the food and the drink taste better.

Part of this pairing stuff is voodoo, admittedly, but there is some method to the madness of matching wine and beer with food. You all know the simplest one: red wines with red meat, white wines with white meat, right? Well, usually, but not always. Fried food with Champagne is a great example: They work great together. Another good rule is the hotter the weather, the lighter the beer. Budweiser or Labatt's at a backyard barbecue? Yes, please. But I'd rather have something more substantial in winter while eating a venison carbonnade.

Next thing to remember: There is no one true venison wine or beer. Yes, most wine drinkers agree that cabernet sauvignon, Italian Barolos or Barbarescos, Spanish Rioja, or French Cotes du Rhône blends are the best overall wines to drink with venison. But that doesn't mean an easier-drinking zinfandel won't be good—if, say, you're barbecuing venison in summertime.

I often hear skepticism when I talk about beer pairings, but beers are in many ways far more varied than wines. After all, even professionals confuse wine varieties with some frequency. But I can pretty much guarantee that you'll never confuse an imperial pale ale with a Scottish ale. As much as I love the good ole' American and Canadian macro-brews we've been drinking for decades, there are now legions of fantastic local beers to be had in every corner of the country, and more and more people are drinking beer with their meals in both the United States and Canada. Other than the tip about lighter beers for hot weather, here are a few others:

- Malty beers (German bocks, Scottish ales, brown ales, porters, and stouts) with heavier dishes, like stews and roasts. Always great in cold weather.

- Hoppy beers (IPAs, pale ales) with spicy foods like venison curry or fried rice.

- More carbonation with fattier foods; for example, pilsner or lager with chicken-fried venison. These are your hot weather beers. German weiss beer (white wheat beer) is great here, too.

- If I could choose just one style of beer for venison, however, it would be a pale ale. You want a bit of hoppy bitterness to balance the richness of the meat, but not so much that it blows it away like a serious IPA would.

There *are* a few beer styles you might not want to bring to the dinner table. For example, barley wines and imperial stouts, which are too strong and syrupy for food; most double or triple IPAs, unless you are a major hop-head and the food is *really* spicy; weird fruit beers, such as lambic, which are just hard to match with any food.

Wines and venison are a natural match. Here are a few good guidelines:

- Go for a full-bodied red, such as cabernet sauvignon, from Bordeaux or California, a good French Cotes du Rhône, an Italian Barolo or Barbaresco, or a Spanish Rioja.

- If you want to drink zinfandel with your venison, be sure it is a drier style, such as one from Italy, or California's Alexander Valley or Amador County. Avoid most Lodi zins, as they tend to be syrupy.

- In summer, a dry rosé is a good idea, as are some whites: Try a viognier or a roussanne from California, especially with grilled venison or tacos.

- In winter, go even darker. I like mourvèdre or a petit verdot with heavy braises and stews. But my all-time go-to wine for venison is a French Châteauneuf-du-Pape. There's just something about it that works with lots of different dishes.

STOCK, BROTH, AND GLACE DE VIANDE

Knowing how to make stocks and broths, or, if you are adventurous, French *glace de viande*, are important skills every deer hunter should have. It's one of the easiest ways to get more out of your animals, and is a great way to make use of the bones and trim left over after butchering. Beyond utility, the satisfaction of making something you simply cannot buy anywhere, perfectly suited to your own tastes, is worth every moment of the time it takes to prepare it. A house where broth simmers on the stove is a happy one. There are several ways to go about making your own stocks and broths, and I'll walk you through them here.

Most cookbooks put discussions of stock and broth at the end; I think this is in error. After all, you make stocks most often when you butcher your own animals—otherwise you'd need to freeze bulky bones, which can take up a lot of space. Not that you can't, but I find myself making big batches of stock when I've finished the fine work of butchering and am letting the meat rest in the fridge for a few days.

Another reason to put these recipes at the front of the book is because they are used in so many of the recipes that follow. Venison broth (a more fully flavored version of venison stock), and the highly concentrated venison *glace de viande* (which is just a heavily reduced stock with added gelatin), will come in handy when you begin to explore the recipes themselves.

That said, you can substitute beef broth or veal stock—even chicken stock in some cases—for homemade venison stock. But there is something special about using homemade broths that will both elevate your cooking, and give you the satisfaction of knowing that you made use of one more bit of the animal you brought home.

Any bones will work for stock, although I always toss the part of the animal that's been destroyed by

More than Just Bones

Great broth is made with meat. But don't think for a second that cooks are tossing backstrap into the pot. What they are doing is collecting trim and odd bits like silverskin, sinewy pieces that are hard to deal with, and in some cases shanks, which are loaded with connective tissue, and using these to enrich their broths. Me? I especially love to add those strips of meat we all cut out between the ribs. It's good meat, with a little connective tissue to add body. I also keep a pile of trim that's too gnarly for the grinder—that, too, goes into the stockpot.

the bullet, especially if I've been shooting with lead rather than copper. Another caveat is to avoid the backbone, neck, and skull of any animal that had lived in an area with chronic wasting disease (see page 16).

The best stock, hands down, is stock that's been made fresh. The quality of freshly made stock is an order of magnitude better than that of frozen stock, although frozen is still good. One step below fresh stock is pressure-canned stock (page 48), which isn't as good as fresh or frozen, but which has the significant benefit of being shelf stable and convenient. I use all three depending on the circumstance.

Fresh broth is best for fancy dinners where broth will serve as the star of a dish, say with venison tortellini swimming in your luxurious homemade broth. It will also make a spectacular venison risotto. Frozen broth will be perfectly good for these dishes, and it's also excellent for soups with other things in it, like the Scotch Broth on page 159. Pressure-canned is best for sauces, braising liquid, and thick stews where there are other big flavors, like the Hungarian Pörkölt on page 164.

A STOCK PRIMER

As well as being a core skill of any good cook, making stock is a labor of love I embrace wholly. Some cooks make stock without vegetables, but I rarely do that. Vegetables add so much to the final flavor of a stock, and can transform it from an additive into a full-fledged broth suitable for drinking on cold days. Incidentally, while I use stock and broth interchangeably, technically a stock is a base, and a broth something you can serve on its own; generally, a broth is more flavorful and better seasoned than a stock.

My essential stock vegetables: onions or leeks, carrots, celery, bay leaves, and parsley. I will add other herbs as appropriate, most often rosemary and thyme. With venison, I add rosemary and juniper berries. Secret weapon for venison stock: parsnips, whose sweetness brings so much to the party.

The first step in making broth is roasting the bones. I like darker, fuller stocks, and this is what does it. The Vietnamese don't roast their bones when making broth for pho, possibly the world's most perfect soup (Vietnamese Pho, page 162), and I occasionally will make stock without roasting, too. But not often. So I roast my deer bones at 400°F for an hour or so, until they are well browned and yummy looking.

Next, cram your bones into the stockpot and cover with cold water. Cold water to start, and slow heating, will help extract the maximum amount of collagen; it is collagen from the joints, cartilage, and skin that builds body in your stock by making it thicker than water. Want to make an even better broth? Go buy a pig's or calf's foot from your local butcher or Asian or Latin market and add it—these cuts have lots of collagen, and are a time-honored secret to great broth.

Bring the stock to a boil (gradually!) and skim off any scum that floats to the surface. After the surface is clear, reduce the heat to a bare simmer. You want it to shimmy, not roil, not even bubble too much (some cooks call this "moving water"). A boiled stock will turn cloudy, and the higher temps can extract bitter flavors from the bones. Let the stock shimmy gently for several hours. How long? From four hours minimum to overnight.

After the meat has infused the water to your liking, add your veggies, roughly chopped. You don't want to use anything spoiled or rotten, but the ends of things like carrots or parsnips make great stock, as do onion skins, which will help turn the broth a lovely brown. Stir in your vegetables and let the broth simmer for another ninety minutes, or up to two hours (but no more; after this point, those bright flavors you added will muddle and become murky).

Now strain everything out. Set a paper towel into a fine mesh sieve. Ladle your venison stock through this into a large bowl or plastic bin. Is all of this fuss really necessary? Yes. Unless you want a mucky, cloudy stock. And it is more than aesthetics: The impurities are just that—impure—and they add off-flavors to your otherwise wonderful brew.

Once your stock is strained, clean the stockpot, or pour the strained liquid into another one. Now you can reduce it if you want to. This is also the time to salt the stock. Stock gets saltier the longer you cook it down because salt does not evaporate with the water. So add the salt close to the end, tasting as you go, and you will know what you're getting. If you're making demi-glace, don't salt at all.

All of this takes time, but not a lot of it is active—and it will make your house smell wonderful. The process is as comforting to me as the reward.

BASIC VENISON BROTH

Makes about a gallon | **Prep Time: 10 minutes** | **Cook Time: At least 6 hours**

This is my go-to venison broth that can stand alone as a broth for pasta or, if you clarify it later, as a consommé. It's stronger in flavor than store-bought stock, so if you use it as a base for stews or soups, remember that, and label your jars accordingly. Making a good stock or broth is an all-day affair. Don't take shortcuts, or your broth will suffer. Relax and let things happen as they will.

4 pounds venison bones (or antelope, moose, or elk bones)

4 tablespoons olive oil

Salt

1 pig's foot (optional)

1 tablespoon crushed juniper berries

2 tablespoons fresh rosemary, or 1 large sprig

1 tablespoon black pepper, cracked or coarsely ground

1 tablespoon dried thyme, or several sprigs of fresh

4 bay leaves

1 large onion, chopped

2 large carrots, chopped

2 celery sticks, chopped

About 1½ cups chopped parsley

Coat the bones with olive oil and salt them well, then roast in a 400°F oven until brown, about an hour. If you can stand it, keep some meat on the bones—shanks are ideal for this. The extra meat will make a better broth. Put the bones in a large stockpot. If you want, saw the bones into large pieces with a hacksaw; this lets you fit more bones into the pot—again, yielding a richer broth. Cover with cold water by an inch or two, add the optional pig's foot, and bring to a simmer over medium-high heat.

While the water is heating up, add more water to the roasting pan and let it sit for a few minutes to loosen up the browned bits on the bottom. Use a wooden spoon to scrape up those bits and pour it all into the stockpot.

Skim the froth that forms on the surface and simmer very gently for at least 4 hours; I let it go overnight on the lowest possible heat. You want the broth to steam and burble a little, not roil.

Add the remaining ingredients and simmer for another 90 minutes.

Using tongs, grab out all the bones and large bits and discard. Set a paper towel in a fine-mesh sieve that is itself set over another large pot or plastic bin. Ladle the venison broth through the paper towel-lined sieve. Discard the dregs in the broth pot, which will be loaded with sediment and other bits.

Add salt to the clarified broth to taste and pour into quart jars and freeze (or pressure can; see page 48). If you freeze, leave at least 1½ inches of space at the top of the jar or the jars will crack when the broth freezes because the stock will expand. Use within a year.

DARK VENISON BROTH

Makes about a gallon | **Prep Time: 10 minutes** | **Cook Time: At least 6 hours**

This is a darker, richer venison broth that is a bit burlier that the previous recipe. It also includes some extra meat for added heft.

4 pounds venison bones (or antelope, moose, or elk bones)

1 pound chopped random venison meaty bits, or ground with no fat

7 tablespoons olive oil, divided

Salt

1 pig's foot (optional)

1 large onion, chopped

2 large carrots, chopped

1 parsnip, chopped

2 celery sticks, chopped

4 tablespoons tomato paste

Skins from the onion

1 tablespoon crushed juniper berries

2 tablespoons fresh rosemary, or 1 large sprig

1 tablespoon black pepper, cracked or coarsely ground

1 tablespoon dried thyme, or several sprigs of fresh

4 bay leaves

2 star anise pods (optional)

About 1½ cups chopped parsley

Coat the bones and meat with 4 tablespoons of the olive oil and salt well, then roast in a 400°F oven until brown, about an hour. Put the bones and meat in a large stockpot. If you want, saw the bones into large pieces with a hacksaw; this lets you fit more bones into the pot—again, making a richer broth. Cover with water, add the pig's foot and bring to a simmer over medium-high heat.

While the water is heating up, add more water to the roasting pan and let it sit for a few minutes to loosen up the browned bits on the bottom. Use a wooden spoon to scrape up those bits and pour it all into the stockpot.

Skim the froth that forms on the surface and simmer very gently for at least 4 hours; I let it go overnight on the lowest possible heat. You want the broth to steam and burble a little, not roil.

When you are almost ready to add the remaining ingredients, heat the rest of the olive oil in a large sauté pan and brown the vegetables over medium-high heat. Stir occasionally. This should take a solid 10 to 15 minutes. Stir in the tomato paste, and let this cook another 4 or 5 minutes. Add it all to the stockpot and ladle some of the broth into the sauté pan to get every last bit of goodness out of it. Return that bit to the pot.

Add the remaining ingredients to the stockpot and simmer for another 90 minutes.

Using tongs, grab out all the bones and large bits and discard. Set a paper towel in a fine-mesh sieve that is itself set over another large pot. Ladle the venison broth through the paper towel-lined sieve. Discard the dregs in the broth pot, which will be loaded with sediment and other bits.

Add salt to the clarified broth to taste. Pour into quart jars and freeze (or pressure can, see page 48). If you freeze, leave at least 1½ inches of space at the top of the jar or the jars will crack when the broth freezes and expands. Use within a year.

VENISON GLACE DE VIANDE

Makes 6 half-pints | Prep Time: 10 minutes | Cook Time: Overnight

Glace de viande, **essentially meat jelly, is a secret ingredient of many professional chefs. It's cooked-down stock that has some added source of gelatin in it. A spoonful here and there makes everything better.** *Glace* **(pronounced glah-ss) freezes really well, too.**

It takes a long time to make, so make a big batch and freeze it for the rest of the year.

4 pounds venison bones (or antelope, moose, or elk bones)

4 tablespoons olive oil

Salt

1 or 2 pig's feet or 1 calf's foot

1 tablespoon crushed juniper berries

2 tablespoons fresh rosemary, or 1 large sprig

1 tablespoon black pepper, cracked or coarsely ground

1 tablespoon dried thyme, or several sprigs of fresh

4 bay leaves

1 large onion, chopped

2 large carrots, chopped

2 celery sticks, chopped

About 1½ cups chopped parsley

Coat the bones with olive oil and salt well, then roast in a 400°F oven until brown, about an hour. If you can stand it, keep some meat on the bones—shanks are ideal for this. It will make a better broth. Put the bones in a large stockpot. If you want, saw the bones into large pieces with a hacksaw; this lets you fit more bones into the pot—again, making a richer broth. Add the pig's feet or calf's foot. Cover with cold water and bring to a simmer over medium-high heat.

While the water is heating up, add more water to the roasting pan and let it sit for a few minutes to loosen up the browned bits on the bottom. Use a wooden spoon to scrape up those bits and pour it all into the stockpot.

Skim the froth that forms on the surface and simmer very gently for at least 4 hours; I let it go 8 hours. You want the broth to steam and burble a little, not roil.

Add the remaining ingredients and simmer for another 90 minutes.

Using tongs, grab out all the bones and large bits and discard. Set a paper towel in a fine-mesh sieve that is itself set over another large pot. Ladle the venison broth through the paper towel-lined sieve. Discard the dregs in the broth pot, which will be loaded with sediment and other bits.

Clean the stockpot and return the clarified broth to it, then set it over very low heat on a weak burner. Put the pot a little off-center to the burner, which sets up a circulation pattern that concentrates all the impurities on one side of the pot. This makes them easier to skim off. Let the stock reduce by half or more, very

(continued)

slowly, skimming the surface from time to time. By the time I am at this point, it's usually nighttime, so I let it go overnight.

The next morning, pour the reduced stock through the same set up you used before—the strainer with the paper towel in it—into a container. Now's the time to pour it into small glass jars, leaving about ½ inch headspace or so (*glace* doesn't expand as much as stock). Set the jars in the fridge to cool for a day.

The next day, if the stock has set up and become gelatin, label the jars and put in the freezer. They'll keep in the fridge for about 10 days, and more than a year in the freezer.

NOTE: If your *glace* has not set up into a gel, reheat it and add more gelling agents: pig's feet, calves' feet, chicken feet, or even a tablespoon or two of Knox gelatin.

"Life in the open is one of my finest rewards. I enjoy and become completely immersed in the high challenge and increased opportunity to become for a time a part of nature. Deer hunting is a classical exercise in freedom. It is a return to fundamentals that I instinctively feel are basic and right."

—FRED BEAR, ONE OF THE GREATEST ARCHERS OF ALL TIME

PRIMAL CUTS

There is something, well, primal, about cooking whole cuts of an animal. A smoky hind leg of venison, a whole backstrap char-grilled, a slow-braised shoulder, or even a whole deer roasting in front of a bed of coals made from the forest where it once lived—all evoke our past the way a burger or a simple venison steak cannot. Big cuts are special and should be reserved for family or parties, and most are best cooked with real fire. These are the cuts of our ancient heritage and should be celebrated.

Primal cuts are the larger hunks of an animal, normally the legs or neck, but also whole backstraps, which, when they're still on the spine, are called saddles. If you have especially small deer, you could even do a baron, which is the saddle plus both hind legs, still attached to the pelvis. I don't work with barons of venison, so you are on your own there. Look into 18th and 19th century cookbooks for more insight.

I do deal with whole legs and necks, however, as well as long lengths of boneless backstrap. I find that these are manageable in most home kitchens, and in some cases produce a better end result than if you'd cut them into smaller pieces. Besides, they're great for holidays and parties.

Cooking large pieces of meat does require some special consideration. When you are butchering, keep in mind how large your oven is, or your smoker, or wherever you think you might cook your big bits. For example, when I want to cut a whole shoulder of venison to braise or barbecue, I make sure it will fit into my largest roasting pan or my smoker. Otherwise, months down the road, when you finally want to cook the thing, you will be sad.

I generally find that primal cuts are best cooked slowly, either with fire or in broth. Slow braises are wonderful because you get the benefit of all the connective tissue enriching the broth, which you would not get with a regular roast. Fire, especially a smoky fire, is even better. The ultimate image of venison, to my mind, is a hind leg studded with garlic and basted with butter or olive oil, hanging from a string next to an oak fire, with a frying pan set underneath to catch the drippings that will soon become gravy. Heaven.

Sadly, I don't have a fireplace in which to do this. But I do have a smoker, and hanging a leg in a smoker does come close.

THE SCIENCE OF CARRYOVER HEAT

One bit of cooking science you should know when roasting primal cuts—especially whole legs—is carryover heat. (Note that carryover isn't a factor in slow braises.)

Serious steak lovers know that for the best results, you should take the meat off the heat while it's still a little underdone. They know that as the meat rests, the internal temperature will continue to climb, and the steak continue to cook just enough to bring it to perfection when it's served. The same is true with poultry and roasts. This remnant heat is called carryover cooking, and there are a few things you need to know in order to master it.

Carryover heat is actually a redistribution of heat throughout a piece of meat. For example, while the center of a roast might be 125°F, the exterior could well be 200°F. It is this heat on the exterior that continues to cook the center; the redistribution of the heat, from the outside in, is called the carryover.

There's a bit of basic physics involved here, though fear not, no equations will be necessary. Simply put, the larger and denser the piece of meat, the greater the carryover, and the more the cooking will continue after removing the meat from the heat source. This is because larger roasts have a lower surface-area-to-volume ratio, so they retain heat better. (This same rule in animals is called Bergmann's Rule, and it's why a whitetail from Alberta will normally weigh a lot more than one from Louisiana.) Also, denser foods normally have more water content; venison happens to be denser than beef. Finally, water has a higher capacity to retain heat than fat, so there is more energy in a lean venison roast or steak to continue the cooking than there would be in a comparable piece of beef or lamb.

How to apply this?

First, you need one more bit of meat science: Meats cooked slow and low don't undergo the carryover phenomenon. Only things cooked in very hot situations do. This is why there's no carryover in barbecue. So for a roast, you will want to actually cook it slow and low first and then sear it brown. I know, this is opposite to what most cookbooks and cooking schools tell you, but they've got the science all wrong.

For starters, you will want to cook your roast at about 225°F until the center hits about 115°F, which can take a couple hours depending on the size of the roast.

You then will want to either sear it well in a very hot pan, or do this: Take the roast out and let it rest while you raise the oven temperature to 475°F or even 500°F. Once the oven hits that temperature, return the roast to the oven to brown the exterior. The advantage here is that you'll have more of a traditional roast, without having to use a second pan. The advantage of searing in the pan is that you will brown the exterior faster (and you'll have more control to prevent burnt spots), and you'll initiate carryover cooking a bit more, allowing you to bring up the interior of the roast a bit higher. Incidentally, doing the finishing sear on a really hot grill is another great option; I use this method all summer.

Regardless of how you cook your roast or steak, you can expect it to carry over at least a little heat. Bigger roasts carry over more, as do leaner roasts; fat is an insulator. So remember this: If the internal temperature of your meat is close to what you want when you eat it, say, 130°F, let it rest uncovered on a cutting board. If the temperature is cooler, say, 115°F, tent the roast with foil. Foil can add as much as 10°F to the internal temperature of the finished piece of meat compared to open resting.

How long? For primal cuts, at least ten minutes, and up to thirty minutes for very large roasts.

In any event, it's rare for the internal temperature of even a large roast to rise more than 15°F. So if you account for that, you're in good shape.

BRAISED SHOULDER OF VENISON

Serves 6 to 8 | Prep Time: 25 minutes | Cook Time: 4 hours

This is one of the few recipes in this book that requires a specific animal: You really need to do this with a young deer or antelope, or at least a small one. Older animals will work, but their shoulders tend to be very large, and they will take almost twice as long to become tender. And I can't imagine someone with a pot large enough to roast an entire elk or moose shoulder in.

You have some options for this braise. If you're in a mood for red wine, use it and a dark stock, like Dark Venison Stock (page 66) or regular beef broth. If it's one of those early spring nights when there's still a chill in the air but it's losing its grip, go with white wine and a light stock, or chicken broth.

What you drink with this depends on how you made it: If you went red, go with a red wine or a dark, malty beer. If you went white, a dry rosé, riesling, or oaked chardonnay are all good choices, as well as weiss beer or a lager.

1 bone-in deer shoulder, about 4 to 6 pounds

Olive oil

Salt

1 bottle red or white wine

1 quart stock (see above)

3 tablespoons minced rosemary

1 tablespoon minced sage

A sprig or two of fresh thyme, or
    2 teaspoons dried

2 bay leaves (optional)

A dozen crushed juniper berries (optional)

Black pepper

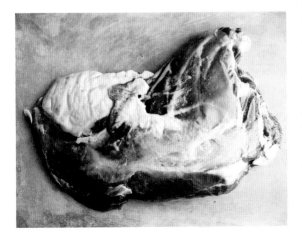

Preheat the oven to 450°F. Coat the shoulder with olive oil and salt it well. Set it inside a roasting pan and roast until it browns, about 30 to 40 minutes.

When it's nicely browned, take the pan out of the oven and set the meat aside for a moment. Drop the oven temperature to 300°F. Pour the wine into the roasting pan and use a wooden spoon to scrape up any browned bits stuck to the bottom. Add the herbs and a little salt into the liquid. Return the venison shoulder to the roasting pan. The liquid should be about halfway up the side of the shoulder. If it isn't, add the stock, and then water if you need to. Cover the roasting pan and braise in the oven for 3 hours.

Check the shoulder at 3 hours. You want it almost falling off the bone. It might need another hour or so, depending on the deer's age. When the venison is ready, remove the cover from the roasting pan and increase the heat to 425°F. Roast until a crust forms on the top of the venison, about 20 minutes or so.

Remove the roasting pan from the oven, and gently remove the meat from the pan. Set the meat aside and tent with foil. Taste the remaining braising liquid. If it is to your liking, just use that as a sauce. If it's too thin, set the pan over two burners and boil down until it tastes right. I strain the liquid to remove the herbs before serving.

To serve, lift away portions of the venison onto everyone's plate and grind some black pepper over it. Serve with lots of sauce over the meat, alongside boiled or mashed potatoes or dumplings.

POLISH POT ROAST WITH A VENISON NECK

Serves 4 to 6, depending on the size of the neck | Prep Time: Overnight for the marinade
Cook Time: 3 to 4 hours, or up to 8 hours for a slow cooker

This is my version of the good ole' pot roast that pretty much everyone ate while growing up. What makes it Polish? Only that I found a similar recipe in a book called *Polish Heritage Cookery* by Robert and Maria Strybel. I like the use of flour and paprika, and the overnight wine marinade, each of which adds a layer of flavor to the final dish.

You could, of course, use other cuts for this recipe, such as a shank or a shoulder, or even a hind leg roast. But a whole neck, boned or bone-in, is the perfect cut. The long, slow simmer melts all that connective tissue and gives you an intensely flavored, yielding piece of meat that can either be torn apart roughly or sliced thick and served. Note that although a boned-out neck will be sliceable, you won't get clean cuts unless you chill the meat overnight before slicing. Why bother with that, though? Eat it messy.

1 bottle red wine

6 to 10 allspice berries, cracked

6 to 10 black peppercorns, cracked

3 bay leaves

A 2½ to 4 pound neck roast, boned or bone-in

Salt

1 cup flour

3 tablespoons paprika

1 tablespoon cayenne (optional)

¼ cup lard, bacon fat, or cooking oil

2 onions, sliced root to tip

2 celery stalks, diced

3 carrots, cut into large chunks

2 parsnips, cut into large chunks

3 Yukon Gold potatoes, cut into chunks

1 rutabaga or 2 turnips, peeled and cut into chunks

Black pepper to taste

Sour cream, for garnish

Bring the wine, allspice, black peppercorns, and bay leaves to a boil. Turn off the heat and let the marinade cool to room temperature. When it's cool, submerge the venison neck in the marinade and keep in the fridge overnight, or up to 4 days.

Mix the flour, paprika, and cayenne (if using) in a large bowl or shallow container large enough to hold the neck roast. Pat the meat dry with paper towels and salt it well. Coat it in the flour-paprika mixture. Heat the lard in a large Dutch oven or other heavy, lidded pot, and brown the meat. With a typical neck roast you will need to cut it into two pieces to get it to fit the pot. Brown one piece and then remove while you brown the other. If you are using a bone-in neck, just turn the meat to brown all sides. When the meat has browned, remove it from the pot and set aside for a moment.

Preheat the oven to 325°F. Add the sliced onions to the pot and brown them well, stirring occasionally. This should take about 8 minutes. Add 2 cups of the marinade and bring it to a boil. Add the venison back to the pot, along with 2 cups of water. Bring to a simmer, cover the pot, and cook in the oven for 1½ hours.

After 1½ hours have elapsed, add the root vegetables and celery and continue to cook for another 1½ hours, or until the meat is falling apart and the root vegetables are tender.

Remove the meat and set on a cutting board. Slice roughly, or pull the meat off the bones. Taste the sauce, and add salt if it needs it. Add black pepper to taste, and serve with the meat and vegetables, with a dollop of sour cream alongside.

WHOLE GRILLED BACKSTRAP

Serves 4 | **Prep Time: 30 minutes** | **Cook Time: 20 minutes**

Grilling meat is one of the basic skills every cook needs to have. This is especially true with venison, which is so lean that you have very little leeway between perfect and overdone—and overcooked venison is gray, dry, and livery. You can grill any venison steak, but whole backstrap or loin is a better cut for fast grilling. With a whole loin, you grill the sides and then, when you cut into it, you get to see that pink perfection.

Start with a piece of backstrap that's at least ten inches long, which is usually about 1 pound. Depending on how wide it is, this will feed two to four people. Note that this works best with small or medium-sized deer.

I like to serve the venison with a side salad like potato, macaroni, or bean salad, plus maybe some tomatoes and basil, corn on the cob, dinner rolls—you get the idea. Nothing overly fancy.

---

1 to 1½ pound piece of venison loin, or elk/moose tenderloin

Olive oil

Salt

YOUR FAVORITE BBQ SAUCE, OR THE FOLLOWING MIXTURE:

Zest and juice of 4 lemons or limes

1 tablespoon ground black pepper

¼ cup minced parsley or cilantro

Coat the venison backstrap in oil and salt well. Set aside for 30 minutes at room temperature.

Get your grill hot, clean the grates, and lay the venison on the grill, fat cap facing down if you've left the fat on your deer. Keep the grill cover open. Let this cook for 5 to 8 minutes without moving, depending on how hot your grill is and how thick your venison loin is. You want a good sear, with good grill marks, on that side of the meat. If you left the fat cap on, keep an eye out for flare-ups; douse flare-ups with a spray bottle of water.

Flip the venison and repeat on the other side. Paint the side you just seared with BBQ sauce, if using. (Note: If you're going with the citrus-pepper-herb combo, wait until the end to use it.)

Do the finger test to check for doneness (see page 79). If the venison needs more time, turn it to the sides that have not had direct exposure to the grill and cook for 2 or 3 more minutes, checking all the way. Paint those sides with BBQ sauce, too.

When the meat has been cooked to your liking, take it off the fire and let it rest for 10 minutes, fat cap facing up if there is one. (If the meat's still a little underdone, tent it loosely with foil.) If you're using the citrus mixture instead of BBQ sauce, roll the meat in the sauce before it rests.

To serve, slice into medallions and serve with BBQ sauce or the extra citrus sauce on the side.

ROAST LEG OF VENISON WITH BAVARIAN DUMPLINGS

Serves 4 to 8, depending on the size of the roast
Prep Time: 45 minutes, mostly to let the meat come to room temperature
Cook Time: 90 minutes, again, depending on the size of the roast.

A whole roast leg of venison is something to behold. It's a perfect holiday roast or celebration dinner. The goal here is to roast the whole leg just to the point where the meat nearest the bone is medium-rare. This isn't hard, but you need to keep your wits about you. Be sure to read my notes on carryover heat (see page 70), and follow the roasting directions below closely.

I typically make this dish with a young deer or antelope, preferably a doe or yearling. This recipe will work with larger, older animals, but the connective tissue that separates the various muscles in the leg can be pretty tough—and this recipe isn't going to melt them.

A note on the oil: I absolutely love the flavor that roasted squash seed oil brings to venison. You can find it in some stores, but your best bet is to buy squash seed oil online. But any good oil will work: good olive oil, walnut oil, even sesame oil. The point is to use something that adds flavor to the roast.

Serve this with classic trimmings: cranberry sauce, something green, and a comforting starch. Mashed, baked, or roasted potatoes are traditional, but I like German dumplings. Oh, and stale bread works great with these dumplings, if you have some lying around.

And should you have leftovers, sliced roast venison is awesome on rye bread sandwiches with some mustard and cheese.

VENISON ROAST

1 hind leg of venison, shank removed

Salt

6 to 8 garlic cloves, peeled and cut into thick slivers

¼ cup squash seed oil or other flavorful oil

About 1 cup of red wine, stock or water

2 tablespoons minced sage

2 tablespoons freshly ground black pepper

BAVARIAN BREAD DUMPLINGS

8 to 10 slices of bread, crusts removed (about 10 ounces)

1 teaspoon salt

1¼ cups tepid milk

3 slices bacon

¼ cup minced onion or shallot

1 tablespoon minced parsley

1 teaspoon dried marjoram

2 eggs, lightly beaten

(continued)

Take the venison leg out of the fridge and salt it well. Let it sit on a cutting board for 30 minutes before proceeding. After 30 minutes have elapsed, preheat the oven to 325°F. Take a sharp knife with a narrow point and jab holes all over the leg of venison, tucking a sliver of garlic into each hole. You can use more or less garlic, depending on your taste.

Pat the venison dry, then massage the oil all over it. Now sprinkle the sage all over the meat, making sure it gets into any nooks and crannies. Set the leg of venison on a rack in a roasting pan and pour enough wine, stock, or water into the bottom of the roasting pan to just moisten the bottom—don't totally cover the bottom or the meat will steam.

Put the venison into the oven and roast until the center of the meat reaches the temperature you want: If you pull the venison at about 110°F, it will be rare once you've seared the outside and it has rested. I pull mine at 120°F, which is closer to medium. Do not let the venison cook past 140°F under any circumstances or it will get tough and gray. How long will this take? At least 25 minutes, and up to 90 minutes, depending on the size of the leg. Check the temperature after 25 minutes, then every 10 minutes after that. A general rule is a little more than 20 minutes per pound at 325°F.

Remove the venison from the oven, and increase the temperature to 450°F. Add a little more wine to the bottom of the pan if it's dry; this will limit the amount of smoke you produce while you're searing the outside of the meat. Drizzle a little more oil over the top of the roast.

When the oven temperature reaches 450°F, set the venison back into the oven and roast until it's nicely browned, about 10 to 20 minutes. Move the meat to a cutting board. If the internal temperature is more than 10 degrees off your target, tent the roast loosely with foil. If not, let it rest uncovered. Don't carve it for at least 10 minutes; I wait a full 20 minutes. Carve and serve.

DUMPLINGS

After you take the venison out of the fridge, break up or chop the stale bread and put it into a bowl. Pour the lukewarm milk over the bread and let it stand while you're getting the venison ready to roast. If it looks like there isn't enough milk, add a little water.

Fry the bacon in a small skillet and remove when crispy. Chop it fine. Sauté the onion in the bacon fat until it's nice and brown. Mix the bacon and onion in a small bowl and allow to cool. Once it's cool, mix in the parsley and marjoram.

When the venison goes into the oven, set a large pot of salted water on the stove to boil. Once it boils, drop the heat to a simmer.

If there is any milk still in the bread bowl, pour it off. Mix the bacon, onions, parsley, and marjoram with the bread. Make sure to break up any large pieces. Wait until the venison is resting to cook the dumplings.

When it's time, add the beaten eggs and mix well to combine. If the batter is too wet to form dumplings, add breadcrumbs a tablespoon at a time until you can roll the batter into a ball with your hands. Make sure your hands are wet when you do this or the batter will stick all over them.

Gently lower each dumpling into the simmering water. Cover the pot. Once they float back to the surface, let them cook for another minute or two, then remove with a slotted spoon. Serve hot with the venison.

Smoke-Roasting a Leg of Venison

Technically, you can't roast meats in an oven—that's baking them. Real roasting requires fire and smoke. While few of us have that ideal fireplace-roasting setup that I mentioned earlier (see page 69), many of us do have smokers. And while most smoking is done at a very low temperature, you can jack up the heat in a smoker to roast meats. Even 225°F will do a good job, but in fire-stoked smokers you can actually get to a proper roasting temperature of 350°F.

You can get to a perfect fire-fueled roast in three ways:

- Roast the leg of venison entirely at 350°F. This works fine, but you don't get that gorgeous crust you'd get from the higher heat in the oven recipe above.

- Cook in the smoker until you get close to your target temperature, then finish the leg in the oven at 450°F, or on the grill until you get that nice crust.

- Stoke the fires of your smoker to get the smoking chamber to 400°F or better, roast the leg in there for 20 minutes, then open the chamber doors to drop the temperature to 300°F or thereabouts.

I roast until the center of the meat hits about 120°F, and then let the leg rest for a full 15 minutes. This gets me to medium-rare. Remember to use foil to tent your roast *only* if your internal temperature is more than 10°F away from target.

I can tell you that fire-fueled roasts are a quantum leap above oven roasts. Fire and smoke and big haunches of meat are primal joys we've been enjoying since long before we were fully human. It's important to carry on that tradition.

BACKSTRAPS, LOINS, AND TENDERLOINS

No matter whether you call it the backstrap, loin, or ribeye, this, along with the coveted tenderloin, is the money cut on a deer, elk, or moose. Lightly cooked tenderloin is often the celebratory meal after a successful hunt, and rare is the hunter who will share this coveted morsel with anyone other than, maybe—*maybe*—their spouse or partner. Poorly cooking these cuts disrespects the animal, although, sadly, I see it all too often. This chapter will help you perfect your methods for cooking venison steaks large and small.

The backstrap, or loin, of a deer, moose, or elk, is the equivalent of a ribeye in beef. The tenderloin, which is all too often confused with backstrap, is actually underneath the loin—analogous to the filet mignon in beef. Both cuts are extremely tender, and are best suited to fast, hot cooking.

Under no circumstances should you cook these cuts beyond medium. To do so is a crime against nature. If you like well-done meat, give the backstraps to someone who enjoys a fine, medium-cooked cut, and cook the leg meat instead. Seriously. If you are worried about food safety, reread the section on page 15.

Cooking backstraps, chops, and tenderloins is pretty much the same as cooking a beef steak. If you can do that, you can cook venison steak. But cooking a steak properly does require some skill, and you do need to know a little about carryover heat (see page 70) and resting meat, and you should have the finger test for doneness memorized. Let's start with that.

THE FINGER TEST FOR DONENESS

The fastest and most effective way to test for doneness is the finger test. Open your right hand loosely. Take the tip of the index finger of your left hand and press down on the fleshy area of your right hand where your thumb connects with the rest of your palm, making sure your right hand is relaxed. That's what raw meat feels like.

Now touch the tip of the index finger of your right hand to the tip of your thumb. With your left hand, press that fleshy part at the base of the thumb again: It should feel a little less squishy. That's how medium-rare meat feels.

Move back one finger on your right hand so you are now touching the tip of your middle finger to

Remember, once the meat is resting, carryover heat will continue to cook it. So I always take meat off the heat a little before it is where I want it, which is on the rare side of medium. Once it has finished resting, the meat is perfectly cooked.

TO REST OR NOT?

It is conventional wisdom that after you cook meats, you let them rest a bit on a cutting board before you serve. And in general, this is a good idea, as it can help many kinds of meat retain a bit more moisture.

But not always. First of all, you should know that some water loss is inevitable; it's part of how meat cooks. You will lose moisture no matter what you do, mostly through evaporation in the oven and while the meat is resting. And you will lose more moisture by tenting meat with foil than by leaving it uncovered, which sounds odd. But think about it: Tented meat stays hotter and cooks longer while it's resting, steaming more, which equals more water loss. Ever look at the underside of your foil? Coated with condensation from your meat.

Interestingly, in steaks that are cooked rare, the final meat temperature of 125°F or thereabouts is barely high enough to cook the connective tissue or collagen in the meat. This means that the utility of the resting step is limited. If you or your butcher have done the job right, there should be no connective tissue in your venison backstrap at all (yet another reason why the infamous "leg steak" is an abomination; see page 30). In practice, this means *you need not rest a venison steak that's been cooked rare*. Medium is another story, since the 140°F temperature of medium-cooked meat is hot enough to affect the collagen within the meat—again, *if* there's any in your steak.

What advantage do you gain by *not* resting a rare steak? The "bark"—the crispy crust on the exterior of the meat—will stay crispy and bacon-y. If you rest it, that bark will soften.

Meat Temperature Chart

Many people have an intuitive notion of when meat is rare, medium, or well-done. But if you are using a thermometer, here are some temperature readings to help you make those determinations. Keep in mind that these temperatures are measured at the center of a piece of meat *after* resting.

Rare: 125°F   Medium-rare: 130°F

Medium: 140°F   Medium-well: 150°F

Well-done: 160°F

your thumb. With your left hand, touch the fleshy part of your right thumb once more: This is medium.

One more finger back (to the ring finger on your right hand) and you get to medium-well. Not so good for any red meat. Finally, touch your pinky to your thumb and feel the base. Rock hard, right? That's well-done, which means you just made cat food from your venison steak, although I am reasonably certain even the cat won't eat it.

What happens if you slice into some venison and you get a juice tsunami?

Fear not. First of all, I'm hoping you have a cutting board with gutters to catch the juices. If not, tip the board into a bowl as you work. Keep slicing, and arrange the slices on a platter. Pour all the juices into a bowl and season with a little salt, a splash of olive oil, some vinegar or citrus, and a few chopped herbs of your choice; parsley, chives, and marjoram work very well with venison. *Bam!* Instant dressing for your steak or roast. What's more, the meat will reabsorb some of that juice.

WHICH ONE: LOINS, STEAKS, OR CHOPS?

How you get your backstrap determines how you cook it. If you have the option, you really want to prep your backstraps in lengths that you'll cook whole, and which will be cut into individual medallions just before serving (remember, backstrap tenderloins are very easy to overcook). The exception to this is backstraps of elk or moose, which are large enough to be sliced into proper steaks first and then cooked. For me, on a typical deer, that means lengths of loin weighing about one to two pounds. If you have a large family, you might want even longer, heavier lengths. Why do this? Because when you cook a length of backstrap, it's a lot easier to cook it to a perfect medium-rare, or whatever temperature you prefer. Then, when you serve, you slice the length of loin into perfectly cooked medallions.

But many butchers don't give you lengths of backstrap, although most will give them to you if you remember to ask before they start on your deer. Many of you reading this have chops or boneless medallions in your freezer right now—and pretty much all commercially available venison (like the stuff you can buy at Whole Foods) will be medallions. What's the difference?

Well, cooking individual chops and medallions is trickier because of the greater surface-area-to-mass

ratio of each piece of meat. (Yep, science. Again.) Think for a moment about a chop or a medallion that's been cut from a length of backstrap: If you cook it, you will do so on the cut side, the widest, largest part of the medallion. The medallion will cook very fast, going from rare to medium to overcooked in minutes or seconds, depending on how thick it is. What's more, you really don't get that lovely sight of perfectly cooked meat when you serve it since the perfectly cooked part is inside the medallion or chop. On the other hand, you get more bark. It's a tradeoff.

If you have medallions from a typical deer, they should be roughly an inch thick and three inches wide. In this case, you'll want to take your meat out of the fridge just fifteen minutes before you start cooking, instead of the thirty minutes I call for in most of these recipes. Unlike a length of backstrap, which you really want at room temperature before cooking, you want the interior of smaller medallions to still be cool—an insurance policy against overcooking.

For larger animals, this equation changes. In the case of elk, moose, really big deer, caribou, or red deer, medallions or chops are actually preferred, since the loin is so wide in diameter that it becomes much harder to cook a length properly; the distance between the edge of the loin and its center is just too great. It can be done, but you need to have the meat out at room temperature for about an hour, and you will likely need to finish the loin in the oven. Easier to do big medallions or chops. Just be sure to make them at least 1 inch thick; I prefer at least 1½ inches. Two inches is even better. After all, this is the ribeye of an elk or moose, a luxury cut that ought to be celebrated.

All of these recipes can be done with any form of backstrap.

VENISON WITH CUMBERLAND SAUCE

Serves 4 | Prep Time: 30 minutes, mostly to let the venison come to room temperature | Cook Time: 15 minutes

If there were one classic way to eat venison, this would be it. Cumberland sauce, which hinges on the tart-and-sweet red currant, is perhaps the oldest wild game sauce still commonly made today. It dates from at least the 1700s, and has been modified only slightly since then. Cumberland sauce has persisted so long in our kitchens because it is a perfect balance of sweet, spicy, savory. and salty.

One thing that really makes this recipe shine is *glace de viande* (page 67), which adds so much to the flavor. But fear not: If you don't have *glace de viande*, use regular, low-sodium stock boiled down by half. Be very careful about adding any other salt to the sauce, though, as the boiled-down stock can get very salty.

What goes well with Cumberland on the plate? I like simple mashed potatoes, but boiled or baked potatoes are just as good. Polenta or fried hominy would be excellent, as would any other mashed root vegetable. Or go simple and just serve it with a green salad and some nice, crusty bread.

VENISON

1 to 2 pounds venison backstrap, in one piece

Salt

3 tablespoons unsalted butter, lard, duck fat, or cooking oil

CUMBERLAND SAUCE

1 shallot or ¼ cup minced onion

½ cup Port wine

½ cup of *glace de viande*, or you can use 1 cup of regular stock, boiled down to ½ cup

A pinch of salt

½ teaspoon mustard powder

¼ teaspoon cayenne

Zest of a lemon or an orange

¼ cup red currant, cranberry or lingonberry jelly (not jam)

Freshly ground black pepper

Take the venison out of the fridge and salt it well. Let it rest at room temperature for 30 minutes.

Melt the butter in a sauté pan large enough to hold the venison backstrap. When it's hot, turn the heat to medium and brown the venison on all sides. Use the finger test (see page 79) to determine the level of doneness that you want. I prefer medium-rare. Remember, the meat will continue to cook as it rests, so take it out a little before it reaches the doneness you want. Move the venison to a cutting board, and let it rest while you make the sauce.

When your meat has come out of the pan, make sure there is at least 1 tablespoon of butter or oil in it. If not, add more. Sauté the shallot over medium-high heat for 90 seconds, just until it softens. Don't let it burn.

Add the Port wine, and use a wooden spoon to scrape up any browned bits stuck to the pan. Let this boil furiously until it is reduced by half. Add the demi-glace (or stock), the salt, citrus zest, mustard, and cayenne, and let this boil for a minute or two. Stir in the red currant jelly and the black pepper. Let all this boil down until it's thick but still pourable. You can strain it if you want a more refined sauce.

Slice the venison into medallions. Pour any juices that have come out of the meat into the sauce and stir to combine. Serve with the sauce either over the meat or alongside it.

STEAK DIANE

Serves 2, and can be doubled | **Prep Time: 30 minutes** | **Cook Time: 12 minutes**

Steak Diane. What can I say? This dish was already passé when I first began going to restaurants as a boy in the 1970s; its heyday in America was in the 1950s and 1960s, when French cooking was all the rage (thanks, Julia!). Most people who remember this dish remember it as beef filet mignon with a piquant sauce of mustard, Worcestershire sauce, demi-glace, cream, and shallots—all flambéed at the table with cognac. Ritzy, eh? Well, my version of steak Diane is a little less flamboyant, and it hearkens back to the dish's roots. Diane, you see, is really Diana, the Roman goddess of the hunt. And Sauce Diane, at least in its proto-form, was first mentioned by Escoffier in his *Le Guide Culinaire* back in 1907. And it was a sauce not for beef, but for venison.

It is a classic for a reason. This sauce is so good that you must have lots of bread around to sop it up. If you don't, you will find yourself licking the plate, and that's not very polite. Steak Diane is absolutely a date-night dish, but it is also so easy to make that you can whip it up on a Wednesday night. So I suppose if you have a Wednesday-night date, it would be perfect.

The best way to cook Steak Diane is with a large piece of backstrap that you then cut into medallions right before you serve (though regular, pre-cut medallions will still work, if that's what you have). While it is important to use heavy cream for this recipe (lighter creams will separate), it's not that important to have fancy brandy for this recipe—just use something you would actually drink, OK?

½ to 1 pound piece venison backstrap

Salt

2 tablespoons unsalted butter

1 shallot or ¼ cup onion, minced

2 garlic cloves, minced

¼ cup brandy

½ cup venison stock or beef broth

2 tablespoons Worcestershire sauce

1 tablespoon mustard

1 tablespoon tomato paste

Enough heavy cream to turn the sauce the color of coffee with cream, about ¼ cup

Minced herbs for garnish (basil, parsley, chives, etc.)

Bring the venison loin out of the fridge, salt it well, and let it come to room temperature, about 30 minutes.

Heat the butter in a large sauté pan over medium-high heat for about 90 seconds. Pat the venison dry with a paper towel and sear it on all sides. Turn the heat to medium so the butter doesn't scorch. Take your time; it should take about 8 to 10 minutes or so to get a nice brown crust on the venison without overcooking the center. Use the finger test for doneness (see page 79) to get the venison where you like it. Remove the meat and let it rest.

Add the shallots to the sauté pan and cook for 1 minute, then add the garlic and cook for another 30 seconds or so. Don't let the garlic burn. Deglaze the pan with the brandy, scraping off any stuck-on bits in the pan with a wooden spoon. Let the brandy cook down almost to a glaze, then add the venison stock, tomato paste, mustard, and Worcestershire sauce, and stir to combine. Let this boil down until a wooden spoon dragged across the pan leaves a trail behind it that does not fill in for a second or so. This should take about 3 minutes on high heat.

Turn off the heat and let the boiling subside. Stir in the cream until the sauce is as light as you like. Don't let the sauce boil again or it could break.

Slice the venison into thick medallions. If you find you have not cooked it enough, let the meat swim in the sauce for a few moments to heat through. If the venison is to your liking, pour some sauce on a plate and top with the meat. Garnish with some chopped herbs. Chives are traditional, but basil and parsley are also nice. Serve with a big red wine such as cabernet sauvignon, Barolo, petit verdot, or graciano.

JÄGERSCHNITZEL

Serves 4 | Prep Time: 20 minutes | Cook Time: 10 minutes

Jägerschnitzel means "hunter's cutlets" in German, and, like Steak Diane, the dish was originally made with venison. A classic jägerschnitzel is a thin cutlet of meat served with a mushroom gravy. Potatoes—boiled, mashed, or in a salad—are the traditional side dish. It is a manly meal, and the only green thing allowed is a garnish of parsley, chives, or chervil. Maybe.

This is an ideal recipe for venison backstrap or venison heart. Yes, venison heart. You open up the heart, trim away any vein-y stuff, then pound the heart thin, the same way you would with any other meat (instructions are on page 232). It is absolutely delicious. Try it. You'll thank me later. You can also do this with a leg steak, but make sure there is no sinew in it.

What mushrooms to use? Historically, you would use regular button mushrooms or chanterelles. I say use anything you want, but use several varieties together if you can. I like those "chef's sampler" packs you can get in the store. This is a great dish to have memorized, as it is perfect for a cold night in camp after hunting.

---

4 venison medallions or 2 venison hearts

Salt (smoked salt if you have some)

About 1 cup rye, or all-purpose flour

½ cup bacon fat, lard, butter, or cooking oil

1 pound mixed fresh mushrooms, cleaned and roughly chopped

½ yellow onion, roughly chopped

¼ cup red wine

1 cup venison or beef stock

A pinch of celery seed (optional)

A pinch of caraway seed (optional)

2 to 3 tablespoons sour cream

Black pepper to taste

Parsley, chives, or chervil for garnish

If you are using venison hearts, follow the directions on page 232 to flatten them out. Place the venison medallions or flattened heart between two pieces of plastic wrap and pound until the meat is about ¼ inch thick or less. Do this firmly, but don't wail on the meat or you will tear it. Trim the cutlets if you want. Dust the schnitzels with the rye flour in a wide, shallow container.

Heat the oven to 175°F and put a baking sheet in it. Place paper towels in the baking sheet.

Put the bacon fat in a large sauté pan and heat it until a little bit of flour sizzles instantly when it hits the oil. Shake off any excess flour from the schnitzels and put as many as will fit in your pan. Fry until nicely browned, about 2 minutes, then flip and cook another 2 minutes. Remove and put on the baking sheet in the oven while you do the rest.

When you're done, pour off all but about 3 tablespoons of the fat. Add the mushrooms and the onion and toss to coat. Stir-fry everything over high until the mushrooms and onions begin to brown, about 3 minutes.

Pour in the wine and boil it furiously for a minute, then add the stock and spices (if using) and boil this down by half, about 4 or 5 minutes. When the sauce has thickened a bit (the stray flour from cooking the schnitzel will do this), turn off the heat, and when the sauce stops boiling, stir in the sour cream. Add salt and black pepper to taste. Top with the sauce and garnish with the herbs.

COUNTRY FRIED VENISON STEAK

Serves 4 | Prep Time: 15 minutes | Cook Time: 30 minutes, if you have the caramelized onions done

This is the American descendent of jägerschnitzel. You'll find it all over the South and especially around Texas and Oklahoma. I learned about this version of country-fried steak from a Mississippi chef, John Currence of City Grocery. Currence's book, *Pickles, Pigs & Whiskey*, is one of my all-time favorite Southern cookbooks, and a version of this recipe is in that book.

Note: Because you are pounding the meat, you don't need backstrap here, although it still makes the best cutlet. I will also use leg steaks that have been stripped of all connective tissue.

I like this with grits, mashed potatoes, or hash browns.

CARAMELIZED ONIONS (*optional*)

1 large onion, sliced thin from root to tip

3 tablespoons butter or lard

A pinch of salt

1 teaspoon dried thyme

1 tablespoon honey

VENISON

4 venison medallions

Salt

2 cups seasoned flour (add salt, black pepper, cayenne, and garlic powder to the flour, or use a commercial "fish fry")

3 eggs, lightly beaten

½ cup heavy cream

Tabasco sauce

3 cups panko breadcrumbs (regular breadcrumbs are fine, too)

Peanut oil or lard (see below for amount)

GRAVY

¼ cup flour

1 cup dark broth, beef or venison (see page 66)

¼ cup cream

The caramelized onions

If you're going to add the caramelized onions to the gravy, you'll need to make them first. It can even be done several days in advance, and you can just keep the caramelized onions in the fridge; it's always a good idea to have some handy, anyway.

Heat 3 tablespoons of the butter in a frying pan over medium-high heat and cook the onions. Toss to coat with the oil and sprinkle the salt over them, then the thyme. As soon as you see some brown edges, turn the heat down to medium-low and cover the pan. Cook, stirring occasionally, until the onions are totally brown. This can take 30 minutes or so. Add a dollop of honey and cook another 10 minutes. Turn off the heat, remove the onions and reserve, then wipe out the pan.

Heat the oven to "warm" and set a baking sheet inside lined with paper towels.

Put the venison medallions between two pieces of plastic wrap and pound them thin with a meat mallet, rubber mallet or empty wine bottle. How thin? Your choice. At least ¼ inch, and as thin as ⅛ inch. Salt the meat and set it aside.

Set up a breading station. Get three large, shallow bowls. In one goes the seasoned flour. In the next go the eggs, cream, some salt, and black pepper, and just a couple dashes of Tabasco. In the third goes the breadcrumbs.

Heat enough peanut oil to come up ¼ inch along the sides of a cast-iron or other heavy frying pan. Heat it over high heat until a tiny bit of flour sizzles instantly when flicked into it. You are looking for 350°F. While the oil is heating up, dredge the venison cutlets in the flour, then the egg mixture, then the breadcrumbs. Fry

> "A dog forced into the woods won't hunt deer."
>
> —DANISH PROVERB

the venison for about 2 minutes per side, just until they are golden brown. Remove each to the baking sheet in the warm oven while you finish the rest.

When the venison is done, pour off all but about 3 tablespoons of the oil. Heat it over medium-high heat. Mix in the flour and cook this, stirring almost constantly, until it turns the color of coffee with cream, about 5 to 10 minutes. Slowly pour in the broth with one hand while you whisk the gravy with the other. It will sizzle and seize up, but keep pouring the broth in slowly until it is incorporated. Stir in the caramelized onions and simmer the gravy for a few minutes. Add the cream, mix well, and add salt, black pepper, and a touch of Tabasco to taste. Give everyone some cutlets and pour the gravy over.

THAI VENISON SATAY SKEWERS

Serves 4 as an appetizer, and can be scaled up | **Prep Time: 4 hours, marinating time** | **Cook Time: 15 minutes**

If you've ever had these, you'll know why I put them in this book. *Satay* ("sah-tay") is a Southeast Asian appetizer that is basically marinated meat on a stick, grilled, and served with a dipping sauce. It's made of awesome.

Don't skimp on the marinating time with this recipe: The aromatic coconut or buttermilk soak goes a long way toward tenderizing the venison. Start with a four-hour soak time, but you can safely go up to eight hours, maybe ten. Too much longer and the meat will get mushy.

1½ pounds venison backstrap, cut into 6-inch strips about ¼ to ½ inch thick

Bamboo or metal skewers, soaked for 1 hour to prevent them from burning

Oil for coating the venison

MARINADE

1 cup coconut milk or buttermilk

2 tablespoons minced fresh ginger (or 2 teaspoons ground ginger)

2 large garlic cloves, minced (or 1 teaspoon garlic powder)

3 tablespoons yellow curry powder (or Thai yellow curry paste)

1 to 3 Thai hot chiles or 1 teaspoon cayenne (optional)

2 tablespoons Asian fish sauce or soy sauce

PEANUT SAUCE

½ cup smooth peanut butter

¼ cup soy sauce

2 tablespoons sriracha hot sauce (or more to taste)

2 tablespoons brown sugar

Juice of 4 limes

1 teaspoon garlic powder

½ cup coconut water (regular water is fine)

2 teaspoons sesame oil (optional)

If you're using bamboo skewers, put them in water to soak. Mix the marinade ingredients together in a bowl or small container; you can put it all in a blender if you want. Coat the venison strips with the marinade. Cover the container and marinate in the fridge for 4 to 8 hours (see note above).

Meanwhile, mix together all the peanut sauce ingredients with a spoon and set aside, covered, at room temperature while the venison marinates. Depending on how thick your peanut butter is, you may need to add more peanut butter or water—you want the sauce to be a little thicker than melted ice cream, a little thinner than pancake batter.

To grill: Take the venison out of the marinade and thread one strip per skewer. Shake off any excess marinade and set on a tray. Get your grill hot and scrape it down with a grill brush. Soak a paper towel in some vegetable oil, and grab it with tongs to wipe down the grates. Brush the venison skewers with a little more vegetable oil and grill over high heat (with the lid open) until the venison is done, about 2 to 4 minutes per side, depending on how hot your grill is.

To broil: Take the venison out of the marinade and thread one strip per skewer. Shake off any excess marinade and set on a broiling pan. Set an oven rack about four inches from the broiler. Heat your broiler for 10 minutes or so. Brush the venison skewers with a little vegetable oil and broil about 4 minutes per side, until the meat is fully cooked and has a little char on it.

Serve on a platter with the dipping sauce.

Velveting Meat, Chinese Style

Ever wonder why the meat in Chinese food is so different from anything you make at home? That no matter what you do, your homemade stir-fry just doesn't taste like what you buy at your neighborhood restaurant? Chances are the reason is that they are velveting their meat, and you are not. Velveting is a Chinese trick that will make any wild game meat tender and juicy. Learn this technique and your homemade Chinese food will shine.

Velveting is the process of coating the meat with a delicate layer of ingredients, usually involving some sort of starch or egg, and then stir-frying it. It's not so much a batter as it is a gossamer layer of protection for what is typically very lean meat. And those of us who cook wild game know all about very lean meat.

I've now velveted everything from venison to rabbit to duck to pheasant, and the trick works on any meat. It's a great way to highlight venison leg meat, but it's best with lean, tender meat such as venison loin.

There are lots of ways to velvet meat. Some are über-simple: Marinate it in soy sauce, cooking wine, and corn starch, and proceed to the stir-frying. This works pretty well. A better way, however, is to "pass through" the coated meat in reasonably hot oil. It is the same general idea as double-frying French fries. A sixty-second bath in 275°F oil sets the velvet coating, and helps the meat hold up better under the ferocious heat of a proper stir-fry.

The downside is that you need to use a couple of cups of oil. But, you can strain and save the oil for several uses, so it's not all that bad.

The result will give you that "ah ha!" moment when you realize that you have cracked one of the secrets of Chinese cooking. No matter what you include in your stir-fry, if you do this velveting trick you will be overjoyed with the texture of the meat. Give it a go. You'll see.

BASIC VENISON STIR-FRY

Serves 4 | **Prep Time: 20 minutes** | **Cook Time: 5 minutes**

Consider this a master recipe for any stir-fry you might want to throw together on a work night. The most important thing is to remember the ingredients and their proportions for the velvet marinade. Everything else is your choice.

When making any stir-fry, the work is in the chopping, so do everything before you heat up the wok. Speaking of which, if you like Chinese food, you really ought to own a wok. A wok can get very hot very fast and uses less oil to do the job. But a large sauté pan will work in a pinch. Also make sure to use your most powerful burner for stir-frying.

MARINADE

2 tablespoons *Shaoxing* wine or dry sherry

½ teaspoon salt

3 tablespoons soy sauce

1 tablespoon potato or corn starch, mixed with 2 tablespoons water

STIR-FRY

1 pound venison, trimmed of all fat and sinew

1½ cups peanut or other high-heat cooking oil

1 to 4 hot chiles, fresh or dried

1 red or yellow bell pepper, sliced

3 garlic cloves, slivered

1 bunch cilantro, washed and roughly chopped

1 tablespoon soy sauce

2 teaspoons sesame oil

Slice the venison into thin slivers of about ¼ inch or less and anywhere from 1 to 3 inches long. Mix with the marinade and set aside while you cut all the other ingredients. Slice the chiles if fresh, or break them up if dried.

Heat the peanut oil in the wok or a large, heavy pot until it reaches 275°F to 300°F. Don't let it get too hot. Add about a third of the venison to the hot oil and use a chopstick or butter knife to separate the meat slices the second they hit the hot oil. Let them sizzle for 30 seconds to 1 minute. Remove with a Chinese spider skimmer or a slotted spoon. Set aside and cook the remaining venison one-third at a time.

Pour out all but about 3 tablespoons of the oil. Save the oil for the next time you cook Chinese food.

Heat the remaining oil over high heat on your hottest burner. The moment it begins to smoke, add the chiles and bell peppers and stir-fry for 90 seconds. Add the garlic and cook another 30 seconds. Add the venison and stir-fry 90 seconds.

Add the cilantro and soy sauce and stir-fry a final 30 seconds, just until the cilantro wilts. Turn off the heat and stir in the sesame oil. Serve at once with steamed rice.

CHINESE TANGERINE VENISON

Serves 4 | Prep Time: 45 minutes, including time to pre-fry the meat | Cook Time: 10 minutes

This recipe is the origin of the ubiquitous "orange" chicken or beef you see all over Americanized Chinese restaurants. But where that dish is all about a puffy batter and a cloyingly sweet sauce, the real version is all about tang, heat, and crunch. It has only a touch of sweetness, although you could sweeten it more if you wanted to, and there are enough chiles to make you notice. There's something more, too: The tangerine peels are ever so slightly bitter, which really adds a layer of complexity to the dish.

Dried tangerine peel is pretty easy to come by. You or your kids are probably addicted to those little mandarins, variously labeled as "Cuties" or "Halos." That's the tangerine I'm talking about. Peel a few, let them dry on the counter for a few days, and you're good to go (though the Chinese prefer to use peels that are at least a year old). Dried peels will keep in a glass jar in the pantry forever.

This recipe is best done with backstrap, but you can use any lean, sinew-free part of the animal. But if you do use tougher cuts, take a tip from the Chinese and marinate it in baking soda overnight first. Sprinkle about two teaspoons of baking soda over the thinly sliced meat, toss to combine and store in the fridge overnight. The next day, rinse off the meat, pat it dry and proceed with the recipe. This process will tenderize tough cuts nicely.

A word on the Sichuan peppercorns: These little dried red buds are floral and wonderful to eat, but they also have the effect of numbing your mouth. A few are nice; too many and you'll think your mouth is in shock. Start with a small bit and work your way into it.

As with all stir fries, you need to have everything in place before you start, as it will all come together very fast.

This recipe works best with a wok. If you don't have one, you will need more oil to fry the venison in. Don't worry; you can strain and reuse the oil several times.

MARINADE

2 egg whites

¼ cup *Shaoxing* wine or dry sherry

2 tablespoons peanut or other cooking oil

½ cup corn or potato starch

Put the sliced venison pieces into a large bowl. Add the egg whites and use your hands to massage the meat with the egg whites, making sure each piece is coated. Now add the wine and oil and do the same thing. Finally, add the corn starch and mix to coat. It'll be a gloopy mess, but that's OK. Put the meat in the refrigerator for 30 minutes while you do the rest of the prep.

Place the tangerine peels into a bowl and pour hot water over them. Cover the bowl. In another bowl, mix all the ingredients for the sauce together (except for the tangerine water, which you'll add in a bit), then do your chopping of the chiles, garlic, and green onions. Slice the tangerine peel into thin slivers and set aside. The peels will still be a little hard, but that's OK. When you've sliced the tangerine peels, add the 3 tablespoons of the soaking water to the sauce.

When you're ready to start, heat the oil in a wok or heavy, deep pan to about 350°F. Set a baking sheet or similar container nearby and get a Chinese strainer or slotted spoon, and either a chopstick

SAUCE

¼ cup venison or beef stock

3 tablespoons tangerine soaking water

2 tablespoons soy sauce

2 tablespoons *Shaoxing* wine, dry sherry, or dry white wine

2 tablespoons rice or cider vinegar

1 tablespoon sesame oil

1 to 3 tablespoons sugar

2 teaspoons corn or potato starch

½ teaspoon salt

½ teaspoon white pepper

STIR-FRY

1 pound venison, sliced into bite-sized pieces 1 inch thick

Dried peel of 1 or 2 thin-skinned tangerines (Mandarins are best)

2 cups peanut or other cooking oil (see above)

2 to 6 dried hot chiles, chopped (Tsien Tsin, Thai, árbol, or cayenne)

4 garlic cloves, minced

A 2-inch piece of ginger, peeled and minced

6 green onions, sliced into 1-inch pieces, green and white parts separated

2 teaspoons crushed Sichuan peppercorns (optional)

or butter knife ready. Put about half of the venison in the hot oil and immediately use the chopstick to separate all the pieces, which will want to stick together. Fry over high heat until the venison turns golden brown and crispy, about 6 minutes. Remove with the strainer and set in the baking sheet to drain. Repeat the process with the other half of the venison

Drain off all but about 3 tablespoons of the oil (you can reuse it). Add the chiles to the hot oil and stir-fry until they turn fragrant, about 30 seconds. Add the ginger and the white parts of the green onions, and stir-fry 1 minute. Add the garlic and tangerine slivers and stir-fry 30 seconds. Add the venison back to the wok and toss everything to combine.

Stir the sauce vigorously (the corn starch will have settled on the bottom of the bowl). Pour it into the wok and toss to combine. Allow this to boil and thicken for 1 minute, then add the green parts of the green onions. Toss to combine. Add the Sichuan peppercorns if using. Serve at once with steamed rice.

VENISON WITH MOREL SAUCE

Serves 4 | Prep Time: 30 minutes | Cook Time: 20 minutes

I don't know what percentage of deer hunters also hunt morel mushrooms, but it has to be more than half. So venison with morels is a natural pairing. The only hitch is that you need to tuck away some backstrap or tenderloin from the fall until spring. Of course, you can make this recipe with dried morels from the previous spring, too.

If you are making this with dried morels, as I sometimes do, you will need about one ounce, a really big handful. Pour boiling water over them and soak while you let the venison come to room temperature. Remove, squeeze out excess water, and chop. Save one cup of the water and strain it through a paper towel. Now, when it comes time to put the mushrooms in the pan, instead of the fresh morels, you will add the chopped, reconstituted morels plus the water.

I did include an early version of this dish in my first book, *Hunt, Gather, Cook*, but this rendition is streamlined and improved.

1½ to 2 pounds of venison steaks or boneless backstrap

Salt

2 tablespoons canola oil, grapeseed oil, or lard

2 cups chopped fresh morels, about 12 ounces (see above for dried)

1 cup minced onion

3 tablespoons butter, lard, or duck fat

1 tablespoon flour

½ cup Port or red wine

1 cup *glace de viande* (page 67), or 2 cups venison or beef stock (page 65) boiled down by half

Black pepper to taste

Take the venison out of the fridge and salt it well. Let it sit on the counter for 30 minutes while you chop the mushrooms and vegetables.

Heat the canola oil in a large sauté pan over medium-high heat. Pat the venison dry with a paper towel and sear it in the pan, about 2 minutes per side, or until the meat is done to your liking; use the finger test for doneness on page 79. Remove the venison and set it on a cutting board to rest.

Add the onion and morels to the pan. They will sizzle for a moment, then the morels will begin to release their water (see above for dried morels). Let almost all this water boil away before adding the butter. Toss the mushrooms and onion to coat with the butter. Sear this hard for a couple minutes without disturbing— you want to get some browning. Sprinkle the flour over the mushrooms and stir it in. Add the Port (it might flame up as the alcohol burns off) and use a wooden spoon to scrape up any browned bits on the bottom of the pan. Let the Port almost boil away, then add the *glace* or stock.

Boil this down a minute or three until the sauce comes together. Pour any juices from the venison that have accumulated on the cutting board into the sauce. Add black pepper and salt to taste to the sauce and serve with the venison.

VENISON WITH SPRING VEGETABLES

Serves 4 | **Prep Time: 20 minutes** | **Cook Time: 1 hour, mostly for the potatoes**

Spring and venison aren't things we naturally put together in our minds, but in this age of plentiful venison, many families find themselves with plenty of venison well into spring and summer. So what follows are two recipes that feature the best of seasonal produce served with venison seared simply.

Keep in mind that the vegetables here are interchangeable and variable. If you don't have ramps, use scallions. No fiddleheads? Use green beans, which are similar in flavor. Store-bought pesto is fine here, but if you want to make your own, see the simple recipe below.

1 to 2 pounds venison backstrap, chops, or
   steaks

Salt

1 to 2 pounds fingerling potatoes, or larger
   potatoes cut into chunks

¼ cup olive oil, divided

½ pound fiddleheads or green beans

½ pound wild onions or scallions

1 cup peas, fresh or thawed

A small bunch of dandelion greens, or arugula,
   turnip greens, or mustard greens

3 tablespoons pesto

Lemon juice to taste

Black pepper to taste

PESTO

3 garlic cloves, chopped

2 tablespoons toasted pine nuts, chopped

2 tablespoons grated cheese
   (I like Grana Padano)

About 2 cups chopped basil

Salt

Olive oil (use the good stuff)

Toss the potatoes with 1 tablespoon of oil and salt them well. Arrange in one layer on a baking sheet and roast at 400°F until nicely browned, turning them every 15 minutes or so. This should take about 1 hour.

Meanwhile, take the venison out of the fridge and salt it well. Let it come to room temperature. Chop the wild onions and greens roughly.

When the potatoes are almost done, heat the remaining olive oil in a large sauté pan over medium-high heat. Pat the venison dry with a paper towel and sear it well until it's the doneness you want, using the finger test for doneness on page 79. This should take about 10 minutes or so.

While the venison rests, lay down the fiddleheads in the sauté pan and sear them hard until you get some browning on the edges, about 3 minutes or so. Add the wild onions, greens, and peas, and toss to combine. Cover the pan and turn the heat to low. Let the greens steam a bit, maybe a minute or three.

Add the potatoes to the pan, then the pesto. Toss to combine and add lemon juice and pesto to taste. Put this on everyone's plate and serve with medallions of the venison.

To make your own pesto, put 3 chopped garlic cloves, 2 tablespoons of chopped, toasted pine nuts, 2 tablespoons of grated parmesan, about 2 cups chopped basil and a pinch of salt into a blender or food processor. Buzz to combine, then, with the motor running, drizzle in ¼ to 1 cup of olive oil, depending on how loose you want the sauce.

VENISON STEAK WITH CHERRY TOMATOES

Serves 4 | **Prep Time: 30 minutes** | **Cook Time: 1 hour, mostly to cook the cherry tomatoes**

The crux of this dish is venison loin or tenderloin, cooked simply, with the freshest produce of early summer. My vegetable suggestions are just that: If you happen to find some wonderful corn, or fennel, or carrots, or greens, by all means mix and match.

You don't *have* to spend the hour slow-cooking the cherry tomatoes if you want to make this a lightning quick weeknight meal; you can just toss them in at the last minute. Drying the tomatoes like this concentrates their flavor, however, and is worth the effort if you have the time for it.

1½ pounds cherry tomatoes, sliced in half

Olive oil to coat tomatoes

Salt

1 to 2 pounds venison loin

2 tablespoons olive oil

3 garlic cloves, sliced very thin

1 cup fresh fava beans, peas, or shelling beans

1 or 2 small yellow zucchini, roughly chopped (optional)

1 teaspoon minced fresh rosemary, or ½ teaspoon minced dried

¼ cup chicken broth

3 tablespoons minced fresh parsley

Black pepper to taste

Coat the halved cherry tomatoes in some oil and salt them well. Place them, cut side up, on a baking sheet and put in the oven at 250°F; no need to preheat. If you have a convection oven, turn the fan on. Or, you can put the tomatoes on a rack in your dehydrator and set it to 145°F. It will take longer for the tomatoes to get semi-dry, but it won't heat up your kitchen. Cook the tomatoes until they are about half dried, about 45 minutes to 1 hour in the oven, a bit longer in a dehydrator. Keep an eye on the tomatoes every 20 minutes or so, as different tomatoes and different ovens will give you different results.

About 30 minutes before the tomatoes are ready, take the venison out of the fridge and salt it well.

When the tomatoes are ready, heat the olive oil in a large sauté pan over high heat. As the oil is heating, pat the meat dry with paper towels. When the oil is hot, sear the venison well on all sides. Cook to medium-rare, using the finger test for doneness (see page 79). Set the meat on a cutting board to rest while you cook the vegetables.

Add the zucchini to the pan and toss to coat with oil. Sprinkle with salt and add another tablespoon of olive oil if things look too dry. Sauté over high heat, tossing and stirring, until the zucchini begins to brown a bit, about 4 to 5 minutes. Add the garlic, beans, and broth and let it boil furiously until almost gone.

Add the tomatoes, rosemary, and the parsley, and toss to combine. Cook for about 30 seconds and turn off the heat. Grind some black pepper over everything. Add any juices that have collected on the cutting board from the venison to the pan.

Serve with bread, potatoes, or rice.

ICELANDIC VENISON WITH BLUEBERRY SAUCE

Serves 2, and can be doubled | **Prep Time: 30 minutes, mostly for reconstituting the dried mushrooms**
Cook Time: 25 minutes

Venison and blueberries, or huckleberries if you live in the West, is an ancient and well-respected combination. One that I'd hated for years. Every version I'd had was cloying, sticky, a weird sweet and not very sour flavor that just didn't suit me. Long ago I told myself that I'd just avoid this particular classic. And then I read a quirky little book on, of all things, the food of Iceland. *Icelandic Food & Cookery*, by the memorably named Nanna Rögnvaldardóttir. She has a version of this dish, done with lamb, that was the first one I'd seen that was not obviously sweet. Her use of mushrooms in a berry sauce was also unusual. So I studied the recipe, made a few changes, and gave it a go.

I'm glad I did. This dish is a knockout. I serve this alongside some Irish colcannon, which is a fancy name for mashed potatoes with a green thing mixed in. I used nettles, but any green will do. Spinach would be easiest, but kale is pretty traditional in Ireland, and the Icelanders eat it, too.

As for the mushrooms, I used some dried morels. Any good dried mushroom will do. You'll want the mushroom soaking water, so I don't use fresh mushrooms here. Port wine can be a nicer kick in the sauce than red wine, but it's strong—if you use Port instead of red wine, use only a quarter cup. Finally, remember that this is a savory sauce, despite the blueberries (or huckleberries). If this is weird to you, add some sugar.

I served this with a really good Spanish red wine, but any full-bodied red will work, or if you are a beer drinker, a malty Scottish ale or porter is the ticket.

Tenderloins from a deer, or ¾ pound venison backstrap

Salt

5 tablespoons clarified butter, regular unsalted butter, lard, duck fat, or vegetable oil, divided

1 small onion, peeled, halved and sliced root to tip

1 garlic clove, minced

¾ ounce dried mushrooms, reconstituted in 1 cup hot water

½ cup venison stock or beef stock

½ cup red wine, or Port

½ cup blueberries or huckleberries, fresh or thawed

1 teaspoon fresh rosemary, minced

Black pepper to taste

Malt or cider vinegar, to taste

Sugar (optional)

Take the venison out of the fridge and salt it well. Let it set on the cutting board while you rehydrate the mushrooms and boil the potatoes for the colcannon.

Put the diced potatoes into a pot of salted water and bring to a boil. Simmer until tender. Drain the potatoes and put them back in the pot. Turn the heat to low under the pot and let the potatoes steam for a few seconds.

Beat in the butter, sour cream, and chopped vegetables. You want nice mashed potatoes with green streaks. Add salt to taste, cover the pot, turn off the heat, and set aside.

Get a large sauté pan and put 2 tablespoons of unsalted butter into it. Turn the heat to high, and when the butter is hot add the sliced onion. Sauté over medium-high heat until browned along the edges, about 4 to 5 minutes. Turn off the heat, remove the onions, and set aside.

(continued)

COLCANNON

2 large russet potatoes, peeled and diced

Salt

2 or 3 three tablespoons unsalted butter

1 or 2 heaping tablespoons sour cream or heavy cream

1 cup chopped, cooked green vegetable (spinach, kale, nettles, etc.)

Wipe the pan with a paper towel. Pat the venison dry and put the rest of the butter into the pan. Set it over high heat until the butter is very hot, but not smoking. Add the venison and sear until medium-rare. If you don't know to tell when the meat is done, use the finger test for doneness (see page 79). When the venison is done, move it to rest on a cutting board.

Return the onions to the pan, add the mushrooms and garlic and sauté over medium-high heat for 2 to 3 minutes, stirring often. Sprinkle some salt over everything and add the wine.

Boil this down until it's almost gone, using a wooden spoon to stir up any browned bits on the bottom of the pan. Add the stock and mushroom soaking water (strain the water if there is any debris in it) and boil this down by two-thirds.

Add the huckleberries or blueberries and cook another minute or two. Add black pepper, salt and vinegar to taste. If you want it sweet, add some sugar now; start with a teaspoon or two until you get things as sweet as you'd like. Garnish with the rosemary.

"The fabled musk deer searches the world over for the source of the scent which comes from itself."

—RAMAKRISHNA

VENISON WITH CARAMELIZED ONIONS AND MUSHROOMS

Serves 4 | Prep Time: 20 minutes | Cook Time: 45 minutes, mostly to caramelize the onions

This recipe is a little like the Venison with Morel Sauce on page 97, but this is more of an autumn recipe, using fall mushrooms and caramelized onions as an accompaniment rather than a sauce. I think you'll like both recipes.

I like to make this with the larger steaks from elk, caribou, or moose, but of course it will work with regular venison backstrap as well.

Hen of the woods mushrooms, *Grifola frondosa*, are very common east of the Great Plains, emerging in the fall with the autumn rains. They're large, grayish, meaty mushrooms that grow at the base of trees. If you're not into foraging for your own mushrooms, hen of the woods is widely available in bigger supermarkets, where they are often called by their Japanese name, *maitake*; these mushrooms are farmed. But no biggie if you can't get them, as regular button or cremini mushrooms work just fine. The porcini powder in which I roll the venison, made by blitzing dried porcini in a coffee grinder, adds a lot of flavor, but if you skip it I won't be mad at you.

I will, however, be mad at you if you don't caramelize your onions. It's what really makes this dish. Follow my instructions below and you'll be fine. Just take your time. Caramelizing onions takes a while; just go with it. And they keep for days in the fridge.

I'd serve this with potatoes of some kind, good bread—black pumpernickel is especially good—or polenta. You'll want a nice red wine, too, or maybe a pale ale or Scottish ale.

¼ cup unsalted butter, divided

3 onions, sliced from root to tip

Salt

1 teaspoon dried thyme

2 teaspoons honey (optional)

1 to 2 pounds venison backstrap,
   preferably in one piece

Porcini powder (optional)

½ pound fresh mushrooms, sliced
   (ideally hen of the woods a.k.a. *maitake*)

3 tablespoons fresh chopped parsley

Dandelion leaves, for garnish (optional)

Start by caramelizing the onions. Heat 2 tablespoons of the butter in a large sauté pan over medium-high heat. When it's hot, add the onions and toss to coat. Cover the onions, turn down the heat, and cook slowly, stirring once in a while. You are looking for them to slowly soften and brown, not scorch on the edges. After 10 minutes or so they'll start to get soft. Sprinkle salt over them and let them cook some more. When they are just starting to brown, add the thyme and honey. Cook until they are a nice brown. Remove and set aside. The onions can be made in advance.

While the onions are cooking, take the venison out of the fridge and salt it well. Let it come to room temperature while you are cooking the onions; this is especially important if you are using elk or moose backstrap, which is thick and will take time to warm thoroughly to room temperature.

When the onions are done, wipe out the pan and add the remaining butter. Pat the venison dry with a paper towel and sear it over medium-high heat, turning it to make sure all sides are well browned. Use the finger test for doneness (page 79) to determine when to take it out of the pan. Let the meat rest on a cutting board. If you have some porcini powder, roll the venison in it as it rests.

While the venison is resting, put the mushrooms in the pan and turn the heat to high. Sear the mushrooms until they release their water; this might not happen with hen of the woods. When the water has almost boiled away, or when the mushrooms begin to brown, add some more butter and sauté hard until the mushrooms are nicely browned. Salt them as they cook.

Once the mushrooms are ready, turn the heat down to medium-low and add back the caramelized onions and the parsley, and toss to combine. Heat through and put some on everyone's plate. Add the dandelion leaves if you are using them. Slice the venison into medallions and serve.

VIETNAMESE SHAKING VENISON

Serves 2 ravenous people, or 4 normal ones | **Prep Time: 20 minutes, not including marinating time**
Cook Time: 15 minutes

I am indebted to my colleague Jenny Nguyen of the website *Food for Hunters* for inspiring me to make this insanely good Vietnamese dish. Nguyen is of Vietnamese descent, and grew up with the beef version of this dish. Shaking beef, *bo luc lac*, originated during the time of the French occupation of Vietnam, and the shaking refers to how you cook the dish by shaking the pan to toss and mix the ingredients. One day, Jenny decided to make *nai luc lac*, shaking venison, and it worked wonderfully. What you see below is not her recipe, but my own take on it.

I use backstrap for this recipe, but you could use leg meat that is absolutely free of silverskin or connective tissue.

This is so good you will want to make more than you think you need: Holly and I ate a pound of backstrap done this way at one sitting.

1 to 1½ pounds venison backstrap or tenderloin

½ teaspoon black pepper

1½ teaspoons sugar

2 garlic cloves, minced

2 tablespoons oyster sauce

2 teaspoons fish sauce (optional)

1 tablespoon soy sauce

4 tablespoons lard or vegetable oil

1 medium red onion, sliced thin

1 to 3 hot chiles, such as Thai, serrano, árbol, or cayenne

2 bunches of watercress or arugula

Salt and black pepper

2 tablespoons rice or cider vinegar

Cut the venison into ½- to 1-inch chunks. Make sure it has no silverskin at all. Mix the chunks with the black pepper, sugar, garlic, oyster sauce, fish sauce, and soy sauce. Let this marinate at least 1 hour, and up to a day.

When you are ready to cook, put 2 tablespoons of lard or oil in a wok or large sauté pan and get it ripping hot. When it smokes, add the onion and stir-fry until it begins to brown around the edges, about 2 minutes. Add the hot chiles and stir-fry 30 seconds. Remove the vegetables from the pan and set aside. Wipe out the wok.

Add the remaining lard or oil and get this hot over high heat. Add about half the venison in one layer in the wok and let it sear for 1 minute without moving. Shake the pan to move the pieces. Use tongs to make sure an unseared side is facing down, and sear without touching for another minute (at this point things are smoking pretty well, so have your stove fan on high). Repeat this one or two more times, depending on how well done you like your venison. When you're ready, turn off the heat, add the onion and chiles back to the wok and toss to combine.

Mix the watercress with the vinegar and add a little salt and pepper. Top with the venison and serve either solo as an appetizer, or with rice for a main course.

Pan Sauce Jazz

This chapter has several recipes for simply seared venison backstrap with specific sauces. But they all follow the same principles, and once you know these principles, you can improvise a pan sauce with whatever you have around. Here are the keys to a perfect pan sauce for four people:

Once you have finished cooking the venison, you will want to have about 2 tablespoons of fat in the pan. In some cases, you will need to drain off fat to arrive at that amount.

With the pan over medium-high heat, add about 2 tablespoons minced shallot or onion to the fat and sauté for a minute or so.

Add about 1 cup low-sodium stock (any kind), or ¼ cup *glace de viande* (page 67).

Add a shot glass of hard liquor (brandy, whisky, ouzo, or the like) or a wineglass of wine, then add a heaping tablespoon or two of something sweet, such as jelly, jam, syrup, honey, or molasses. If you don't drink alcohol, substitute fruit juice or a nice vinegar for the liquor.

Mix well, bring to a boil, and boil furiously until the mixture reduces by half or more. Finish by removing the pan from the heat, seasoning the sauce with salt, and then swirling in 2 tablespoons of unsalted butter.

SOUVLAKI

Serves 4 | Prep Time: 2 hours marinating time, at least | Cook Time: 15 minutes

Souvlaki was one of my go-to lunches when I lived back East. A staple of any decent Greek diner (a redundant term in New Jersey), you'd also see good souvlaki at the "roach coaches" all over town, and especially on street corners in Manhattan. (A roach coach, if you've never heard the term, is what everyone used to call a "food truck." It was a rougher time.) What is souvlaki? Grilled pieces of meat on a pita with cucumbers, onions, tomatoes, and "special sauce," which was either some sort of tomato-based red sauce that I've yet to decipher, or the more typical *tzatziki* (tsat-seekie), which is a yogurt-cucumber-dill-garlic sauce. Greek mayo.

Basically this is a Greek taco. Really good, super fun to eat. The diners and roach coaches made the sandwiches for you, but I like to lay everything on the table and let people make their own.

Making this dish is straightforward, but you do need to remember one thing: Your grill or flattop or frying pan or whatever needs to be really damn hot. The reason is that the meat is in small pieces so it needs to cook fast in order not to dry out. Blasting it with the grill cover open will get you there pretty well. But keep an eye on your venison, as it can go from rare to medium to "aw crap I wrecked it" in about two minutes. Remember, it is better to have nice, tender meat than pretty grill marks on the outside—this is a sandwich, after all. You can't see the grill marks, but you sure can tell if the meat's overcooked.

There are a bunch of make-ahead steps here, so if you are pressed for time, you can make the *tzatziki* sauce up to a few days ahead, and marinate the meat a full day ahead of time, too.

Oh, if you are using them, be sure to soak the wooden skewers in water for an hour, otherwise they'll burn on the grill.

MARINADE

1½ pounds venison backstrap or leg meat, cut into 1-inch chunks

½ cup olive oil

¼ cup lemon juice

Zest of a lemon

2 tablespoons dried oregano

2 teaspoons dried thyme

2 teaspoons black pepper

When you're cutting your venison, make sure it's free of all silverskin and sinew. This will make the meat easier to eat in the pita. Cut the meat into smallish chunks—remember, you are going to eat this as a sandwich of sorts, not as a big kebab. Add the meat to all the marinade ingredients in a sealable plastic bag, mix well, and put in the fridge for at least 2 hours, and up to a full day ahead.

Meanwhile, make the *tzatziki* sauce by mixing all of those ingredients together. Keep that in the fridge until you are ready to serve. This can be done a day in advance.

Chop all your accompaniments: tomatoes, cucumbers, lemons, and red onion. If eating raw red onion isn't your cup of tea, soak the sliced onion in lemon juice or white wine vinegar while the meat is marinating. This quick pickle will pull the harshness right out of the onions.

(continued)

TZATZIKI SAUCE

2 tablespoons olive oil

2 tablespoons lemon juice

7 ounces of Greek yogurt

½ cup diced cucumber, peeled and seeded

1 tablespoon dill

2 garlic cloves, minced

Salt and black pepper to taste

OTHER STUFF

Tomatoes

Cucumbers

Red onions

Lemon wedges

Pita breads

Skewers

When you're ready to rock, get your grill very hot. Make sure the grill grates are clean. Salt the venison liberally, and skewer the venison pieces together—this is not how I normally do meat skewers, but jamming them all together helps keep these small pieces of meat from overcooking. Lay the skewers on the hot grill and cook them with the grill cover open until they are medium, about 4 minutes per side depending on how hot your grill is. I use the finger test for doneness (see page 79) to determine when to pull the meat off. Keep it on the skewers while you take it to the table.

To serve, lay everything out and let people make their own little pita sandwiches. Serve with a nice light Greek red wine, a dry rosé, or a crisp beer or three.

ETHIOPIAN TIBS

Serves 4 | **Prep Time: 20 minutes** | **Cook Time: 10 minutes**

Tibs is the unusual name for one of the cooler Ethiopian dishes out there. It's a hybrid stir-fry and stew that comes together in an instant, is meaty and rich, and can be spicy as hell. Served with bread, rice, or, more properly, *injera* flatbread, it was and is my favorite Ethiopian dish. Many years ago I worked in an Ethiopian restaurant where I always made this dish with lamb, but it's great with venison.

This dish is super easy to make, but you do need a few unusual ingredients and spices, and you need to have everything set to go before you start cooking because it comes together quickly.

First, you must get yourself some Ethiopian *berbere*. It comes as either a spice mixture or a paste. You can buy it online, or in places like Whole Foods or Cost Plus World Market, or you can make it yourself. You'll also need clarified butter, although tibs tastes more authentic if you make your own Ethiopian spiced butter. Of the many spices listed in the ingredients, the most important is the fenugreek.

I know it sounds like a lot for a simple plate of food, but if you do this, you will not be sorry. The flavors are exotic, mesmerizing, and addictive. And once you have the basic ingredients, they all last for months. So you can make it again. And again.

1 large red onion, sliced thin (about 2 cups)

¼ cup *niter kebbeh* (spiced butter) or clarified butter (ghee)

2 pounds venison, lamb, or beef, cut into bite-sized pieces

2 tablespoons *berbere* powder

1 teaspoon ground fenugreek

½ teaspoon cardamom (optional)

½ teaspoon ground ginger

¼ teaspoon cumin

¼ teaspoon ground clove

1 teaspoon black pepper

3 to 4 garlic cloves, sliced thinly

2 cups whole, peeled tomatoes, broken into bits

1 to 5 green chiles, such as jalapeños or serranos, sliced thin

½ cup red wine

Get the sauté pan or wok very hot. Stir-fry the onions without the butter for a few minutes, until they char just a little on the outside. Add the spiced butter and the venison. Stir-fry hot and fast until the outside of the meat is brown but the inside of the meat is still very rare. You need to do this on as hot a burner as you have.

The moment the meat has browned, add the spices, garlic, and chiles. Stir-fry another 30 seconds or so, then add the tomatoes and the wine. Toss to combine and let this cook for a minute or two. Serve at once with bread, rice, or *injera*.

Ethiopian Spiced Butter

Makes about 2 cups

If you want to make your own *niter kibbeh*, here's how we did it at the restaurant.

1 pound unsalted butter

2 minced shallots, about ¼ cup

2 minced garlic cloves

2 tablespoons minced fresh ginger

12 to 15 crushed cardamom pods

2 or 3 whole cloves

A cinnamon stick

1 tablespoon dried oregano

½ teaspoon ground turmeric

1 teaspoon ground fenugreek

Toast the cardamom, cloves, and cinnamon in a dry pan over medium heat until they are aromatic. Cut the butter into cubes. Toss everything into a heavy pot and turn the heat on low. Let this come to a bare simmer and cook for at least 30 minutes. We cooked ours at least an hour. *It is vital that the milk solids do not burn.* If they do, you have ruined the butter. Watch for browning, and as soon as you see it, remove from the heat.

Strain through cheesecloth and store in a clean glass jar. It'll last 6 months in the fridge, at least a week on the counter, and forever in the freezer.

VENISON TARTARE

Serves 4 | Prep Time: 20 minutes

Beef or venison tartare is the "trust fall" of the culinary world: raw meat and a raw egg yolk. If your ingredients are not impeccable, things can go very, very wrong. But done right, this is at once a primal and exciting little appetizer.

Tartare is all about texture. Raw meat has a savory slipperiness that causes many people to argue within themselves. It seems so wrong, almost dangerous, yet something deep within urges you to take another bite. It's our inner Australopithecine talking. Beyond the meat, the silky richness of the broken yolk acts as a sauce, flecks of herbs or other flavors sparkle here and there, and the decided crunch of raw shallot punctuates each bite.

Some people, notably Wisconsinites, seem to like their tartare ground. I don't. I prefer it minced, which I think has a better texture. Use a large, very sharp chef's knife to mince the venison. Take your time and don't chop it like you would herbs: It will get all stringy. If you are going to make this recipe for more than four people, my advice is to cut the venison into manageable pieces first, then keep them all in the fridge. Mince one piece at a time and then return it to the refrigerator; this keeps everything cold.

After that, it's all just a question of seasonings. Mine are woodsy, with juniper and caraway. The garnish is wood sorrel, which tastes lemony; it's a hat tip to Chef Rene Redzepi of Denmark, who uses wood sorrel in his tartare.

Any species of venison will work, as will any cut of meat that is free of fat and sinew. Backstrap is best, I find, but I also really like using the heart.

I use some esoteric ingredients here, but there are easy substitutions for most of them—but not all. You really do need the juniper berries, which you can find in many supermarkets or buy online. Or, if you have Eastern red cedar in your neighborhood, that's actually a juniper; harvest these berries when they are deep bluish purple. The other key ingredient here is smoked salt. Any finely-ground smoked salt will work, but the one I prefer is the alder smoked salt from The Meadow in Portland, Oregon.

If you want to use quail eggs here, as I do, look for them at farmer's markets or Asian markets.

Serve this on crackers or in little bowls with crackers alongside. Remember, a little tartare goes a long way.

---

1 shallot, about 1 heaping tablespoon, minced

3 tablespoons red wine vinegar

1 heaping teaspoon juniper berries (about 6 berries)

1 level teaspoon caraway seeds

1 teaspoon black peppercorns

½ to ¾ pound venison

Smoked salt to taste

4 egg yolks (quail egg yolks are cool if you have them)

Wood sorrel or grated lemon zest, for garnish

Soak the minced shallot in the vinegar in a small bowl. Toast the juniper berries, caraway seeds, and peppercorns in a small pan over medium-high heat (shaking often to prevent them from burning) until they are fragrant, about 2 minutes. Move the spices to a grinder or mortar and pestle and grind to a coarse powder.

Mince the venison with a sharp knife. I prefer to cut it into ⅛ inch dice or smaller. If you are not terribly skilled with a chef's knife, partially freeze the meat, which will make it easier to dice small. Put the minced venison in a bowl and sprinkle over the ground spices. Drain the shallots and add them to the bowl. Add about ½ teaspoon of smoked salt, and mix the tartare together. Add more salt to taste.

(continued)

To serve, give everyone some tartare and make a little depression in the center. Separate the egg yolks from the white and discard the whites (or use in another recipe). Put the yolks in the little depression. Garnish with the wood sorrel or lemon zest.

"The weather was fine and moderate. The hunters all returned, having killed during their absence three elk, four deer, two porcupines, a fox and a hare."

—MERIWETHER LEWIS

Eating Raw Venison

I know what you're thinking: No way I'd eat raw venison! It's not a crazy concern. But here's what you need to know to eat raw venison as safely as possible:

Shoot straight. Seriously. If you've gut-shot the animal, think twice about making it into tartare or carpaccio. *E. coli*, both the really nasty O157 variety as well as the nasty-but-non-lethal O103 strain, have been found in venison (and all other ruminants). It mostly lives in the digestive tract. So if you break that tract and get gut gunk all over the inside of your deer, you'd better cook it well.

Cut cleanly. This is an extension of Rule No. 1. If you break the guts while eviscerating the animal, it's nearly as bad as gut-shooting it.

Freeze your venison first. This should kill any larval parasites that might be in the venison, as well as tapeworm and *Toxoplasma gondii* (which causes toxoplasmosis), which are known to exist in deer. Freezing the meat below 0°F (some sources recommend -4°F) for at least two days will go a long way toward making any raw meat safer to eat.

Avoid any possible cross-contamination. Your venison might be perfectly fine, but if you have a dirty cutting board or knife or even hands, you can wreck the whole thing. Sanitation is very important when preparing and serving raw food.

Keep it cool. Just as sushi should be served cold, so should tartare. Work quickly, and keep the venison in the fridge when you are not cutting or mixing it.

Even so, this is not a 100% risk-free recipe. But then again, neither is a trip to your neighborhood sushi bar. Or your breakfast—you are far more likely to get salmonella from eggs than you are from getting sick from raw venison, if you follow the steps above. Needless to say, your egg needs to be of the finest quality to use for tartare.

VENISON STROGANOFF

Serves 4 | Prep Time: 20 minutes | Cook Time: 20 minutes

This one is a classic. I mean, really, who hasn't eaten beef stroganoff? I've seen (and eaten) so many versions of it that I've lost track. They've ranged from horrible—cream of mushroom soup and hamburger—to sublime renditions done with care and with great ingredients. I think you'll find this recipe to be among the latter.

Stroganoff has traditionally been made with quality meat, sliced thin. With venison, thinly sliced pieces of loin mixed with mushrooms, shallots, dill, and sour cream are the ticket. This is filling, easy-to-eat, cool-weather food of the first order.

What to eat it with? Well, historically it's been French fries, believe it or not. But here in America, stroganoff is almost always served with egg noodles. I went with Austrian spätzle, which are a lot like egg noodles. You can do whatever, but I really like the way the stroganoff matches with the little spätzle dumplings. Spätzle makers are cheap and easily available online.

STROGANOFF

4 tablespoons butter

1½ pounds venison backstrap, in one piece

2 large shallots, minced

2 minced garlic cloves

¼ pound sliced cremini or button mushrooms

¼ pound sliced shiitake mushrooms

1 teaspoon ground nutmeg

2 tablespoons chopped fresh dill

¼ cup Madeira wine (or white wine)

1 cup sour cream at room temperature

Dill pollen to garnish (optional)

Heavy cream, to loosen sauce (optional)

SPÄTZLE

2 cups flour

¼ teaspoon nutmeg

¼ teaspoon black or white pepper

1 to 2 teaspoons salt

1 egg, lightly beaten

½ cup sour cream

Up to ¾ cup heavy cream

I make the spätzle first. These can be made up to a day ahead and stored in the fridge. Mix all the ingredients except the heavy cream together in a bowl. Now thin the sticky dough into a batter that is a bit like really thick pancake batter with the heavy cream. I use a spätzle maker to make my spätzle, but you can either use a colander with wide holes or just flick the dough/batter off a cutting board with a knife.

Get a kettle of salty water going over high heat. Once it boils, make the spätzle. Boil them hard until they float, then 1 minute more. Skim off with a slotted spoon or a spider skimmer. Move them to a baking sheet. When they are all made, toss them with a little oil so they don't stick together.

To make the stroganoff, salt the venison well and let it sit on the cutting board for 20 minutes or so. I do this while I make the spätzle. Get 2 tablespoons butter in a large sauté pan good and hot over medium-high heat. Pat the venison dry and sear all sides well in the butter. Cook it until it's rare to medium-rare. If you don't know how to determine this, use the finger test for doneness (page 79). When the meat is ready, move it to a cutting board and let it rest.

Add the mushrooms to the pan and turn the heat to high. Soon they will give up their water, and when they do, use a wooden spoon to scrape up any browned bits from the bottom of the pan. When most of the water has boiled away, add the rest of the butter to the pan along with the shallots and sauté everything for 3 to 5 minutes, stirring often. Add the garlic, toss and cook over high heat for another 3 minutes or so. Sprinkle some salt over everything.

Add the Madeira and toss to combine. Let this boil down furiously. While it is doing so, grate some nutmeg over the mixture. When the Madeira is mostly gone, turn the heat down to low. Slice the venison thinly and return it and any juices that have collected on the cutting board to the pan. Stir to combine and add most of the chopped fresh dill.

Stir in the sour cream and turn off the heat. Stir to combine and let it heat through, using the heat in the pan. Do not let this boil, or even simmer, or Very Bad Things will happen. Think nasty and curdled. To serve, spread out over the spätzle and top with any remaining dill and the dill pollen, if using.

ROASTS

Not everyone can roast a haunch of venison over an open fire, but we can all cook a great hunk from the hind leg in our ovens. Venison lends itself to the homey pot roast as well as the prettier roasts sporting that deeply brown "bark" on the outside and perfectly cooked, medium-rare meat inside. Baking, which is what cooking a roast in the oven actually is, technically speaking, requires a bit of knowledge to get right.

Roasting large hunks of meat is more of an art than a science. In few other areas of cookery are recipes more suggestion than prescription. It's not brain surgery, but you do need to be watchful. True roasting requires the radiant heat of an open fire, and if you are ever lucky enough to eat a haunch of venison properly roasted over such a fire, you will never forget it (see page 78). Texas barbecue comes close, but only in a galactic sense. What most of us do is technically baking, but it still creates wonderful results if you know what you are doing.

What follows is what I know about roasting meat. I've been doing it for many years, but keep in mind that roasting is like life: It's the journey that's important, and it never ends. I learn new things about roasting every year.

I begin any roast by bringing the meat toward room temperature. Roasting a cold joint of meat is a bad idea. Doing so gets you a charred exterior with a cold center, and unless you enjoy this, you will be sad. I also salt early and often. Salt when the meat is resting before cooking; use salt in whatever rub you happen to be using, and salt when you serve. Adding salt little by little as the meat roasts makes it taste more of itself; adding it all at the end makes the meat taste of salt.

Venison is lean, so you need some sort of fat. I prefer rubbing the meat with oil, but you could drape bacon over it if you wanted to. I've also smeared lard or duck fat over the meat, too.

Like roasting primal cuts, I prefer to start my roast in a low oven and sear the hell out of it at the end. I may begin with something like 300°F or 350°F, but occasionally I'll start even lower if time is not an issue. I roast the meat this way until the center hits about 110°F, and then I remove it to rest while I jack up the heat in my oven.

How high an oven? Somewhere between 450°F and 500°F. The smaller the roast, the hotter the oven. I roast the venison this way for at least fifteen minutes, and up to twenty-five minutes.

Tips on Roasting

Either bury an oven-proof thermometer in the meat so you can read it periodically, or make sure you keep using the same hole you punch into the venison each time you test the temperature. This will minimize the amount of juice that will run out.

When taking the temperature of the interior of the meat, be sure the meat thermometer does not touch bone. Bone will be hotter than the meat.

Baste the venison every 10 to 15 minutes with oil. Oil conducts heat better than water, and it will moisten the meat.

Finishing the roast requires attention and an eye for doneness, however. For whatever reason, heat does not seem to increase in a linear fashion with roasting meat. I've tested the center of a roast and have had it at 110°F and then a mere ten minutes later have seen it jump all the way to 140°F. So be vigilant.

I've used those fancy probe thermometers—the kind you jam into the center of the meat, with an attached wire connected to the read-out sitting outside the oven. They *are* quite useful—you can pretty much stand there and watch the temperatures rise at the center of your roast. But if you don't have one, you just need to be watchful. When in doubt, pull the meat early. You can always put it back in the oven. Roasts, no matter what meat they're from, are serious, expensive pieces of meat. Letting one get away from you can ruin a holiday meal.

Finally, for the love of all that's holy, rest the roast thoroughly. If you do not, all the juices will flow out of the meat and onto your cutting board. In the case of a roast, this is an unforgivable sin (see "To Rest or Not," page 80). Wait, and you shall be rewarded. How long? At least ten minutes, even in an emergency. For a typical roast of between four and six pounds, fifteen minutes is about right. Even thirty minutes is not too long.

As for carving, I find that bone-in roasts are best carved in large hunks—take a big hunk off the roast first, then carve into serving slices. Boneless roasts can just be sliced.

BASIC ROAST VENISON

Serves 4 to 8, depending on the size of the roast
Prep Time: 45 minutes, mostly to let the meat come to room temperature
Cook Time: 90 minutes, again, depending on the size of the roast.

This is my master roast recipe. If you've read my general pointers on roasting venison on the previous page, this is the recipe you should start with. It is the venison equivalent of roast beef. The older your animal was, the more important it will be to use single-muscle roasts. This recipe will not melt any connective tissue separating muscle groups, and the finished roast would have tough veins of still-hard connective tissue running through it.

Many single-muscle roasts benefit from trussing with kitchen twine. Doing this helps keep the roast compact, which means it will cook more evenly (see the tutorial on page 122).

A note on the oil: I absolutely love the flavor that roasted squash seed oil brings to venison. You can find it in some stores, but your best bet is to buy squash seed oil online. That said, any good oil will work: olive oil, walnut oil, even sesame oil—the point is to use something that adds flavor to the roast.

Serve this with something green and whichever starch you fancy. Mashed, baked, or roasted potatoes are traditional, but I like German dumplings (page 255).

A 2- to 4-pound venison roast

Salt

¼ cup squash seed oil or other flavorful oil

3 or 4 celery stalks

About 1 cup of red wine, stock or water

2 tablespoons minced sage, rosemary, or
    thyme, or a combination of these

2 tablespoons freshly ground black pepper

Take the venison roast out of the fridge and salt it well. Let it sit on a cutting board for 30 minutes before proceeding. After 30 minutes have elapsed, preheat the oven to 350°F.

Pat the venison dry, then massage the oil all over it. Coat the roast with the minced sage and black pepper. Pour enough wine, stock, or water into the bottom of the roasting pan to just moisten the bottom—don't totally cover the bottom or the meat will steam. You just want to limit the amount of smoke you will eventually be producing. Set the celery stalks in the roasting pan and put the venison on them to keep the meat up off the liquids.

Set the pan in the oven and roast until the deepest part of the meat reaches the temperature you want; if you pull the venison at 100°F, you are on the way to rare. I pull mine at 110°F, which will ultimately be closer to medium. Do not let the venison cook past 130°F under any circumstances or it will get tough and gray. How long will this take? A general rule is about 20 minutes per pound at 350°F.

Remove the pan and jack the oven up to 450°F. You might want to drizzle a little more oil over the roast at this point. When the

(continued)

oven hits temperature, set the pan back in and roast until the venison is nicely browned, about 20 minutes. Be vigilant about temperatures here: For rare, you want the temperature at the meat's center to be 110°F, medium about 125°F or so.

When the venison has hit the temperature you want, move it to a cutting board and let it rest. If the meat is more than 10°F lower than you want it (see temperature chart on page 80) tent it with foil. Don't carve it for at least 10 minutes; I wait a full 15 minutes. Carve and serve.

How to Truss a Roast

Trussing a roast helps keep the meat in a compact shape, which in turn helps it cook evenly so you avoid odd pointy ends that get cooked to hell. You will want a long length of kitchen twine for this, longer than you think you need. A typical venison roast will need about three feet of twine—and it's better to have too much twine than not enough. Drape the twine over your shoulder while you work so it doesn't fall on the floor.

You want to work with the shape of the roast, not against it. Most roasts are rectangular or cylindrical: You want to reinforce that shape.

Start by running the twine underneath the roast lengthwise. Leave about four inches of twine on the end of the roast nearest to you. Working on the end of the roast farthest from you, press the twine down on the roast about an inch down it with one thumb, then sweep a loop of twine under the roast and back to your thumb. Tuck the long length of twine under the bit of twine you held down with your thumb and pull it all the way through. Pull it tight. Repeat this process every inch of the roast all the way down the roast until you get to the end closest to you. Pull everything taught and tie off the two ends of twine.

SAUERBRATEN

Serves 6 to 8 | Prep Time: 5 days, almost all passive marinating time | Cook Time: 5 hours

I think there's a law somewhere that if you write a venison cookbook, you must include a recipe for German sauerbraten. This is a fair and just law, as sauerbraten is one of the great pot roasts of all time. This Teutonic classic comes in as many varieties as there are cooks. I've seen all sorts of variations on the sauce, on the cut of meat, on the cooking temperature. At its core, however, sauerbraten involves a large piece of meat that has been marinated a long time and slowly cooked in a vinegar-based marinade, which is then turned into a sauce.

My use of ginger snaps in the sauce comes from the sauerbraten I once ate as a child at a New York restaurant called Lüchows, a bastion of German cooking in the NYC area until it closed in 1982. They used ginger snaps in their sauce, and I loved it. Still do.

A word on the marinade. You must boil the marinade before using it for two reasons: first, to burn off much of the alcohol in the wine (otherwise the meat gets a weird metallic taste); and second, the heat extracts more flavor from all the spices you put in it. Let the marinade cool completely before submerging the venison.

Oh, and use an inexpensive wine you might think about drinking on a Wednesday night; nothing fancy. Can you use something other than wine? Yes, but then it is not a sauerbraten. It is a pot roast. Still good, though.

3- to 4-pound roast of venison

MARINADE

1 bottle of red wine

½ cup red wine vinegar

2 cups water

1 tablespoon black peppercorns

1 tablespoon juniper berries

1 tablespoon mustard seed

6 to 8 cloves

3 bay leaves

1 tablespoon dried thyme

2 celery stalks, chopped

2 carrots, peeled and chopped

1 medium onion, chopped

TO FINISH

¼ cup melted butter or sunflower, pumpkinseed, or walnut oil

8 ginger snap cookies

3 tablespoon butter

2 tablespoon flour

Salt

Bring marinade ingredients—wine, vinegar, water, peppercorns, juniper, mustard, cloves, bay leaves, thyme, celery, carrots, and onion—to a boil and turn off the heat. Allow to cool. Submerge the venison in the marinade and let it sit in the fridge for at least 24 hours, and up to 5 days. Three days is a good length of time. When you're ready to cook, take the roast out of the marinade and salt it well. Set it aside for 20 minutes or so.

Preheat the oven to 275°F. Actually, 225°F is a better temperature, but the roast can take up to 8 hours to properly cook then; this is what I do at home on weekends. At 275°F, the roast will probably take about 5 hours to cook. You can go up to 300°F—a typical

(continued)

venison roast will be ready in 3½ hours at this temperature—but you will get gray, not pink, meat. It will still taste good, though. Another option is to cook sous vide (see sidebar).

Pour the marinade into a pot and bring it to a boil. Pour it into a Dutch oven or other lidded pot and place the venison inside. Cover and put in the oven. If the venison is not submerged by the marinade, turn the roast over every hour. This is also a good way to test for doneness—you want the roast to be almost falling apart. When the roast is done, take it out of the pot and coat it with some of the ¼ cup oil or melted butter. Reserve the rest of the oil or butter for later. Wrap it in foil.

Now you make the sauerbraten sauce—and sauerbraten is all about the sauce. Strain the cooking liquid through a fine-meshed sieve into a bowl. Take the ginger snap cookies and pulverize them in a blender. You want it to look like rough cornmeal or coarse flour.

In a medium-sized pot, melt 3 tablespoons of butter over medium-high heat. When it is frothing and totally melted, whisk in 2 tablespoons of flour. Cook until it is the color of coffee-and-cream, stirring often. Slowly whisk in the cooking liquid, one cup at a time. The mixture will turn to clay at first, then loosen into a silky sauce. Taste for salt (it will probably need it),and add enough to your taste.

Whisk in 4 tablespoons of the pulverized ginger snaps. They will not dissolve completely at first, but keep stirring and they will disappear. Taste the sauce. Add another tablespoon of ginger snaps if you want, or add a tablespoon of sugar. The sauce should taste sour, warm (a pumpkin pie sort of spicy warm), and a little zippy and sweet.

To serve, slice the roast into ¼ inch-thick slices. Venison can be dry—it has zero internal fat—so one trick I use is to paint each slice in melted butter or oil before I serve it. You'll need about half a stick of melted butter to do this. Serve with lots of sauce, some braised onions, and either mashed potatoes, egg noodles, Bavarian dumplings (page 76) or spätzle (page 118). A hearty red wine would be an ideal match here, as would a dark, malty beer.

ITALIAN POT ROAST

Serves 4 to 6 | Prep Time: 20 minutes | Cook Time: 4 hours

This is a pretty classic recipe, with lots of renditions from both native Italians and Italian-Americans. The flavors are similar to osso buco made with shanks (page 213) but this is best done with a shoulder roast from an old animal, a neck roast, or a whole-muscle hind leg roast.

If you have a large piece of meat that you are pot roasting, you will want to add a little more tomato, wine and broth so you have more sauce. The reason is that after all those hours of slow cooking, the meat, while tender, can dry out a bit and will need the sauce to keep things moist.

A 2- to 4-pound venison roast

Salt

2 tablespoons olive oil

1 onion

1 large carrot

1 celery stalk

A handful of dried mushrooms, crushed (optional)

1 tablespoon tomato paste

1 cup red wine

One 32-ounce can whole, peeled tomatoes

1 cup venison or beef broth

½ teaspoon dried thyme

1 teaspoon dried oregano or marjoram

1 teaspoon chopped rosemary

1 bay leaf

½ cup chopped fresh parsley

Black pepper to taste

Salt the roast well. Heat the olive oil in a Dutch oven or other heavy, lidded pot and brown the roast on all sides. This will take a little while, so take your time. While the roast is browning, roughly chop the onion, carrot, and celery and put the pieces into a food processor. Buzz until the vegetables are small, but not pureed.

When the roast has browned, remove it for now. Add the vegetables and mushrooms (if using) and cook them until the onion is soft and nicely golden, about 6 minutes. As the vegetables cook, use a wooden spoon to scrape up any browned bits that have stuck to the bottom of the pot.

Stir in the tomato paste, then add all the herbs except for the parsley. Nestle the roast back into the pot and pour the wine over the roast. Bring this to a boil and let it cook for a minute or two. Now add the juice from the can of tomatoes. As for the tomatoes themselves, take each one and crush and shred it with your fingers, then add them to the pot. If the liquids have reached halfway up the sides of the roast, you're good to go. If not, add the stock.

Cover the pot and cook over very low heat until the venison is very tender, about 3 to 5 hours, depending on the roast's size and how old the animal was.

Gently remove the roast and set it on a cutting board. Taste the sauce and add salt and black pepper to taste. Stir in the parsley and let the residual heat wilt it. Slice the roast and serve with the sauce and either grits or polenta, or pasta.

BARBACOA

Serves 6 to 8 | **Prep Time: 15 minutes** | **Cook Time: 3 hours, more or less**

This is perhaps my favorite recipe for a deer's front shoulder, with the possible exception of the Braised Venison Shoulder on page 71. Mexican *barbacoa*, a mildly spicy, long-braised variant on barbecue, works perfectly with the tough, sinewy front legs of a deer. The meat cooks very slowly, and all that connective tissue dissolves into the broth, making everything richer and just a little slick. Keeps your lips shiny.

Barbacoa is more warming than *picante*. Yes, there are *chipotles en adobo* in it, but not so many that your head blows off (*chipotles en adobo* can be bought in every Latin market I've ever been in, and even in some "regular" supermarkets). The cloves are a stronger element, as are the cumin and bay. If you want to test this recipe before making it, go to your nearest Chipotle restaurant and try their barbacoa: This recipe is virtually identical.

Serve it in tacos, burritos, or tostadas, or over rice. And be sure to have at least a few of the traditional accompaniments, like cilantro, crumbled *queso seco* (a feta-like Mexican cheese), chopped onions, sour cream, fresh or pickled chiles, avocados—basically anything that works well on a taco.

Still not convinced? Well, barbacoa may well be in the Top Five Easiest Recipes in this book. It's literally a crock-pot-it-and-go dish. Minimal chopping, and the only thing you need to do as a cook is to shred the meat. Stupid crazy easy. Try it and you will not be sad.

No front shoulder? You can also use shanks, roasts, neck, or even the head of the animal; barbacoa is traditionally done with a cow's head, after all.

2 to 3 pounds venison, from the shoulder
    or legs

2 to 4 canned *chipotles en adobo*

1 red onion, chopped

5 garlic cloves, chopped

2 bay leaves

1 teaspoon smoked paprika (optional)

1 teaspoon ground cumin

1 teaspoon ground cloves

1 tablespoon kosher salt

½ cup lime juice

½ cup cider vinegar

1 quart beef or venison stock

¼ cup lard or vegetable oil

Smoked salt (optional)

Cilantro, shredded cheese, sour cream,
    avocados, and hot sauce for garnish

Put everything in a slow cooker or Dutch oven and cook, covered, until the meat falls off the bone, which will be between 2 hours (for a young deer) and 6 hours if you have a very old animal. If you use a slow cooker, set it to "high." If you use a regular pot, put it into the oven set to 300°F.

Pull all the meat from the bones and shred with forks or your fingers. Stir in the lard, and add smoked salt to taste. You want the lard or oil to coat the shreds of meat. Pour over some of the juices from the pot and put the meat in a pan for the table. Serve with tacos, in a burrito, or on a bun.

Variation: DZIK DE VENADO (YUCATÁN VENISON)

This version of barbacoa uses a braise similar to the Barbacoa recipe, but you then toss the shredded venison with radishes, chiles, cilantro, and sour orange juice (or a combination of orange and lime juice) into a sort of mashup of barbacoa, *cochinita pibil*, and ceviche. It is a traditional venison dish of the Yucatán.

BRAISE

2 to 3 pounds venison, from the shoulder
    or legs

1 red onion, chopped

5 garlic cloves, chopped

2 bay leaves

1 teaspoon ground cumin

1 teaspoon ground cloves

1 tablespoon kosher salt

1 quart beef or venison stock

Salt

TO FINISH

¼ cup lime juice

½ cup orange juice

2 tablespoons minced green onion or chives

1 cup chopped red onion

2 diced plum tomatoes
    (only if they are in season)

½ cup chopped radishes

½ cup chopped cilantro

1 to 3 minced habaneros

Pickled red onion and sliced radishes
    for garnish

To pickle the onions, slice them thinly from root to tip and soak them in lime juice while the venison is cooking.

Put all the ingredients for the braise into a pot and mix together. Bring to a boil and then simmer gently until the venison begins to fall apart. When it's tender, shred it with two forks and toss it with the salad ingredients. Garnish with the onion and radishes.

Serve with tostadas or corn tortillas.

VENISON CONFIT

Serves 4 to 6 | Prep Time: 24 to 72 hours, passive curing time | Cook Time: 6 to 12 hours

Confit, pronounced "con-fee," is an old French method of preserving meats, usually duck. Basically, you salt a piece of meat, then cook it very slowly in fat. The idea is that poaching the meat in fat for hours and hours will not only give you meltingly tender meat, but it will be bathed in fat, keeping otherwise dry meats silky.

It's perfect for venison. Shoulder, neck, or hind leg roasts—even shanks—are excellent cooked this way. And since it's salted, the finished meat will also keep for more than a week in the fridge.

The easiest way to make this recipe is with a vacuum sealer and a large pot. You salt the meat down, pat it dry, and then put it into a vacuum bag with some fat and herbs. Then you cook it very slowly in hot water. Note I said "hot," not simmering or boiling water. You want the heat to be at a steam, not a simmer. A big pot of water is the easiest thing to use for this because water holds its temperature well. A sous vide water oven is perfectly designed for this task.

If you don't have a vacuum sealer, you can of course do this the old school way: Submerge the venison in lard, butter, or duck fat and cook in a 190°F oven all day. This requires a lot of fat, so I rarely do it this way. But it works well.

When you're done, you shred the meat and eat it in all sorts of ways. My favorite? Either as a taco filling or like pulled pork barbecue, with my favorite mustard-based South Carolina-style BBQ sauce and some coleslaw.

BRINE

¼ cup sugar

½ cup kosher salt

2 teaspoons dried thyme

2 teaspoons dried rosemary,
   or 1 tablespoon fresh

2 bay leaves

2 star anise pods (optional)

4 garlic cloves, smashed

6 allspice berries

10 juniper berries (optional)

OTHER INGREDIENTS

A 2- to 4-pound venison roast

1 cup unsalted butter, lard, or duck fat

3 sprigs fresh thyme

3 sprigs fresh rosemary

2 bay leaves

Put all the brine ingredients in a pot with 2 quarts of water and bring to the steaming point—just enough to dissolve everything. Let this come to room temperature, then chill it. When the brine is cold, submerge the venison in it and store in the fridge for 24 to 72 hours. The longer you brine the meat, the saltier it will get. Larger roasts need an extra day.

Take the venison out of the brine; discard the brine. Pat the meat dry and, if you have time, let it air dry uncovered in the fridge for an hour or two, or up to 48 hours if you put it into a covered container. When you are ready to cook the venison, seal it in a vacuum bag with the lard and the herbs. If you happen to have a sous vide water oven, cook it at 150°F for as long as 24 hours, and at least 10 hours. Most of you won't have a sous vide machine, however, so instead, fill your largest pot with water and heat it to a bare simmer, about 180°F. Drop the bag with the venison in it and hold the water temperature at the steaming point—do not let it simmer, let alone boil—for about 6 hours.

How you serve your confit is up to you. You can shred and eat it on the spot. Or, shred and mix in a salad, with pasta, spätzle, on a burger bun, in a taco . . . you get the point. But even better? Before you actually eat your confit, shred it roughly and put it under the broiler until one side gets a little charred. That bit of char and caramelized goodness makes a good dish great.

South Carolina BBQ Sauce

This mustard-based sauce goes well with pretty much everything from poultry to pork to venison, and even full-flavored fish like amberjack, tuna, and king mackerel.

4 tablespoons butter

1 medium onion, grated on a box grater

½ cup yellow "ballpark" mustard

½ cup cider vinegar

½ cup brown sugar

1 heaping tablespoon powdered mustard

Hot sauce to taste

Salt to taste

Heat the butter in a small pot and cook the grated onion over medium heat for 4 to 5 minutes, until soft but not browned. Add the remaining ingredients, stir well, and let this cook over very low heat for 20 minutes. You can puree it in a blender if you want a smooth sauce. Once made, this BBQ sauce will keep in the fridge for a month or more.

TRI-TIP-STYLE VENISON ROAST WITH CHIMICHURRI

Serves 6 to 8 | **Prep Time: At least 1 hour** | **Cook Time: 1 hour**

Tri-tip is a very West Coast cut of beef, a triangular muscle taken from the bottom of the sirloin at the top of a cow's hind leg; technically it's known as the *tensor fasciae latae*. But you need not worry about that because unless you are dealing with moose or a really big bull elk, you won't bother isolating this muscle. Mostly, tri-tip is a style of barbecue from Santa Maria, California, that, well, isn't actually barbecue. It's an indirectly cooked roast. But it's damn good, and it's a great method of cooking whole-muscle venison roasts from anywhere on the hind leg.

A 3- to 5-pound venison roast (see above)

SANTA MARIA RUB

1 tablespoon kosher salt

1 tablespoon ground black pepper

1 teaspoon garlic powder

1 teaspoon onion powder

1 teaspoon cayenne

CHIMICHURRI

2 garlic cloves, minced

1 cup fresh chopped parsley, lightly packed

½ cup fresh chopped mint, lightly packed

1 small hot chile, minced (I use Thai, árbol, or mirasol chiles)

2 to 3 tablespoons lime juice

½ cup olive oil

Salt and black pepper to taste

Mix together the rub ingredients and massage it into the venison. Let the meat sit at room temperature for an hour, or, alternatively, wrap the roast in plastic and refrigerate overnight.

This roast is best cooked over wood or charcoal, but gas will be OK in a pinch. You need to set up the grill so the heat is only on one side, for example, by piling the charcoal in one corner of the grill. You want to add smoke somehow, ideally from oak, which is traditional for Santa Maria BBQ. Get the grill pretty hot, about 325°F, and set the roast on the side of the grill with no coals. If you've kept a fat cap on the roast, put the fat side up. Cover the grill and roast the venison until the interior hits about 115°F, which will take between 30 minutes and an hour, depending on how hot your grill is and how thick your roast is.

When the venison hits this temperature, move it to the direct side of the coals and sear it until it develops a nice crust, about 3 or 4 minutes per side. Watch for flare-ups from any fat that has not rendered out from the roast. Spray them down with a spray bottle of water.

Remove the venison from the grill and let it rest for 10 minutes. Slice against the grain and serve with the chimichurri.

There are two ways to make the chimichurri. In a food processor, buzz to combine the garlic, herbs, chile, lime juice, and a little salt. Do not puree. With the motor running, drizzle in the olive oil. Add more salt and black pepper to taste. Let steep for an hour or so before serving. Or, you can do the traditional method, which is to mince the garlic, chile, and herbs by hand, then pound it all in a mortar and pestle. Slowly add the lime juice, salt, and pepper, pounding all the time, then mix in the olive oil slowly by hand, stirring all the while. Let steep for an hour or so before serving.

MARINATED VENISON KEBABS

Serves 4 | **Prep Time: 24 hours, almost all of it marinating time in the fridge** | **Cook Time: 15 minutes**

Kebabs are perhaps the best summertime preparation for meat from the hind legs of the deer. And after all, who doesn't love to eat a good kebab? There is a certain jazz-like quality to them: You can vary the veggies to suit your preference, and you can marinate the kebabs in anything from a vivid green herb sauce to Italian dressing to teriyaki. Or try this marinade, which is a mixture of red wine vinegar and harissa, which is to North Africa what ketchup is to North America.

Harissa is a condiment whose main flavors are chiles and caraway. And while it's supposed to be spicy, it's not supposed to be blow-your-head-off spicy. You'll note in my recipe below most of the chiles are milder varieties like poblano, pasilla, and ancho. If you are not into hot food, go easy on the really hot ones like the cascabels or Aleppo. You can buy harissa in places like Cost Plus World Market or Whole Foods, too.

I like to serve these kebabs with something simple, like grilled potatoes or bread, or, if I'm feeling like a low-carb day, coleslaw.

HARISSA

8 dried guajillo, ancho, pasilla, or New Mexican chiles

4 to 8 dried hot chiles, Aleppo if you can get them

1 teaspoon caraway seeds

½ teaspoon coriander seeds

½ teaspoon cumin seeds

1 teaspoon dried mint

¼ cup olive oil

2 teaspoons kosher salt

4 to 6 garlic cloves, mashed and minced

Lemon juice

KEBABS

2 pounds venison, trimmed of sinew and cut into 1½- to 2-inch chunks

¼ to ⅓ cup harissa (see above)

¼ cup red wine vinegar

Salt

Various vegetables cut to the size of the venison, such as mushrooms, onions, bell peppers, or zucchini

If you're making your own harissa, start by removing the stems and seeds from the dried chiles. Tear the chiles into pieces and pour enough hot water over them to just barely cover. Weigh the chiles down with a small plate or something similar and let the chiles soak for an hour or two, until they're soft.

Once the chiles are soft, put them and the remaining ingredients into a blender or food processor and process into a paste—it can be smooth or rough, depending on how you like it. You might need a little bit of the soaking water to loosen things up. You can make the harissa days or even weeks in advance and store it in the refrigerator; it lasts for months that way.

To marinate the venison, mix the harissa and the red wine vinegar into a slurry in a bowl. Massage the marinade into the venison and pour the whole shebang into a lidded container. Refrigerate for at least a few hours, and as long as 2 days.

When you are ready to cook, remove the venison from the marinade. Cut the various vegetables into pieces roughly the size of the venison. Carefully skewer them onto two skewers—doing this makes it much easier to turn the kebabs. I say carefully because you want to watch out for the pointy ends; I've stabbed myself a couple times when I got distracted. When you've made all your skewers, salt everything well and put them back into the fridge.

(continued)

Get your grill nice and hot. Now make sure the grill grates are clean by scouring with a wire brush. When your grill is ready, soak a paper towel in some vegetable oil and use tongs to wipe down the grates. Lay the skewers on the grill so they are not touching. Grill for 6 to 10 minutes on the top and bottom of the skewers, plus another 1 to 2 minutes on each side to "kiss" the edges. Use the finger test for doneness (page 79) to determine how well-cooked you want your venison.

Let the kebabs rest for 5 minutes, then pull the meat off the skewers and serve.

A Kebab Primer

The real key to great kebabs is how you cook them. If you follow these general directions, you'll make a better kebab—no matter what meat or marinade you are using:

Cut the meat into chunks no smaller than 1 ½ inches and not much bigger than 2½ inches. Too big and the outside gets charred before the inside cooks. Too small and you get shoe leather in a hurry.

Trim out all silverskin and connective tissue. Grilling will tighten up these tissues and leave you chewing and chewing and chewing . . .

Vegetables need to be about the same size as the meat. Otherwise they won't cook properly.

Use bamboo skewers, or freeze your metal ones. Metal conducts heat, which can cook your kebabs from the inside. It's *much* harder to get a medium-rare kebab with a metal skewer.

Use two skewers instead of one. Yes, it's harder to set them up, but you will have a far easier time turning them with two skewers. Meat and especially veggies tend to spin when you only have one skewer.

Leave a little space between everything on the skewers. If you pack the skewers, the space where one item meets another will take a long time to cook.

Start with cold meat! Doing this is insurance against overcooking the center of the venison.

Hot fire, open grill. Don't be tempted to close your grill. That creates an "oven effect" which can overcook your meat in no time. Better to have a really hot fire on one part of the grill, and a cooler section off to one side in case things get too hot too fast. Remember: kebabs are supposed to be cooked over open fire, with no cover.

Follow those general rules and you'll be in business.

KENTUCKY SMOKED VENISON BARBECUE

Serves 6 to 8 | **Prep Time: 20 minutes** | **Cook Time: 4 to 7 hours**

I really wanted to do a proper barbecue for this book—barbacoa (page 127) is kinda-sorta BBQ, but not really. None of the "normal" styles of barbecue worked well with venison. They all just seemed, well, like I was subbing in venison for what the dish really wanted to be, which was pork. But there is at least one barbecue style almost tailor made for venison: an obscure, Western Kentucky style that revolves around mutton. Yep, adult sheep, which is considerably gamier than any venison I've ever eaten.

This is a really unusual barbecue. No tomato, no chile. It hinges on the ingredients: brown sugar and Worcestershire sauce, and hickory smoke. Hickory is a major element in the flavor of this barbecue, which is dark, pungent, smoky, and sweet. It tastes almost Old World. My recipe is based on an extensive eating tour of Western Kentucky mutton barbecue, with a little help from Steven Raichlen's *BBQ USA: 425 Fiery Recipes from All Across America*.

Serve this on buns with coleslaw on top—a Virginia thing, admittedly—and all the picnic fixins', like potato salad, mac and cheese, and lots and lots of beer.

VENISON

A 3- to 5-pound venison roast

Salt and freshly ground black pepper

MOP

1 cup cider vinegar

½ cup Worcestershire sauce

Juice of a lemon

Salt and black pepper to taste

Salt the venison and grind about a tablespoon of pepper over it. Set aside to come to room temperature while you make the sauces and build your fire.

All you need to do for the mop, the thin sauce you baste the meat with while it cooks, is to whisk all the ingredients together. For the barbecue sauce, bring everything to a simmer and cook for about 5 to 10 minutes, just to meld the flavors. This is supposed to be a thin sauce, almost a dipping sauce. Turn off the heat and set aside for now.

Get your smoker going. You want to preheat it, if you can, to about 200°F, but no hotter than 275°F. Put a pan under where the meat will go to catch drippings. If you don't have a smoker, set up a charcoal grill with the coals on one side and a cheap foil roasting pan on the other. Don't make a raging fire—you want a slow burn here. You'll also need to add coals at least once while you cook the venison. Put a little water in the roasting pan. Set some hickory chips on the coals when you're ready to start. Place the venison over the roasting pan, cover the grill and you're off!

(continued)

BBQ SAUCE

¼ cup Worcestershire sauce

¼ cup cider vinegar

1 cup water

Juice of a lemon

5 tablespoons brown sugar

1 teaspoon black pepper

¼ teaspoon ground allspice

½ teaspoon garlic powder

½ teaspoon onion powder

Salt and black pepper to taste

6 to 10 hamburger buns

Coleslaw

Pop open a beer, 'cause it's gonna be a while. Let the venison cook for 30 minutes, then paint it with the mop. Do this every half-hour until the venison is fall-off-the-bone tender, which will take at least 4 hours, and 8 hours is not unheard of. Slow and low is your mantra. Keep an eye on the temperature every 30 minutes or so and do whatever it takes to not top 300°F; anywhere from 200°F to 225°F is your sweet spot. If you're looking for an internal meat temperature, shoot for 185°F to 190°F.

If using a charcoal grill, keep an eye on the coals, and add a few more every hour or so, along with some more hickory, until you're done.

When the venison is ready, move it to a cutting board and let it rest for 5 minutes or so. Now you can either slice it and serve on a plate with the BBQ sauce, or shred it and serve it on the burger buns, again, drenched in the sauce and topped with coleslaw, which is, I admit, not traditional in Kentucky.

"Every morning in Africa, a gazelle wakes up. It knows it must run faster than the fastest lion or it will be killed. Every morning a lion wakes up. It knows it must outrun the slowest gazelle or it will starve to death. It doesn't matter whether you are a lion or a gazelle . . . when the sun comes up, you'd better be running."

—SOURCE UNCERTAIN

VENISON PIEROGIS

Serves 2 gluttons or 4 to 6 normal people | Prep Time: 4 hours, most of it to braise the venison
Cook Time: 15 minutes

Pierogis are one of the world's many little filled dumplings, addictive and homey. The Chinese version, potstickers, is on page 197. Pierogis are Eastern European in origin, and here in America, immigrants from these places carry on that tradition: Cleveland, Pittsburgh, Chicago, various parts of Michigan, Wisconsin, and upstate New York are all cogs in the Great Pierogi Machine.

True to form, a friend of mine from Pittsburgh is the inspiration for this recipe. Her name is Casey Barber, and her book *Pierogi Love* is a must-have if you like these little bundles of happiness. Her original recipe calls for beef short ribs, but I substituted venison here—and I made a few changes to the filling, too.

FILLING

3 tablespoons butter, lard, duck fat, or the cooking oil of your choice

2 pounds venison shoulder, shank meat, or neck meat

Salt and black pepper

1 teaspoon caraway seed

2 celery stalks, chopped

1 onion, chopped

1 carrot, chopped

2 garlic cloves, chopped

A handful of dried mushrooms

1 tablespoon tomato paste

2 tablespoons Worcestershire sauce

A 12-ounce bottle of dark malty beer, such as stout, porter, or a brown ale

1½ cups venison or beef stock

1 tablespoon cornstarch

Heat the butter in a heavy, lidded pot large enough to hold the venison. Salt the meat well and brown it on all sides. Don't crowd the pot, and do this in batches if need be. As the venison browns, remove it from the pot and set aside.

Add the vegetables and cook over medium heat until they begin to brown on the edges, about 10 to 15 minutes. Stir in the tomato paste, then add the Worcestershire sauce, beer, and about ½ cup of broth. Return the meat to the pot and add more stock until it comes halfway up the sides of the meat. Cover the pot and simmer gently over medium-low heat until the meat is very tender. This could be anywhere from 90 minutes to 3 hours, depending on how old your animal was.

When the meat is ready, shred it roughly. Put 1 cup of this meat into a food processor and add 2 tablespoons of cooking liquid. Pulse until coarsely ground.

Depending on what sort of cuts you use, you may have extra meat. You can eat the rest of the meat as a cook's snack, use it to fill agnolotti (page 215), or drop it into soup. Strain the cooking liquid and reserve it to make gravy later. All of this can be done up to a day or two before you make the pierogis.

To make the dough, mix 1 egg, the sour cream, and melted butter into one bowl, and the remaining ingredients into another bowl. Stir the wet into the dry, then knead until the dough comes together—this should only take a minute or three. Cover the dough and let it rest for 15 minutes.

(continued)

DOUGH

2 large eggs

½ cup sour cream (4 ounces)

3 tablespoons melted butter (unsalted)

1 teaspoon salt

1 cup all-purpose flour (4¼ ounces)

1 cup dark rye flour or pumpernickel flour
(3¾ ounces)

Cut the dough in half. Cover one half while you work with the other. Roll the dough into a snake and cut it into 12 pieces. Roll each piece into a ball and set aside, covered. Repeat with the second half of the dough.

Ideally, you have a tortilla press; they are cheap and available online or in any Mexican market. It makes the process of forming all sorts of dumpling wrappers (and, of course, tortillas) so much easier that it's worth the $20. If you have one, line the press with cut pieces of a heavy plastic bag (like a freezer bag), and press each ball of dough into a flat disk.

If you don't have a tortilla press, flatten each ball of dough with your hands, keeping it as round as possible. Finish rolling out the wrappers out on a well-floured surface with a rolling pin. You want them as thin as possible, like ⅛ inch. Alternately, you can roll out the whole batch of dough, and cut out 3-inch circles with a cookie cutter.

Beat the remaining egg for the dough with some water to make an egg wash. Get out a baking sheet and either line it with parchment paper or dust it with semolina flour or cornmeal.

Fill each circle with about a heaping tablespoon of the venison. Using your finger, swipe a little bit of the egg wash along the edge of the dough circle, then fold the dough over the filling to make a half moon. Seal the dumplings with your fingers and set them on the baking sheet.

When you're done, you have a choice: Fry your pierogis or boil them. If you boil them, get a large pot of water boiling and add enough salt to make the water taste a little salty. Boil the pierogis until they float, then boil a minute or two more. If you fry them, get a wide frying pan and add 3 or 4 tablespoons of your favorite fat—duck fat and butter are mine—and fry the pierogis over medium-high heat in one layer until nicely browned, about 2 minutes.

You can eat them all this way, with sour cream and caramelized onions, or you can make a gravy with your cooking liquid by heating it up to steaming, then adding the cornstarch. To do this without clumping, mix the cornstarch with about 1 tablespoon of water to make a slurry, then stir it into the hot liquid. Keep stirring, and bring the gravy to a boil. That will set the corn starch. Drop the heat back to a simmer and you're ready.

SOUPS AND STEWS

Even though I no longer live in a place with truly cold winters, I still eagerly await what cool weather we do have here in Northern California because it's then that I finally get a chance to put a pot of something wonderful on the stove and let it stew there while I write or watch football or do chores around the house. Soups and stews are, at their core, amalgamations of good things to eat, cooked just so in one big pot. Some are simply collections of ingredients tossed in at once and simmered, but the finest soups and stews are built like houses, with foundations, structure, and lots of delicate touches added at precisely the right moment. A stew such as this needs nothing other than good crusty bread to accompany it.

SOUPS VS. STEWS

Soups, put simply, are bowls of goodness where the broth itself is the star, and the things in it play backup. Broth is equally important in a stew, but stews tend to be heartier, and all about the things floating around in it. Most of the recipes in this chapter are stews, but there are a few soups here, such as Scotch Broth (page 159) and Pozole Rojo (page 145), as well as a couple of wonderful soups in the chapter on the wobbly bits that rely on a clear, dark, venison broth with either marrow or liver dumplings (page 240).

Most of these recipes are very easy, but almost all require time. They are intended to be made on a weekend, a day off, or a holiday. The good news is that all stews are better in the couple of days after they're made, so make a pot and eat it for lunches or easy dinners during the week. A few, notably the Thai Curry and the Vietnamese Pho, can be done in a hurry if you're using premade curry paste or premade broth. But for the most part, relax and enjoy the process. Making soup is comforting, nourishing and will perfume your house all day.

CAJUN SAUCE PIQUANTE

Serves 6 to 8 | **Prep Time: 15 minutes** | **Cook Time: 3 hours**

A few years ago, I found myself in southern Louisiana, near Houma. I was down there to catch some redfish near Grand Isle, and en route I stopped for lunch at a place called Bayou Delight.

It was exactly what I'd hoped it would be. A little grubby, very lived-in, and dotted with sugar cane farmers and other random Cajuns, some speaking French. I had just sat down in a booth when a gigantic man wearing a foot-long Bowie knife on his belt walked in with his petite, dark-haired wife, and sat down in the booth next to me. Turns out he was a gator hunter. We got to talking, and when he learned I'd never eaten gator—although, oddly, I'd eaten crocodile in South Africa—he suggested I order the alligator sauce piquante. I'd never eaten a sauce piquante (sauce pee-kahnt) before, and when it came it looked like red gumbo.

It was about as thick as a gumbo and very tomatoey, with an island of white rice in the center and lots of diced gator floating around. It was spicy, but not blow-your-head-off spicy. I'd never eaten anything like it. Gumbo meets chili. Well, venison sauce piquante is a thing in Cajun Country, and here is my homage to Bayou Delight's specialty.

What's unique about a sauce piquante is that the meat is diced small. This works great for venison, which has a tendency to become dry in stews. Always serve this with white rice. And remember, like all good stews, this one is better the day after it's made.

⅔ cup peanut oil or lard

¾ cup all-purpose flour

2 cups chopped onion

1 cup chopped green pepper

1 cup chopped celery

5 garlic cloves

One 6-ounce can of tomato paste

1 tablespoon Cajun seasoning, or more to taste

3 pounds venison, diced small

1 cup red wine

One 28-ounce can tomato puree or crushed tomatoes

2 bay leaves

Salt, black pepper and hot sauce to taste

Chopped green onions or parsley for garnish

In a large, heavy pot, heat the peanut oil over medium-high heat for a minute or two. Stir in the flour, then turn the heat down to medium. Cook this roux, stirring often, until it turns the color of peanut butter, at which point you will need to stir it almost constantly to prevent it from burning. Keep cooking the roux until it turns the color of chocolate, about 15 to 20 minutes.

While the roux is cooking, bring 6 cups of water in another pot to a boil, then drop it to a simmer.

When the roux is ready, add the onions, celery, and green pepper and stir to combine. Turn the heat to medium-high and cook, stirring often, until everything is soft. Sprinkle in some salt. Stir in the garlic, Cajun seasoning, and tomato paste. Drop the heat to medium. Cook, stirring occasionally, for 3 minutes.

Stir in the venison, then add the cup of red wine, the can of crushed tomatoes and the hot water. Add the bay leaves and bring everything to a gentle simmer. Add salt and hot sauce to taste. Simmer very gently until the meat is tender, 2 hours or more.

When the sauce piquante is ready, add any more salt, black pepper, hot sauce, and/or Cajun seasoning you want, then serve it with white rice and lots of green onions or parsley. Make sure you have hot sauce at the table; I use Tabasco, but use whatever variety you prefer.

POZOLE ROJO

Serves 6 to 8 | Prep Time: 30 minutes | Cook Time: 3 hours

Pozole (poh-ZO-lay) is a classic Mexican soup that relies heavily on dried chiles, some form of meat, and hominy corn. Any combination of ancho, mulato, negro, pasilla, or guajillo chiles will work. None are terribly spicy, and all are easily found in any Latin market; anchos are often found in regular supermarkets these days. You could use dried red Hatch or other New Mexico chiles, but they are a little spicy, so only use six chiles.

Hominy in this context is a giant corn kernel that has been nixtamalized, an ancient process that opens up the whole array of nutrients in the corn. It has a distinctive flavor—it tastes like corn tortillas smell—and is indispensable in a true pozole. Hominy is also easily found in Latin markets dried or in cans.

The fun of pozole is its interactivity. The soup itself is pretty basic, but everyone at the table gets to put on whichever toppings they want; it's very much like eating Vietnamese Pho (page 162). The stew will keep for more than a week in the fridge once you've made it.

4 ancho chiles

2 mulato or chile negro chiles

3 guajillo chiles

6 garlic cloves, chopped

2 pounds venison, cut into 4- to 5-inch hunks

3 tablespoons lard or cooking oil

Salt

5 cups water

2 teaspoons Mexican oregano

2 teaspoons ground cumin

Two 28- to 32-ounce cans white hominy

GARNISH

Hot sauce

⅓ head of cabbage, shredded

1 sliced radish per person

2 diced avocados

Chopped cilantro

1 red onion, chopped

Lime wedges, preferably Key limes

Tear the dried chiles into a couple large pieces. Discard the stems and seeds. Heat a comal or other heavy frying pan (cast iron is best) over high heat and toast the dried chiles until they're fragrant and start popping, which only takes a few seconds. Watch carefully and do not let the chiles burn; they will become bitter. When they're all toasted, put the chiles in a bowl. Cover the chiles with hot water and place a smaller bowl or plate on them to weigh them down. Soak for 30 minutes.

When the chiles are soft, chop roughly and then put into a blender with the garlic cloves and enough of the soaking water to let the blades run. Puree until this is very smooth.

Heat the lard in a large, lidded pot. Pat the venison chunks dry with a paper towel and brown them well. Don't crowd the pot, and take your time with this step. Do it in batches if need be.

When the meat is browned, add a little water to the pot so you can scrape up any browned bits on the bottom with a wooden spoon. When that's done, add the chile puree and the rest of the water. Bring to a simmer. Add the oregano, cumin, and salt to taste. Return the venison to the pot and simmer gently until the meat is tender.

Once the meat is ready, remove it to a plate or pan to cool. Rinse the hominy under cold running water, then add it to the soup. Shred the meat with two forks and return it to the soup. Ladle some pozole into everyone's bowls and let them choose which toppings they want.

STIFADO

Serves 4 to 6 | **Prep Time: 30 minutes** | **Cook Time: 90 minutes**

Stifado is the chili of Greece: Everyone's got their own version, and they range from beef to lamb to rabbit to venison. Stifado tastes like the Orient, in its classical sense. It must have been quite the treat when it was invented, most likely in the Middle Ages when Greece was under Venetian rule. Any combination of sweetness with exotic spices such as cinnamon and allspice in an otherwise savory dish fairly screams 14th century.

Stifado uses a lot of olive oil, which keeps the venison moist as it slowly cooks until it is about to fall apart. The spices give the stew zing without heat, and the tomatoes, which are obviously a post-1492 addition, add a bit more sweetness as well as needed acidity.

You'll want either a nice Greek red wine, a lager beer, or ouzo with a glass of water as a chaser to go along with this stew. And don't forget to have lots of good crusty bread around, too.

1 to 2 pounds venison, cut into bite-sized pieces

Kosher salt

¼ cup olive oil

2 large red onions, sliced about ¼-inch thick, root to tip

5 cloves chopped garlic

10 allspice berries

1 cinnamon stick

4 bay leaves

1 tablespoon dried oregano

2 tablespoons tomato paste

4 large tomatoes, grated, or one 14-ounce can of crushed tomatoes

1 cup sweet red wine, such as mavrodaphne or Port

1 quart venison or beef stock

1 to 4 tablespoons red wine vinegar (to taste)

Freshly ground black pepper

Salt the venison well and set it aside, then chop the vegetables.

Heat the olive oil in a Dutch oven or other heavy, lidded pot. Pat the venison dry with paper towels and brown it in batches, making sure to not crowd the pot. Remove the pieces as they brown and set aside.

Sauté the onions for 8 to 10 minutes over medium-high heat until they begin to brown. Add the garlic and sauté for another minute. Sprinkle with salt. Do not let the garlic burn.

Pour in a little water and use a wooden spoon to scrape up any browned bits on the bottom of the pot. Add the bay leaves, oregano, allspice berries, and cinnamon stick to the pot. Mix in the tomato paste, then the canned or grated tomatoes, sweet wine, 1 tablespoon of vinegar, and stock. Return the venison to the pot. Cover and bring to a simmer. Cook slowly for 90 minutes, then check. The meat may need to cook for as much as one additional hour.

When the venison is tender, add salt, black pepper and more red wine vinegar to taste, and, if you have some, drizzle a bit of really good olive oil over everything right when you serve.

ICELANDIC VENISON STEW

Serves 6 to 8 | **Prep Time: 20 minutes** | **Cook Time: 3 hours**

This unusual stew evokes the dead of winter in a very cold place, which is appropriate as this is an Icelandic recipe called *kjötsupa*. I first learned about this dish from Magnus Nilsson's *Nordic Cookbook*, and it struck me as interesting because of its use of barley (or rye, or oats) and dried vegetables. His version uses rolled oats, but I like rye, barley, or steel cut oats better as they are more interesting to eat.

As for the dried vegetables, they're a holdover from tougher times when Icelanders could not get fresh vegetables in winter, but I like the texture of rehydrated vegetables with this soup. Of course, you can skip them if you want. Which vegetables to use? Think of things that you'd grow in a cool summer, like green beans, leeks, kale, or chard, that sort of thing. A healthy dose of dried herbs such as parsley, lovage, dill, or thyme completes the effect.

As for the meat, you want something with connective tissue. Ideally neck meat or shanks, but also hunks from the front shoulder as well. Cut them into largish pieces about three inches across.

2 to 3 pounds venison (see above), cut into large pieces

1 rutabaga, peeled and cut into chunks

4 large carrots, peeled and cut into chunks

4 Yukon Gold potatoes, cut into chunks

1 large onion, sliced root to tip

3 to 5 tablespoons dried herbs and vegetables (see above)

½ cup steel-cut oats, rye, or barley

Salt and black pepper

Put the chunks of meat in a soup pot and cover with cold water. Turn the heat to high, and when the water boils, remove the meat and dump the water. Return the meat to the pot and cover with about 2 inches of new water. Bring to a gentle simmer, add some salt and let the meat cook very gently until it is beginning to get tender; this should take an hour or two.

Add the fresh and dried vegetables and cook for another hour. If you are using rye berries, add them with the vegetables. If using barley or oats, add them about 30 minutes after the vegetables. Add more salt and some pepper, and serve.

"A wounded deer leaps highest"

—EMILY DICKINSON

MINESTRA MARITATA

Serves 6 to 8 | Prep Time: 20 minutes | Cook Time: 3 hours

This is the original Italian wedding soup. The name means "married," not "wedding," and refers to the fact that bitter greens and rich meats are such a good match they ought to be married. As you look through the ingredient list, you'll quickly notice that this is something of a Mulligan's stew. You can vary it as much as you want; you just need a bunch of different meaty things, a variety of greens, and some cheese.

Be sure to include some bitter greens when you make this soup. Choices include dandelion greens, chicories, escarole, parsley, turnip greens, collard greens, kale, chard, arugula, and mustard greens. Just wash them well and chop into pieces that you'd want to eat in a soup, and enjoy!

Some venison bones (optional)

1 to 2 pounds random venison bits: neck or stew meat, ribs, flank, shanks, tongue

A pig's foot or small smoked hock (optional)

A Parmesan rind (optional)

3 bay leaves

A rosemary sprig, or 2 teaspoons dried

1 large carrot, chopped roughly

2 celery stalks, chopped

1 onion, chopped

Salt

½ pound small soup pasta such as orzo, ditalini, or pastina (optional)

1 or 2 Italian sausages

¼ pound diced salami (optional)

2 to 4 pounds of chopped greens (see above)

Black pepper to taste

Grated pecorino or Parmesan to taste

Place the venison bones, bits of random venison, and pig's foot into a large soup pot. Cover with water by 4 inches and bring to a boil. Use a large, shallow spoon to skim all the froth that collects, and when it's all gone, drop the heat to a bare simmer. Barely let this bubble for the rest of the way. Add the Parmesan rind, bay leaves, and rosemary. Simmer for 2 hours. Add the carrot, celery, and onion, and simmer until the meats are all tender, probably another hour.

Fish out all the meats and let them cool a bit. Fish out the rosemary and Parmesan rind and discard. Pick off all the meat from the various bits, including the pig's foot; discard all the bones. Chop the pig's foot into small pieces and return it to the pot with all the meats. Add salt to taste.

Add the greens, pasta, sausage, and salami, and simmer until the pasta is done, about 15 minutes. I like to remove the sausage and slice it into rings at this point, returning it to the soup. Add black pepper to taste, and serve with the grated cheese.

UKRAINIAN BORSCHT

Serves 4 to 6 | Prep Time: 15 minutes | Cook Time: 2½ hours

This version of borscht is hearty and slightly tart, and seems to contain pretty much everything in a typical Eastern European produce aisle. Borscht in America is a polarizing dish. For some reason, some people think that its vivid crimson color somehow means this soup is sweet. It's not. It's basically a rich vegetable soup based on meat broth with some meat in it—in this case, venison. The red of the beets is for show, although you certainly can taste them in the stew. Use any cut of venison here: Roasts, stew meat, neck, shanks, and shoulder are all fine.

1½ pounds venison, cut into 1-inch chunks

1 quart venison or beef stock

½ ounce dried mushrooms

Salt

3 beets, about 1 pound

2 tablespoons unsalted butter

1 large carrot, cut into ¼-inch slices

1 onion, sliced from root to tip

1 large parsley root or parsnip, cut into ¼-inch slices

1 small celery root, diced (optional)

2 tablespoons tomato paste

1 large potato, peeled and diced

⅓ head of cabbage, roughly shredded (about 2 cups)

Juice of 2 lemons, or 2 to 3 tablespoons red wine vinegar

2 tablespoons chopped parsley

1 tablespoon chopped dill

Black pepper

Sour cream for garnish

Preheat the oven to 375°F.

In a large Dutch oven or other heavy, lidded pot, just barely cover the venison with water and bring to a boil. Immediately turn off the heat, drain the water, and reserve the venison. This removes any scum that might otherwise rise to the surface of your broth. Return the venison to the pot, and add the stock and 1 quart of water. Bring to a gentle simmer and add salt to taste. Crumble the dried mushrooms into the soup, cover, and let it cook gently while you turn to the rest of the soup.

As soon as you put the lid on the soup, move to the beets. Coat them in the oil and wrap loosely in foil. Roast in the oven for 1 hour to 90 minutes, until reasonably tender. Remove from the oven and let the beets cool enough to handle. (If you have latex or nitrile gloves, put them on—beets stain.) Peel the beets and then shave them on a coarse box grater.

Heat the butter in a sauté pan. When it's hot, add the sliced onion and sauté over high heat until the edges brown, about 6 minutes. Drop the heat to medium-high and add the beets, carrot, celery, and parsley root. Cook for 10 minutes, stirring often.

Stir in the tomato paste, adding a ladle or two of the simmering soup to help blend everything and to scrape up any browned bits on the bottom of the sauté pan. Turn off the heat.

When the venison is tender, add the diced potatoes to the soup pot and simmer for 10 minutes. Add the cabbage and simmer another 10 minutes. Add the contents of the sauté pan to the soup and cook another 5 minutes.

When the potatoes are ready, add the lemon juice or vinegar, parsley, dill, and a healthy grinding of black pepper. Serve with a dollop of sour cream in the middle of the soup.

CARBONNADE

Serves 4 to 6 | Prep Time: 15 minutes | Cook Time: 3 hours

Belgian *carbonnade flamande* is one of the few dishes from that little country to gain wide renown. Cousin to the more-famous French beef Bourguignon, this is a sort of hybrid stew-braise that relies on beer, not wine. It's hard to say when this dish was invented, but I'd guess sometime in the Middle Ages because it relies on a little bit of sweet-and-sour that is characteristic of that era of cooking.

Regardless of its history, *carbonnade* (carbon-ah'd) is a damn good dish to make with any cut of venison—stew meat, shoulder, neck, or shank. You can eat this dish in one of two ways: as a full-on stew; or as a braise you eat with a knife and fork alongside a starch and a vegetable—the "stew" here becomes the sauce. Either way, you're in for a treat.

What does it taste like? Well, I use the hard-working, sinewy cuts of meat because when they finally do get tender, they get super silky and nice. But it's the sauce/gravy/stew that makes this dish: dark and rich, with a very European version of that magic combination of sweet-spicy-sour-salty from mustard, cider vinegar, and a little bit of red currant jelly mixed in (you can use brown sugar if you can't find red currant jelly).

The beer matters here. Make this with a real Belgian abbey ale and you will understand why this is such a famous dish. Make it with Budweiser and you might wonder what all the fuss is about. The mustard is also important, although not as much as the beer. Try to get a mustard like Dijon, not one with turmeric added for extra yellow. You don't need color here, you need flavor. As for the mushrooms, I use dried morels or porcini. Any good dried mushroom will do.

Like all stews, this one is even better the next day, and it reheats beautifully—perfect to make on a Sunday for lunches or quick dinners during the week.

3 pounds shank, shoulder, neck, or stew meat

¼ cup duck fat or unsalted butter

Salt

3 onions, peeled and sliced root to tip

1 ounce dried mushrooms, rehydrated in 1 cup
    warm water and chopped

2 teaspoons dried thyme

3 or 4 tablespoons flour

2 tablespoons mustard (Dijon is best)

1 cup venison or beef broth

1 or 2 bottles of beer; Belgian abbey ale
    is traditional

2 tablespoons cider vinegar

1 heaping tablespoon red currant jelly,
    or brown sugar

Black pepper

Chopped parsley for garnish

If you are using elk shanks, cut the shank off the bone in large pieces, about 2 to 4 inches across; same thing if you are using shoulder meat. If you are using venison shanks, you can leave them whole if they will fit into your pot.

Heat the duck fat or butter in a large Dutch oven or other heavy lidded pot over medium-high heat. Pat the meat dry and brown it well on all sides. Salt them as they cook. You might need to do this in batches. Remove the pieces as they brown and set aside in a bowl.

When all the meat has browned, add the sliced onions and mix well. Turn the heat down to medium and cook the onions until they are nicely browned and soft, which can take a solid 20 minutes. About halfway through, salt the onions and add the chopped mushrooms and thyme.

When the onions are ready, return the meat and all juices from the bowl into the pot. Mix in the mustard, then add enough flour to dust everything in the pot.

Stir in the mushroom soaking water (strain it if there is debris in it), the venison broth, and at least one bottle of the Belgian beer. You want the meat to be just barely covered. Pour in more beer if need be. Bring to a simmer, add salt to taste, cover, and cook slowly until the meat is really tender, from 2 to 4 hours depending on the age and cut of the animal.

Once the meat is tender, whisk in the red currant jelly and vinegar, and add black pepper to taste. Garnish with the chopped parsley. Serve with spätzle, egg noodles, or potatoes.

KENTUCKY BURGOO

Serves 6 to 10 | Prep Time: 30 minutes | Cook Time: 3 hours, or more if your game is old and tough

Every region of the United States has its big, burly stew, from gumbo to chili to cioppino. This is burgoo, a Kentucky classic, done with a menagerie of wild game: pheasant, squirrel, and venison. This is a stew thick enough to stand your spoon in. How you get there is more a matter of personal taste. There are as many versions of burgoo as there are cooks throughout the Greater Burgoo Diaspora, which is basically Kentucky, southern Illinois, and Indiana, as well as parts of the Ohio River Valley.

When you cook this stew, don't mess around: Make enough for leftovers. A particularly grand burgoo party written up in the *New York Times* in 1897 included "400 pounds of beef, six dozen chickens, four dozen rabbits, thirty cans of tomatoes, twenty dozen cans of corn, fifteen bushels of potatoes, and five bushels of onions." My recipe is a bit more modest, but it will still get you through a few lunches at work.

Don't worry if you don't have squirrel, venison, and pheasant on hand all at once. The only true rule in burgoo seems to be that you need at least three different meats, so let your imagination wander: Chicken is obvious, as is pork. But lamb, rabbit, hare, other game birds, duck, muskrat, whatever is in this stew, they'll all get hammered into submission regardless.

3 tablespoons vegetable oil

1 to 2 squirrels or rabbits, cut into serving
   pieces

2 to 3 pounds venison, cut into large pieces
   (3 to 4 inches wide)

3 to 5 pheasant legs/thighs (bone-in)

1 green pepper, chopped

1 large onion, chopped

2 carrots, chopped

2 celery ribs, chopped

5 garlic cloves, chopped

1 quart pheasant or chicken stock

1 quart beef or game stock

One 28-ounce can crushed tomatoes

2 large potatoes

1 bag of frozen corn (about a pound)

1 bag of frozen lima beans (about 14 ounces)
   or canned black-eyed peas

Salt and pepper

¼ cup Worcestershire sauce

Tabasco or other hot sauce on the side

Pour the oil into a large Dutch oven or soup pot and set the heat to medium-high. Working in batches, brown all the meats. Do not crowd the pan or the meat will not brown well. Salt the meat as it cooks. As they brown, move the various meats to a bowl.

Add the onions, carrots, celery, and green pepper to the pot and turn the heat to high. Cook the vegetables until they are well-browned; you might need to add a little more oil to the pot. When the vegetables have browned, add the garlic and cook for 1 minute. Add back the meats, along with the chicken and beef broths and the tomatoes. Stir to combine, and add salt to taste. Bring to a simmer, cover, reduce the heat, and simmer gently for 2 hours.

Fish out the meat pieces. Strip the pheasant and squirrel off the bone. Tear the large pieces of venison into bite-sized pieces. The reason you did not do this right at the start is that venison will stay moister when it's cooked in larger pieces. Return all the meat to the pot and return the stew to simmer.

Peel and cut the potatoes into chunks about the same size as the meat pieces. Add them to the stew and simmer until they are tender. Add the Worcestershire sauce, mix well, and taste for salt. Add more Worcestershire sauce to taste if needed.

Finally, add the corn and lima beans. Mix well and cook for at least 10 minutes, or longer if you'd like. Serve with cornbread and a bottle of hot sauce on the side.

Another Way to Brown Meats

For every recipe that calls for you to brown meats before stewing or braising, I will normally ask you to brown them in some sort of fat or oil in the pot they will ultimately cook in. But there's another way, one we use in restaurants or when cooking giant batches. You can cut the meat into pieces, coat with a little oil and salt, and then roast them in a very hot oven, turning them once or twice. I do this on big baking sheets or roasting pans at about 450°F. Make sure the oven is well preheated and your meats are loosely set in one layer in the pan—don't pack everything close together. This way, the meats will brown, not steam.

MASSAMAN CURRY

Thai-style massaman curry is a great curry for people who don't normally like curry: It is a stolid, meat-and-potatoes meal that doesn't taste as exotic as it really is. And if you use a premade curry paste, available online or in many decent supermarkets, you can make this in the time it takes to cook the potatoes.

There are many versions of massaman curry. Mine is an adaptation of a recipe I found in what may be the first Thai cookbook in English, Jennifer Brennan's *Original Thai Cookbook*, written in 1981. And since Brennan first wrote that book, the ingredients required to make a good Thai curry from scratch have become pretty easy to find: *galangal* and turmeric (both relatives of ginger), lemongrass, coconut milk, and fish sauce. So I've included a recipe for homemade curry paste, but the premade curry pastes are actually quite good.

Because this curry does not stew for hours and hours, you need to treat the venison or other meat in a special way. First, make sure the meat is completely free of all silverskin or connective tissue. Second, drop it into the curry maybe five minutes before you serve—just enough time for the chunks of meat to cook through, yet still be pink inside. If you cut it into thin strips, put the meat in as you serve; the curry's carryover heat will cook it through like a Vietnamese pho (page 162).

CURRY PASTE

7 to 10 dried hot chiles, Thai, Tabasco, or piquin

6 cloves

A 2-inch stick of cinnamon

12 cardamom seeds, or ½ teaspoon ground

½ teaspoon ground nutmeg

4 bay leaves, crushed fine

1 teaspoon salt

8 garlic cloves, minced

½ cup onion, minced

1 tablespoon lard or vegetable oil

1 tablespoon minced *galangal*, fresh or pickled

A 2-inch piece of fresh turmeric,
   or 2 teaspoons powdered

1 lemongrass stalk, minced

CURRY

1 tablespoon lard or vegetable oil

1 large onion, sliced

1 pound potatoes, peeled and cut into
   2-inch chunks

One 14-ounce can coconut milk

3 tablespoons fish sauce or 2 tablespoons
   soy sauce

A 2-inch piece of cinnamon

4 tablespoons yellow curry paste
   (homemade above or store-bought)

2 pounds venison, trimmed of fat and silverskin
   and cut into 1-inch cubes

Chives or cilantro for garnish

If you're making your own curry paste, heat the tablespoon of lard and sauté the onion and garlic until soft and translucent. Let cool a bit and put into a bowl. While the onions are cooking, grind the chiles, cloves, cinnamon, cardamom, nutmeg, bay leaves, and salt into a powder. Put the spice mix into a sturdy bowl or mortar and pestle with the onions and garlic. Add the *galangal*, turmeric, and lemongrass and mix everything well. Pound everything into a rough paste and set aside.

In a large sauté pan or wok, heat the other tablespoon of lard or vegetable oil and sear the onions over high heat. Toss well to combine, then don't move the onions for a minute or two—you want some char on them. Toss again and let sear one more time.

Add the potatoes, coconut milk, fish sauce, cinnamon, and enough water to just barely cover the potatoes. Mix in the curry paste one tablespoon at a time, stopping when it's spicy enough for you. Cover and simmer until the potatoes are tender, about 20 minutes. When the potatoes are tender, mix in the venison and cook gently for 5 more minutes. Serve at once with chives, Thai basil, or cilantro, and a cold beer.

VINDALOO

Serves 4 to 6 | Prep Time: 30 minutes | Cook Time: 2 hours

Originally a lamb dish from the western Indian province of Goa, vindaloo is a stalwart of Indian menus all over the world. It's a sharp, spicy stew that will make you grab for your beer and a spoonful of *raita*, that Indian yogurt and cucumber sauce that seems to make the heat all better, at least for a moment.

Traditional vindaloo doesn't have tomato or potato in it, but I like both. This version is closer to what you'd get in an Indian restaurant in America.

CURRY PASTE

4 garlic cloves, chopped

2 tablespoons chopped fresh ginger

2 to 8 red chiles, fresh or dried (serrano, cayenne, or árbol are good choices)

2 teaspoons ground cumin

2 teaspoons ground coriander

2 teaspoons turmeric

1½ teaspoons ground fenugreek (optional)

¼ cup malt vinegar

¼ cup water

MARINADE

1 teaspoon salt

1 teaspoon sugar

½ teaspoon ground cardamom

½ teaspoon ground cloves

1 teaspoon black pepper

1 tablespoon chopped fresh ginger

¼ cup malt vinegar

¼ cup water

VINDALOO

¼ cup peanut oil

1½ pounds venison stew meat

1 large onion, sliced root to tip

Salt

1 tablespoon tomato paste (optional)

1 pound small potatoes, cut into chunks

Cilantro for garnish

Blend all the ingredients of the marinade in a blender, then pour into a non-reactive container or sealable plastic bag with the venison and marinate in the fridge for at least 1 hour, and up to a day.

Blend all the curry paste ingredients in the same blender; no need to clean it beforehand. Spoon out the paste and set aside. Don't clean the blender yet.

Heat a deep sauté pan or wide pot over medium-high heat. Add the peanut oil. When it's hot, sear the onions until they brown at the edges, about 6 to 8 minutes. Salt them as they cook. Mix in the curry paste and bring to a boil. Stir in the tomato paste if using. Pour about 1 quart of water into the blender, swishing it around to capture all the leftover good stuff.

Mix the venison and the marinade into the sauté pan, and let this cook a minute or so. Pour in the spicy water from the blender. Cover the pan and let this simmer gently until the venison is tender, anywhere from 2 to 3 hours. Remove the lid from the pan, add the potatoes, and cook uncovered until the potatoes are tender, about 20 minutes. Garnish with cilantro and serve with long-grain rice.

SCOTCH BROTH

Serves 6 to 8 | **Prep Time: 30 minutes** | **Cook Time: 3 hours, 35 minutes**

This is a traditional Scotch broth, a simple lamb and barley soup with carrots, turnips, and other wintry things for which I substitute venison for lamb. Venison is still widely eaten in the United Kingdom, and Scotland is home to one of the largest remaining herds of red deer (they're like our elk) left in Europe. So it seems appropriate.

My special ingredient? Nettles. Blanched and chopped, nettles, a wild vegetable adored by both Irish and Scots cooks, add a vivid spring green to the soup. If you can't get nettles, use spinach or any other leafy green.

There is one vital key to my version of this soup: Never ever let this soup boil. If you do, the soup will still be OK, but you will wonder what all the fuss is about. Keeping the venison cooking below a simmer—about 170°F—breaks down the connective tissue of the meat but keeps the venison tender and still pretty pink. If the soup boils, the meat will tighten up and turn gray.

The recipe keeps well in the fridge for up to a week, although the barley will swell over time. It is best eaten the day after it is made.

---

2 pounds venison stew meat

1 quart venison or beef broth

2 quarts water

Salt

1 medium yellow onion, sliced

2 or 3 turnips, peeled and cut into chunks

5 or 6 small carrots, peeled and trimmed

2 celery stalks, chopped

1 cup barley

1 cup blanched and chopped nettles or spinach

Black pepper to taste

Pour the water and broth into a large pot and add the venison chunks. Bring this to a bare simmer, just to the bubbling point. You will notice lots of scum collecting on the surface of the soup; skim it as best you can. I let the venison gently simmer for 20 minutes, then fish out the venison pieces and put them in a bowl. I then pour the broth through a paper towel set in a sieve over another pot or large bowl. This strains out all the scum. If you skip this step, your soup will be cloudy, but still perfectly edible. I just like clear soup.

Add salt to this new broth, and return it and the premade venison stock with the venison chunks to the heat—only this time, do not let it even simmer. Cover the pot and set it on low heat. You are shooting for about 160 to 175°F. Cook the meat this way until tender, which will take 2 to 3 hours.

After 2 hours have passed, add all the vegetables and the barley, cover, and cook for another hour or so, or until the barley is tender.

Stir in the chopped nettles, add some black pepper, and just heat this through, about 5 minutes. Serve at once with a dark ale or red wine.

CHILINDRÓN

Serves 8 | **Prep Time: 20 minutes** | **Cook Time: 2 hours**

Chilindrón (chill-in-DRONE), is a Spanish stew dominated by roasted red peppers, paprika, and onions. Most recipes also call for rosemary, olive oil, garlic, some tomatoes, good stock, and wine. It is rich, woodsy, and bright, a perfect combination of the "red food" many of us crave, like spaghetti sauce and chili (think about the colors in your favorite foods and you'll find many of them are reddish), with the slightly austere, piney flavors that mark European wild game cooking. I love this stew so much that it has become a standard I repeat on a regular basis.

3 pounds venison stew meat, neck, shank or shoulder, cut into bite-sized pieces

2 large onions, sliced root to tip in half-moons

1 whole head of garlic, chopped

2 tablespoons sweet paprika

1 tablespoon hot paprika

1 jar (15 ounces or so) or 5 roasted red sweet peppers, chopped

1 cup crushed tomatoes

2 cups red or white wine

Venison or beef stock (see below)

½ cup diced cured meat such as bacon, pancetta, or ham

1 tablespoon chopped fresh rosemary

4 bay leaves

½ cup chopped fresh parsley

¼ cup olive oil

Salt and pepper

A large handful of dried mushrooms (optional)

If using, put the mushrooms in a container just large enough to hold them and pour hot water over them. Cover and set aside.

Salt the meat and set aside for 20 minutes at room temperature. Use this time to chop the vegetables.

Pat the meat dry and pour the olive oil into a large Dutch oven or other heavy pot that has a lid. Heat the pot over medium-high heat. Brown the meat on all sides in batches. Do not overcrowd the pot. Set the meat aside in a bowl when browned. Take your time and do this right. Add more oil if needed.

When the meat is browned, add the onions and stir to bring some of the browned bits up off the bottom of the pan. Sprinkle the onions with a little salt. Cook until they begin to brown, then add the garlic, the cured meat, and the mushrooms. Cook until fragrant, then add the meat back to the pot and mix well.

Pour in the wine and turn the heat up to high. Stir and boil furiously until the wine is half gone. Turn the heat back down to medium and add the tomatoes, the roasted red peppers, and all the spices and herbs (except the parsley). Stir well. The level of liquid should be about two-thirds the way up the sides of the meat. If it is low, add the venison stock. I typically need about 2 cups.

Cover and cook at a bare simmer—just barely bubbling—until done. How long is that? Depends on the meat. Rarely is any venison done within 90 minutes, and old animals can take 3 hours or more to get tender. Use your judgment.

Right before serving, test for salt and add some if needed. Add black pepper and the parsley and stir well. Serve with mashed potatoes, rice, polenta, or bread. Simple sautéed greens are a good accompaniment. A big red wine is also a must, ideally something Spanish, like a Rioja.

VIETNAMESE PHO

Serves 8 to 10 | **Prep Time: 3 hours** | **Cook Time: 30 minutes**

Pho is quite possibly the best soup in the world. Typically made with beef broth, venison broth is an excellent stand-in. In that soup, you get a host of meats, ranging from thinly shaved tender meat to meatballs to slow-cooked fatty brisket—even tendon and tripe make an appearance.

Everything hinges on the broth, which is sweet-smelling from ginger, star anise, and other spices. It's a special broth: You do not roast the bones; pho broth must be light. Also, it needs body, which is why it is traditionally made with knuckle bones. Give the broth all day to simmer and you will be rewarded. You can make it ahead, and it freezes well—you can even pressure can it if you want (page 48).

Once you have the broth, pho comes together quickly. Have everything set out beforehand, and bring it all together quickly.

BROTH

3 to 5 pounds venison bones or scraggly meat

1 pig's foot or calf's foot

2 sliced onions

A 6-inch piece of ginger, sliced

10 cardamom pods

5 star anise pods

1 tablespoon coriander seed

6 cloves

1 tablespoon fennel seed

3 tablespoons sugar

1 tablespoon salt

¼ cup fish sauce

To make the broth, put all the bones and meat into a large stock pot, cover with water by 1 inch, and bring to a boil. Skim the scum that rises to the top, then turn the heat down to a bare simmer. Do not let it boil from here on in.

While the water is coming to a boil, toast the coriander, cloves, fennel seed, cardamom, and star anise in a dry frying pan until fragrant. Stir often to keep it from burning.

Once the water in the stockpot is pretty much scum-free, add the onion, ginger, toasted spices, fish sauce, sugar, and salt and stir well. Move the pot off the center of the burner a little and simmer for 2 to 3 hours. Moving the pot a little off to the side allows you to periodically skim the top. You want to remove most of the fat this way. When the broth is ready, turn off the heat and discard all the solids. Ladle the broth through a paper towel placed in a fine-mesh strainer that is set over a large bowl. Discard the last dregs of the broth, which will have sediment in it.

If you want to be fancy, cool the broth now, and once it has been refrigerated for a while, pick off the fat cap that may form.

TO ASSEMBLE

¼ pound venison backstrap, sliced as thinly as
possible

A few Japanese Venison Meatballs (page 191)
(optional)

Some leftover venison pot roast (optional)

2 tablespoons sesame oil

2 pounds Vietnamese rice noodles (spaghetti
will work in a pinch)

2 thinly sliced onions

A 4-inch piece of ginger, peeled and sliced

½ pound bean sprouts

A large bunch of cilantro or Asian basil

4 hot chiles, thinly sliced

To serve, heat the broth gently(do not let it boil) with the sliced 4-inch piece of ginger and the sliced onions. Cook until the onions are wilted, about 10 minutes. Taste and add salt if you need to. If you are using the meatballs and leftover roast venison, add it now.

Set out an array of condiments: herbs, bean sprouts, sliced chiles, fish sauce, hot sauce, and hoisin sauce. This is traditional, although you can improvise if needed. The one thing you must have is fresh herbs, however.

Boil water, salt it, and cook the noodles. Traditional pho noodles (available at Asian stores) are best, but if you absolutely can't find them, spaghetti will work. When the noodles are done, gather up portions and put them in serving bowls.

Lay the thinly sliced venison on the noodles. Pick the ginger out of the broth, then pour some broth over the noodles and venison. Be sure to give everyone some onions, brisket, and meatballs, if using. Serve at once. Let everyone add whatever condiments they want.

"My wife can't cook at all. She made chocolate mousse.
An antler got stuck in my throat."

—RODNEY DANGERFIELD

HUNGARIAN PÖRKÖLT

Serves 6 to 8　|　Prep Time: 30 minutes　|　Cook Time: 3 hours

Goulash. Love the name. Sounds so mysterious, like something warriors in the Dark Ages would have wolfed down to make them strong before battle. I grew up eating my mum's goulash, and it was good. But, sadly, it wasn't actually goulash. It was chili. I only learned this years later, after I ordered goulash at a Hungarian restaurant in Wisconsin. What they served me looked nothing like chili, and everything like what you see in the picture: A thick, meaty stew, heavy on the paprika, served with little pasta dumplings on the side.

But guess what? Even *that* wasn't actually what the Hungarians would call *gulyás*. It was *pörkölt*. Wha? Yeah, I know, all those umlauts over the "o's" make my head hurt. Best I can tell this word is pronounced something like "purr-cult."

Making an authentic Hungarian dish is like running a gauntlet. There really is no single "authentic" goulash, as every Hungarian cook makes it her own way. Tomatoes? Green peppers? Verboten in some recipes, required in others. Sour cream? Typically only allowed as a tableside condiment, if at all (although there is dish, *paprikash*, that includes sour cream mixed into the stew itself and is usually done with chicken). Vegetables? Sometimes, and most often carrots, parsnips, and potatoes, which are in an actual *gulyás*. Wine? Only with venison, apparently. Stock? A little. Beans? Hell, no! After no small amount of research, the only constants I can determine are paprika and onions. Lots of onions and lots of paprika. More than you think you'd need.

What to serve with your goulash is also variable. Mashed, boiled, or smashed potatoes are all common, as is spätzle. This, I think, is an Austrian touch (those of you who remember your history might recall that there was once this thing called the Austro-Hungarian Empire). So here we have the Hungarian version of Austrian spätzle, called *nokedli*.

You will want fresh paprika for this recipe: the stuff that has likely been sitting around in your pantry since the Pleistocene won't cut it. Paprika needs to be bright red and smell wonderful. Oh, and don't freak out about the huge amount of onions. They cook down.

NOKEDLI DUMPLINGS

2 cups flour

1 teaspoon salt

4 eggs, beaten

A little water or milk

PÖRKÖLT

¼ cup lard, bacon fat or sunflower oil

2 pounds venison stew meat, cut into
   3- to 4-inch hunks

Salt

5 cups chopped onions

¼ cup sweet paprika
   (Hungarian if at all possible)

2 teaspoons hot paprika

2 teaspoons caraway seed

1 teaspoon dried marjoram

1 cup crushed tomatoes

2 cups venison or beef stock

1 cup red wine

Heat the lard or bacon fat over medium-high heat in a large Dutch oven or stewpot and brown the venison in batches. Salt the venison as it cooks. It will take 20 minutes or so for all the meat to brown. Remove the venison as it browns and set aside.

Add all the onions and caraway seeds and turn the heat to medium. Sauté the onions, stirring often, until they are browned. This will take a solid 30 minutes if you do it right. I cover the pot about halfway in. Add the venison back, then all the other ingredients. Mix well and bring to a simmer. Cover and cook over low heat for 2 hours, or until the meat wants to fall apart.

When the meat is ready, make the *nokedli* dumplings by mixing all the ingredients in a bowl until you have a thick batter. Get a large pot of water boiling and add enough salt to make it salty. Push the batter through a spätzle maker or a colander with large holes into the boiling water. Boil the *nokedli* dumplings until they float, then 1 minute more. Drain and set aside.

Use a pair of forks or a potato masher to shred the meat in the pot. Add salt if needed. Serve the pörkölt alongside the dumplings with some sour cream at the table to mix in.

FOOD PLOT

Serves 6 to 8 | Prep Time: 90 minutes, mostly soaking time for the rye and beans | Cook Time: 2 hours

Whenever you are winging it in the kitchen, designing your own dishes and stretching your creative muscles at the stovetop, there is one ironclad maxim to live by when you are deciding what should and should not go into the pot: If it goes together in life, it will go together on the plate. Rabbits and carrots. Striped bass and crab. Duck and wild rice.

This dish follows that maxim. A food plot is an invention of the whitetail deer hunting industry (and it is most definitely an industry) that basically takes what a whitetail deer loves to eat (and that will promote antler growth) and puts it in a big sack o'seed. Landowners plant huge fields of this stuff solely for the purpose of attracting deer. They then set up a blind or tree stand and wait for Mr. Big Rack to amble by.

Look at the ingredients of any of these big bags of seed and you might be surprised at what you find. It's a smorgasbord of grains, greens, roots, and beans: rye, barley, millet, wheat, and buckwheat; cowpeas, vetch, and broad beans; turnips, rutabagas, radishes; chicory, alfalfa, and other green things

Crazy, eh? Almost everything in this list can be found in a deer food plot, and is easily available even in small, rural supermarkets. The secret to the stew is the sequence of when you put things in it, so you have everything cooked perfectly when you are ready to eat. All stews are like houses: They require a foundation, rooms of flavor, and accents of color and texture.

Nothing in this stew is especially difficult to find, although you really do want some sort of high-quality finishing oil to drizzle on at the end. I use a roasted pumpkinseed oil that really adds a lot to the dish, which is otherwise pretty low-fat. Other good choices would be walnut oil, unrefined canola or sunflower oil, or a good olive oil.

Be sure to cook the rye separately, as it can take a full hour of boiling to get tender. Rye has its own earthy flavor, but barley, oat groats, or wheat berries also work well—and cook faster.

¾ cup black-eyed peas

¾ cup rye berries (or barley, oat groats, or wheat berries)

Salt

3 tablespoons unsalted butter

2 to 3 pounds venison stew meat

1 large onion, sliced thin from root to tip

6 cups venison broth, beef broth, or water

1 teaspoon dried thyme

¼ teaspoon celery seed

1 pound turnips or rutabagas, peeled and cut into chunks

4 cups chopped dandelion greens, chicory leaves, kale, or chard

Put the black-eyed peas and rye berries in separate bowls. Bring a quart or so of water to a boil and pour it over the rye and black-eyed peas. Let this sit for at least 1 hour. You can also just soak them in cool water overnight.

Bring a small pot of water to a boil and salt it well. Add the rye berries and simmer them until tender, 45 minutes to 1 hour. If you use barley or oats, it will take a lot less time, maybe 20 minutes. When the grain is tender, drain, cool and set aside.

Meanwhile, get a large Dutch oven or other heavy pot and set it over medium-high heat. Heat the butter. While the butter is melting, take a few pieces of the venison and pat it dry with paper towels. Brown the venison in the hot butter, salting it as it cooks. Do this in batches so you don't crowd the pot, and pat dry each new batch before you put it into the pot. Set aside the browned venison pieces in a bowl.

(continued)

4 to 5 red radishes, thinly sliced

Black pepper

Roasted pumpkinseed oil, walnut oil, or other flavorful oil for drizzling

Vetch or pea flowers (optional)

When the venison is all browned, add the onion and cook over medium-high heat, stirring often, until the edges of the onions begin to brown, about 5 to 6 minutes. Return the venison to the pot and add the broth, thyme, and celery seed. Bring this to a simmer and cook gently for 90 minutes.

Add the rutabagas or turnips and the black-eyed peas. Simmer this for another hour or so.

About 5 minutes before you want to serve, stir in the chopped dandelion greens and cooked rye berries. To serve, ladle out some stew—it should be a thick stew, with lots of stuff and not too brothy—grind some black pepper over it, sprinkle the thinly sliced radishes and vetch flowers (if using) on top, and drizzle with the oil. I'd serve this with a strong beer, such as a good IPA.

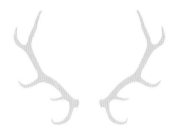

MEATBALLS, BURGERS, AND OTHER GROUND MEAT DISHES

Burger, that catchword for those endless pounds of ground deer or elk or moose you get when you bring your animal home from the butcher, is almost always the last thing remaining in the freezer. What's more, it can be something of a mystery meat: Was there fat ground in with your venison? Was it ground coarsely or fine? Is it even from your own deer? Better to grind your own meat to suit your own needs. Meatballs are best ground one way, burgers another. Most of the time, you want to add fat, but not always. And if you do add fat, which fat? I'll walk you through the nuances of the grind. Follow my lead and you might find that your ground meat is the first to go, not the last.

A DISCOURSE ON BURGERS

It has occurred to me that the single most consistent ingredient in the Great American Hamburger is testosterone. The chest-thumping that surrounds the making and cooking of burgers is matched only by that of chili in winter or barbecue in the South. This is especially true of men who have grown up eating wretched fast-food patties, or had mothers who

made, as comedian Eddie Murphy so memorably put it, "brontosaurus burgers." There is something validating about being able to rectify a childhood wrong, as a bad burger seems to be in America.

Ideas about the "perfect burger recipe" are as varied as there are minds to contemplate such weighty matters. I've seen complicated equations involving exact percentages of this cut of meat or that one, including such horrors as including hanger steak or skirt steak in a burger. These are noble cuts, not something to be ground into a Wednesday gut filler. Might as well grind a ribeye. And yes, I am certain at least one person reading this has done so.

Meat-to-fat ratio is a big area of contention, too. So is the timeless debate over whether to salt the meat as you make the patty or just salt the outside. A few errant souls even add things to the meat itself, which to purists is anathema. (I am one of those souls: My Mushroom Burger recipe on page 177 includes powdered dried mushrooms in the patty itself.) To flip once or many times? Toast the bun or no?

Get into the Toppings War and you can have some fun, too. Cheese or no cheese? Cooked or raw onions? Is it nobler to use hothouse tomatoes on your burger in winter or not to do so, and by opposing this outrageous arrow against seasonality, end the debate forever? (Sorry, Hamlet.) Well, here is where I stand.

I will preface all this by saying that this is, to me, a perfect burger. To you, it may not be. And you are free to believe so. That's why this is America (or Canada, or wherever it is you happen to be reading this). I like other sorts of burgers, and I have a couple of recipes for them below, but this is my Once and Future Burger.

1. All burgers, venison or no, need fat. Period. My preferred ratio is 80 percent meat, 20 percent pork fat. I dislike beef fat; it's too strongly flavored for me. Lamb fat is too waxy.

2. Grind your own if at all possible. This is the secret to virtually every great burger joint's meat. Grinding your own takes less than ten minutes (unless you are feeding an army), and gives you ultimate control over texture and composition. And in the world of venison burgers, this is what I've come to like best: venison meat from the shoulder, ribs, neck, or hind leg, ground with bacon ends. If you've never tried this, do it. It's amazing. What's more, I vary my grind. (Exact proportions are in the recipe below.) Why? Because it makes the burger taste more interesting.

3. Gently patties must you make, young padawan. So Sayeth Yoda. These aren't meatballs, folks. Think of a burger as you would a crabcake, which is supposed to just barely hold together. It's a fine line between perfect and too crumbly, but a dense, packed patty is depressing and somehow un-American.

4. Salt only the outside of the burger, right before you cook or even when you flip the patty. This one matters. Salt denatures proteins, which is why sausage binds so well and, incidentally, has a very different texture from a good burger. Add salt to the meat mixture and you have a sausage patty, not a hamburger. And yes, people have done experiments proving this. (As for my bacon ends, which contain salt, I use them only when I grind and cook, not when I grind lots of burger in advance and freeze it.)

5. Grilled burgers are only better when there's wood or charcoal involved. Yes, I cook burgers over gas grills, and they are nice, but not qualitatively better than those done in a pan inside. Unless of course you add smoke chips to your gas grill. Meat + woodsmoke = awesome.

6. Flip once, or several times. It apparently doesn't matter in the final judgment. And again, yes, people have done experiments proving this. I flip only once because I want a hard crust on the outside of the burger, which I find helps hold it together.

7. Rest thine burgers. It's the little-known Twelfth Commandment, lost in the making of Mel Brooks's classic film *History of the World Part I*. Why? Remember the original name of a hamburger: hamburger steak. You rest steaks, right? Right? Please tell me you do.

8. Let all else be free. Let your burger freak flag fly when it comes to toppings. Just let the meat be the star, OK?

When to Skip the Fat

I include fat in almost all my grind. But there are a few instances where you can not only get away with 100 percent meat, but your final dish will actually be better that way. Here are three places where you might want to skip the fat:

1. Ground meat jerky. Fat will go rancid far faster than meat. So if you make ground meat jerky, like my Pemmican Style Jerky on page 269, it will last longer if you don't have added fat. The jerky stays moist because of all the dried berries in it.

2. Spaghetti, chili, and taco meat. All are great with added fat, but when you use 100 percent meat, you can alter the fat to match the dish, for example, olive oil with a spaghetti sauce or lard with taco meat. Nothing wrong with using ground meat that has fat included, but you can get a better result when you match the fat to the dish.

3. Base meat for sausage. You get a better bind on sausage and salami when you mix the ground meat and salt and let it sit in the fridge overnight. The presence of fat hinders this process, so if you have a lot of 100 percent ground meat, you can go right into the binding process, skipping the initial grind.

A BASIC VENISON BURGER

Serves 4 | Prep Time: 20 minutes, a little more if you are grinding your own meat | Cook Time: 10 minutes

Keep in mind that what's important here is the technique and the grind, not so much my additional ingredients. Of course, I love my venison burgers like this, so I am biased. But so long as you follow general guidelines on toppings—mix something rich (cheese) with something sharp (tomato) and something slightly bitter or cleansing (lettuce or sorrel leaves) and a touch of sweet (ketchup)—you will be in good shape.

I know many of you get your venison pre-ground from the butcher shop. Go ahead and use what you've got for now, but next time make sure that a) the butcher grinds your venison with pork fat, and/or b), just ask him for more stew meat so you can grind the meat yourself.

1½ pounds venison meat, from the shoulder, ribs, or hind leg

½ pound bacon ends or regular bacon, chopped roughly

Salt (smoked salt if you have it) and freshly ground black pepper

3 tablespoons butter, lard or vegetable oil

1 large or 2 medium onions, sliced thin

Burger buns

Something green, like Bibb lettuce, arugula, sorrel, or spinach

Slices of fresh tomato (summer), or canned, fire-roasted peppers (winter)

Slices of cheese of your choice

Condiment of your choice (ketchup, mustard, remoulade, mayo, etc.)

Make sure the meat and bacon are very cold. Cut the venison into chunks that will fit into your grinder. Do the same for the bacon. Mix the two together roughly so you can add a bit of each into the grinder as you go. Grind one-half to two-thirds of the mixture coarsely and the rest with the fine die. NOTE: If you are grilling your venison burgers, flip this so you grind two-thirds of the mix fine and only one-third coarse—the reason is because grilled burgers tend to cook better and stay juicier when the grind is fine.

Make between 4 and 6 patties, depending on how large you want your burgers. I like big burgers. Form the patties with only as much force as absolutely needed—you want the patties to hold together only loosely. Make them about ½ to 1 inch thick. Use your thumb to press an indentation into the center of each patty—this prevents the burgers from turning spherical when you cook them. Set the burgers aside.

Heat the butter in a frying pan over medium-high heat. When it's good and hot, add the sliced onion and cook until it's done to your liking. Some people like juicy onion with a little char on the edges; some people prefer to go the full caramelized onion route. When finished, put the onions in a bowl so you can have them ready.

I prefer grilled burgers, so I'll go through that method. Heat your grill (charcoal, wood, gas) on high, and be sure to scrape down the grates with a wire brush. Only salt your burgers right before you cook them, and if you are salt-sensitive, you might not need to with these because of the bacon. Place the patties on the grill and cook them without disturbing them with the grill cover open for

(continued)

3 to 5 minutes, depending on how well done you like your burgers. Flip and cook for the same amount on the other side. I prefer 3 minutes per side with a really hot grill.

When you flip the burgers, grind some black pepper over them, then spoon a little caramelized onion on each one if you'd like. With about 90 seconds to go on the second side, lay the cheese on top of the onions and cover the grill until the burger's ready. If you like toasted buns, toast them on the grill in this last 90 seconds. When everything's done, move the burgers and buns to a sheet tray or plate so the meat can rest for 5 minutes, while you build the burgers.

You can do this any way you want, but I start with a green thing (sorrel leaf), then some ketchup or mayo or whatever, then the burger patty that has the onions and cheese already on it, topped with a slice of tomato (or roasted red pepper), and finally some more of whatever condiment I happen to be using. My method is just how I do things; you can do anything you'd like.

VENISON SMASHBURGERS

Serves 4 and can be scaled up | Prep Time: 20 minutes | Cook Time: 20 minutes

Usually it is considered a sin to mash your burger patties with a spatula while you cook them. This allows the juices to escape and can break apart your burger, which will make you sad. But as in all things in life, there is an exception to this rule: the smashburger.

Now the headliner in a successful chain of fast food burger joints, this was the standard way many greasy spoon diners made burgers decades ago. You get a juicy burger with a great crust that cooks in just a couple minutes.

There are some tricks to doing this successfully. First, you need finely ground venison. Second, that meat needs to be fatty—I prefer a full 20 percent fat content in my burger for this. And the pressing is important, too: When you smash your burger, hold it down for thirty seconds, then *slide* off whatever you squashed the meat with; if you lift, chances are you will break your burger.

Needless to say, my toppings are standard, and you can vary them at will. Use your imagination.

1 to 1½ pounds finely ground venison
 (must have fat in the grind)

3 tablespoons vegetable oil, lard,
 or clarified butter

Salt

Black pepper

Burger buns

Sliced tomato

Lettuce

Ketchup

Smashburgers need to be fairly large, so ¼ pound is about as small as you want to make them. Form the meat into four equally sized "hockey pucks" and set aside. Preheat the oven to 185°F and put a baking sheet inside; this is to collect the finished burgers while you cook the rest.

Get a large frying pan, or even two if you have them, and set them over high heat. I prefer cast iron here, but anything other than non-stick will work; non-stick pans don't do well at high heat. When the pans are hot, put 2 teaspoons of oil or lard in the center of the pan. When it melts, put a puck of meat on the melted fat and use another, smaller pan to squash it down until the patty is about ½ inch thick or so. Err on making them a little thicker until you get it right. Hold this down for 30 seconds, then remove the top pan. Salt and pepper the exposed side of the burger.

Turn the heat down to medium-high and cook the burger for 90 seconds. When you see red juice percolating up in the center of the uncooked side, you're pretty much ready to rock. Use a metal spatula—the toughest and stiffest one you have—and scrape the burger off the pan. It's likely that it will be sticking in several places.

Flip the burger, salt and pepper the exposed side, and add cheese if you're making cheeseburgers. Cook another 30 seconds for rare, and no more than 2 minutes for well-done, then remove and put on the baking sheet in the oven and repeat until you've done all the patties. You might need to scrape down the pan a few times to remove debris that collects, and keep adding fat as needed to lubricate the pan. When you're done, just build your burger as you wish.

MUSHROOM BURGERS

Serves 6 | Prep Time: 15 minutes | Cook Time: 20 minutes

This is where I break my own law of including nothing inside the burger patty itself. I just like the hit of savory umami flavor from the mushroom powder in these burgers. Consider this the exception that proves the rule. It's a wild game version of the classic mushroom burger you see in hamburger joints all over the country: A big ole' meat patty, topped with grilled or sautéed onions and mushrooms, served with cheese, usually Swiss. Mustard is the traditional accompaniment here, but nobody dies if you use ketchup, too.

I use wild mushrooms here because I am a mushroom forager. If you have access to morels in spring, or dried morels for the powder in the patties, by all means use it. If not, no worries. Any fresh mushroom will do, and most supermarkets sell those little dried packets of porcini or "forest mix" mushrooms. They're perfect for this recipe.

2 pounds ground venison

A small handful dried morels or other mushrooms, about ½ ounce or 3 tablespoons once ground

2 teaspoons dried thyme

½ teaspoon celery seed

12 ounces fresh morels or other mushrooms, chopped

1 medium onion, sliced thin into half-moons

2 tablespoons olive oil

Hamburger buns

6 slices of Swiss or Provolone cheese

Mustard

Grind the dried mushrooms to a powder in a coffee grinder. Mix the dried mushroom powder, celery seed, and thyme with the meat. Shape the meat into patties. When you do this, don't overwork your meat or your hamburgers will become tough and chewy. Crumbly is better than tough, to my mind. Also, press a little indentation into the center of each patty. This helps the patty keep its shape once cooked, because when meat cooks, it tightens up and will turn into a ball shape if you don't have that indentation.

Heat a large sauté pan over high heat, and add the fresh mushrooms. Shake the pan frequently so they don't all stick, and cook the mushrooms until they release their water, about 2 to 4 minutes. As soon as the water has mostly bubbled away, add the olive oil, some salt, and the sliced onion, and sauté until everything has nicely browned, about 6 to 8 minutes. Turn off the heat and set aside.

Salt your burgers and grill them (or cook them in any other way) to your liking. I like mine medium, so I grill over medium-high heat about 3 to 5 minutes per side. I only flip my burgers once. When you flip the burger, let it cook about halfway on the second side before slapping a slice of cheese on the patty. Close the grill lid to let it melt.

To build the burger, first toast the buns (if you want them toasted). Paint with mustard or whatever, then lay down a patty. Top with the mushrooms and onions and have at it! Serve with a salad and a cold beer.

VENISON CHILI

Serves 8 to 10 | **Prep Time: 1 hour** | **Cook Time: 3 hours**

Who doesn't love chili? And what hunter doesn't love venison chili? Keep in mind that chili has endless variations: Beans or no beans? Ground meat or chunks? Or no meat at all? Tomato products or no tomato products? Add coffee? Chocolate? Cinnamon? In fact, so far as I can tell, the only things that really must be in chili to make it chili are red peppers of some sort, cumin, and onions.

This is my version and I am pretty proud of it. It hinges on ground venison, but I've made it with all kinds of meats, even ground turkey. What makes my chili unique is the huge amount of dried chiles I use. I will typically use twelve to sixteen dried chiles of all sorts, reconstituted and then pureed with a cup of weak coffee to make the backbone of the dish. My advice is to use at least four kinds of chiles, and not all of them should be super hot. I like a mix of ancho, chipotle, guajillo, chile negro, chile mulato, cascabel, New Mexican, and pasilla chiles. As you get to know these chiles—some are smoky, some hot, some sweet—you can adjust the mix to your taste.

You can find these chiles in any Latin market, and even in many regular supermarkets where there is a Latino population. They're not as hard to find as you might think.

Serve this over rice or polenta, garnished with cilantro, raw onions, and maybe some Mexican *queso seco*, jack cheese, or American cheddar.

1 pound pinto beans or kidney beans

4 each, dried ancho, guajillo, pasilla (ancho), cascabel, mirasol, or mulato chiles

½ pound bacon or Mexican soft chorizo

1 large onion, diced

6 to 8 cloves garlic, chopped

2 to 3 pounds ground venison

2 tablespoons paprika

2 tablespoons cumin

1 tablespoon ground coriander

2 tablespoons tomato paste

2 large tomatoes, peeled, seeded, and chopped, or one small can

1 cup of weak coffee

3 tablespoons molasses

Beef or venison broth (have a quart ready)

At least 2 tablespoons salt

Cilantro and shredded cheese to garnish

Soak the beans in water overnight. If you forget to do this the night before, pour boiling water over the beans and soak for 4 hours, changing the water after 2 hours. Break up and seed the chiles, and cover with hot water. (If your hands are sensitive, wear gloves while doing this.) Let stand for an hour or so. Grind to a thick puree, adding about 1 cup of the soaking water and the coffee.

Chop bacon, and fry over medium heat in a Dutch oven or other large, lidded, oven-proof pot. Once the bacon is crispy, remove it and set aside.

Add the ground meat and brown over high heat. You want the highest heat on your most powerful burner here, otherwise the meat will want to steam and stew and not brown. Stir occasionally.

Once all the meat is browned, add onion to the pot and cook for 4 to 6 minutes, stirring often. Add garlic, stir, and cook for 2 minutes. Add the beans, paprika, cumin, coriander, and salt, stirring to combine.

Add chile puree and tomato paste, and stir to combine well. Add chopped tomatoes, molasses, and enough beef broth to cover everything—you want it a little loose now; it'll cook down. I typically need at least a pint of broth, sometimes a quart.

Stir to combine, plunk the lid on and simmer very gently for 2 to 3 hours. Check after 2 hours to see if you need more salt and broth, and to see how the beans are doing. When the beans are tender, you're ready. Use the reserved bacon for garnish . . . or just eat it.

VENISON LASAGNA

Serves 8 to 10 | Prep Time: 30 minutes | Cook Time: 3 hours

Lasagna was a bedrock staple of my childhood in New Jersey. I grew up around a lot of Italians, and everyone's mother or nonna made lasagna for special occasions, like Sunday nights. I've eaten more versions of lasagna than any man has a right to. Even my own decidedly non-Italian mother made a version of the dish. And it was good. Really good. It hinged on mum's meat sauce, which cooked all day on the stove while I was at school and she was at work. Other than that, it was pretty standard: lotsa meat, lotsa cheese, and those wavy noodles that seem to serve no other purpose. Of course, mum's lasagna is the best in the world. How could it not be? That's the thing about lasagna. It is one of those classics everyone makes that are so evocative of warm moments in our past. This is a riff off my mother's lasagna

Lasagna seems like such a commonplace lunch in a cafeteria. But think for a moment: It's loaded with cheese and meat, making it deceptively expensive. For preparation of this dish, I spent $12 just on the cheese—and I already had pecorino at home. All told, the recipe had three pounds of meat and two pounds of cheese. This may be a familiar form, but lasagna New Jersey style is festival food, make no mistake.

- 1 pound ground pork or wild boar
- 2 pounds ground venison
- 1 chopped onion
- 1 head of garlic, chopped
- One 28-ounce can of crushed tomatoes
- One 8-ounce can of tomato sauce
- 1 can of tomato paste
- 1 cup red wine
- 1 teaspoon fennel seeds
- 2 tablespoons sugar
- ¼ cup chopped fresh basil leaves
- 2 tablespoons dried oregano
- One 15-ounce container of ricotta cheese
- 1 pound mozzarella cheese, shredded
- 1 cup grated pecorino cheese
- ½ nutmeg, grated, or 1 teaspoon ground
- ½ cup chopped parsley leaves
- 12 lasagna noodles
- Salt and pepper

Make the sauce. Brown the meat in a large Dutch oven. Take your time and do this in batches. It could take as long as 20 minutes. Put all the browned meat back in the pot and then add the chopped onions and cook for another 3 to 4 minutes, then add the garlic and cook for another 2 to 3 minutes. Add seasonings—fennel seeds, oregano, basil—and mix well.

Mix the wine and tomato paste and pour into the pot. Bring to a boil over high heat, stirring often. Add the tomato sauce and the can of crushed tomatoes and mix again. Bring to a simmer, and cook slowly for 1 to 2 hours. This can be done as much as two days ahead of time.

Prepare the lasagna. Soak the lasagna noodles in hot water for 15 to 20 minutes. Preheat the oven to 350°F.

Meanwhile, mix the parsley with the ricotta cheese in a bowl. Grate the pecorino and shred the mozzarella. Grate half a nutmeg into the ricotta. If you can't find whole nutmegs, use 1 teaspoon.

To assemble, spread a good amount of the meat on the bottom of a standard 9-inch by 13-inch casserole pan. Remove the lasagna noodles and lay on the meat sauce. Spread half the ricotta cheese mixture on the noodles, then half the mozzarella cheese, then half the pecorino.

Add another layer of meat sauce—you will have one final layer after this—then the rest of the noodles. Add the remaining ricotta and mozzarella, plus half of the remaining pecorino. Spread the remaining meat sauce on this, then sprinkle with the last bit of pecorino.

To cook, cover the lasagna with foil. You might want to spray the underside first with non-stick spray so the cheese doesn't stick to it. Bake covered for 25 minutes. Carefully take off the foil and bake for another 25 minutes. Let the lasagna rest for 15 minutes before serving with a strong red wine.

ITALIAN VENISON MEATLOAF

Serves 4 to 6 | **Prep Time: 30 minutes** | **Cook Time: 1 hour, 15 minutes**

Unlike my mum's lasagna, which I loved, the word "meatloaf" in answer to "what's for dinner"? struck fear into my very core. Mum made lots of good things to eat, but her meatloaf was not one of them. I remember it as a desiccated block of unhappy beef, laced with veins of melting cheese of unknown origin. The only thing I could do to choke it down was to submerge each piece in Worcestershire sauce. And choke it down I did, because mum was not the sort of mother to make special meals for finicky children. Interestingly, my sisters don't remember the family meatloaf being so inedible, so either mum changed the recipe at some point, or I was simply born with an animus against great loaves of ground meat.

My fear and loathing of meatloaf endured for many years until one day when I was at a pork store—Long Island slang for Italian deli—with a friend ordering lunch. I happen to love meatball sandwiches, and Del Fiore's in Patchogue had some of the best. My friend wanted a meatloaf sandwich instead. I must have wrinkled my nose or something. "What? What's wrong with a meatloaf sandwich?" he asked. "It's nasty," I said, conjuring childhood images that made me shudder visibly. My friend was exasperated. "You do know that all meatloaf is just a big meatball, right? Just try it. Tell you what: I'll order the meatball sandwich and you order the meatloaf. If you don't like it, we switch. Deal?" Deal.

The sandwiches came and I immediately noticed something: The meat looked the same, as did the marinara sauce on top. Only the meatloaf sandwich was easier to eat—no meatballs rolling off the back end of the hoagie roll and onto my jeans. I took a bite, and dammit if my friend wasn't right: Meatloaf, at least this incarnation of meatloaf, was basically a big slab of the same meatballs I knew and loved. It was a revelation.

Meatloaf is more of an art than a science, and the loaf's final consistency depends on a few things: how much stuff you put into the mix that isn't meat, how thoroughly you work the meat, and what sort of binder you use. I like a meatloaf that will hold together, but loosely—cake-ish, not dense. The recipe method that follows will do that.

A couple of tips: First, when you're chopping the Italian bread, wherever you have a piece with crust, cut it smaller than crustless pieces. I like having the crust in there though, as it adds texture and flavor. Second, although this recipe calls for marinara sauce, any simple tomato sauce will do, so long as it's not too chunky.

This meatloaf keeps well, and is great as a sandwich filling during the week.

1½ cups Italian bread, cubed (see recipe headnotes)

1 cup milk

1 medium carrot, sliced

1 small fennel bulb, chopped roughly

1 celery stalk, chopped

3 garlic cloves, chopped

2 pounds ground venison (see headnotes)

1 cup grated Italian cheese (parmesan or pecorino)

⅓ cup marinara sauce

¼ cup chopped parsley

1 tablespoon kosher salt

2 teaspoons dried oregano

3 eggs

More marinara sauce for painting the top and serving

Soak the bread cubes in a bowl with the milk for 30 minutes while you chop the vegetables and get everything else ready. Put the roughly chopped vegetables into a food processor and blitz them until it begins to form something of a paste. This will keep the meatloaf super moist.

Preheat your oven to 375°F. When the bread has softened, squeeze out the excess milk and chop and mash the soaked bread on a cutting board until it too forms something of a paste. Toss it and the vegetable mixture into a large bowl. Add the ground venison, cheese, marinara sauce, parsley, eggs, salt, and oregano and combine. I like to work the meatloaf mix well because the bread and vegetable mix will keep it moist and tender—normally you don't want to overwork meatball mixes, but this is an exception. It will help the meatloaf bind together better.

Grease a loaf pan. I used a Pyrex 1½-quart pan that is 8½ by 4½ by 2½ inches. Something more or less this size will be fine. Or, you can set the mixture on a greased baking sheet and mold it into a loaf. Pack the meat mixture into the pan and bake it until the center reads about 160°F, which will take roughly 1 hour and 15 minutes. I put the loaf pan on top of a baking sheet to catch any overflow of fat or tomato sauce.

About 30 minutes before the meatloaf is ready (shoot for the 45-minute mark), paint the top of the loaf with marinara sauce. Have some more sauce warming in a small pot to serve with the finished meatloaf.

Once the loaf is ready, set it on the countertop for 5 to 10 minutes to rest before popping out of the loaf pan. Do this carefully. Slice and serve with sauce.

VENISON BOLOGNESE SAUCE

Serves 8 to 10 | Prep Time: 20 minutes | Cook Time: 4 hours

Have you ever had pasta with Bolognese sauce? I mean a real, honest-to-goodness Bolognese? Probably not. A true Bolognese is different from a typical meat sauce: smoother, meatier, mellower, and a lot richer than a typical ragu or sugo. A little goes a long way.

There is a reason that the guardians of this sauce are so strict about what is and what is not an authentic Bolognese. This is a sauce with rules. It is built on a base of onion, carrot, and celery. No garlic. Nor does it have lots of herbs in it. The sauce contains dairy products. Tomato, while present, is not the star of the sauce. Meat is. And to make a real Bolognese, it must cook a long, long time. Every cook has a personal version. This is mine.

Don't try to make this sauce on a weeknight. It takes a long time to come together, and the time spent slowly simmering really makes this sauce special. But fear not, it keeps in the fridge for up to ten days, and freezes very well.

Porcini mushrooms are my first choice here, but any dried mushroom will work; I know that a lot of deer hunters also pick morels, so use them if you have them. One tip on getting the onion, carrot, and celery minced well enough: Chop roughly, then buzz a few times in a food processor.

4 tablespoons unsalted butter

1 cup minced onion

1 cup minced carrot

1 cup minced celery

2 pounds ground venison

1 ounce dried mushrooms, reconstituted in 2 cups hot water and chopped

One 6-ounce can tomato paste

1 cup venison or beef broth or water

1 cup white wine

1 cup milk

½ nutmeg, grated, or ½ teaspoon ground

Salt and black pepper to taste

Pasta (tagliatelle, penne, etc.)

Grated cheese for garnish

Heat the butter over medium-high heat in a large, heavy pot like a Dutch oven. Add the onion, celery, and carrots and cook gently for 5 to 8 minutes, stirring often. Do not brown them. Sprinkle a little salt over the veggies as they cook.

When the vegetables are soft, stir in the chopped mushrooms and tomato paste and allow everything to cook for 3 to 4 minutes, again, stirring often. When the tomato paste begins to turn the color of brick, add the ground meat, the mushroom soaking water, and the broth. Bring to a simmer.

Allow this to cook down over medium-low heat. Take your time here and resist the urge to do this over higher heat. Stir from time to time. When the liquid has mostly evaporated, add the wine and repeat the process. When that has mostly evaporated, add the milk, nutmeg, and black pepper, and stir well. Bring back to a simmer and add salt to taste. Let this cook until it is the consistency you want.

When you add the milk to the sauce, bring a large pot of water to a boil. Add enough salt to make it taste like the sea. Once the Bolognese sauce has thickened, add the pasta and cook until it's al dente.

To serve, put the pasta in a large bowl and add a healthy ladle of sauce. Toss to combine. Give everyone their portion, then top with a small ladle's worth of sauce. Grate the cheese over the top and serve.

SWEDISH MEATBALLS

Serves 8 to 12 | Prep Time: 2 hours | Cook Time: 45 minutes

This is a version of my mum's recipe for Swedish meatballs, also known as *köttbullar*. Also known as crack. My grandmother was of Swedish extraction, and while I can't remember her ever making Swedish meatballs, I do have several strong memories of mum making these little balls of yum long ago, in the Seventies. *Of course* we ate Swedish meatballs in the 1970s—everyone did. They were right next to the fondue. Can't you just see the chafing dish, the Sterno, and the meatballs nestled in that slowly-congealing-yet-somehow-irresistible gravy? Groovy, baby, yeah!

Serve these little meatballs in the sauce over mashed potatoes. A salad or sautéed greens would round things out.

Lingonberry jelly can be tough to find, although the Swedish furniture store IKEA carries it. Red currant jelly is in most supermarkets, and makes a good substitute. I've used highbush cranberry jelly, too.

4 slices of stale bread, crusts removed

⅔ cup milk

2½ pounds ground venison

2 eggs

2 teaspoons kosher salt

2 teaspoons ground allspice

1 teaspoon caraway seeds

1 teaspoon black pepper

1 grated yellow onion

Flour

1 quart beef or venison stock

½ cup sour cream

½ cup red currant or lingonberry jelly

Salt

Butter or oil for frying

Pour the milk into a pot and set it on low heat. Cut the crusts off the stale bread and break it into pieces. Add it to the pot. It will begin to absorb the milk. When it does, turn off the heat and mash everything into a paste. Let it cool to room temperature.

Add the ground venison and the salt and spices to a large bowl. Crack the eggs into the bowl, then pour the bread-milk mixture in. With clean hands, mix everything together. Work the mixture gently—think cake, not bread. When it's mostly combined (you need not get everything perfect), grab a tablespoon and scoop some up. Roll it into a little ball with your palms, not your fingers. Gently roll the meatballs in the flour; you'll probably need about a cup. Put them onto a baking sheet.

When the meatballs are all made, get a large pan ready; I use a big cast-iron frying pan. Fill it with a little less than a quarter inch of oil. I use canola oil with a little butter tossed in for flavor. Bring it up to temperature over medium-high heat. When a bit of flour splashed in the oil immediately sizzles, drop the heat to medium and add the meatballs. Do not crowd them.

You want the oil to come up halfway on the meatballs. Add a little oil if need be; don't worry, you can reuse the oil for another dish. Fry on medium heat for 3 to 5 minutes. You are looking for golden brown. Turn only once. The other side will need about 4 minutes.

When cooked, set the meatballs on a paper towel or wire rack to drain. They can be used right away, cooled and then refrigerated for a week, or frozen for several months.

THE SAUCE

Once the meatballs are cooked, drain all but about 4 tablespoons of butter/oil from the pan. Over medium heat, add an equal amount of the flour left over from dusting the meatballs. Stir to make a roux and cook slowly until it turns a nice golden brown. Think coffee with cream.

Add the stock gradually, then turn the heat up to medium-high. Stir well to combine, and add more stock or some water if need be—you want this thicker than water, thinner than Thanksgiving gravy. Taste for salt, and add if needed.

Put the meatballs in the pan, cover, and cook for 10 minutes over medium-low heat.

Add the lingonberry or highbush cranberry jelly to the pan. Let it melt and then mix it in gently. Coat all the meatballs with the sauce. Cover and cook another 10 minutes over very low heat. Add the cream and just warm through, maybe 3 minutes. Serve over mashed potatoes, or with German egg noodles.

ALBÓNDIGAS AL CHIPOTLE

Serves 4 to 6 | Prep Time: 20 minutes | Cook Time: 40 minutes

Meatballs are universal. Every culture in the world makes some kind of meatball. They are little balls of comfort. This is a simple meatball recipe from Mexico that comes together in an hour or so, making it easy enough to do on a work night. Kids love making meatballs, too, so shanghai them into helping you out.

I mostly like eating these with rice while watching football or nature shows, but they also make a damn good party appetizer.

The only thing even remotely challenging about this recipe is finding the chipotles in adobo, but pretty much every Latin market in America sells it, as do most larger supermarkets. In a pinch, you could buy chipotles in adobo online.

MEATBALLS

2 pounds ground venison

4 garlic cloves, minced

2 tablespoons dried mint

2 eggs

1 cup breadcrumbs

2 teaspoons ground cumin

2 teaspoons salt

1 teaspoon black pepper

Bacon fat, lard, or other high-heat oil for frying

SAUCE

2 tablespoons lard, bacon fat or oil

1 onion, minced

4 garlic cloves, minced

2 cups tomato puree

2 cups broth (chicken, beef, venison, whatever)

3 to 6 chipotles in adobo, chopped

2 teaspoons ground cumin

2 teaspoons dried oregano

Salt to taste

Put all the meatball ingredients together in a large bowl. Mix with your very clean hands until the mixture comes together. Don't overwork the mix or the meatballs will get tough. Roll into meatballs of whatever size you want. I like to make them by the tablespoon. If you have the time, let the meatballs sit in the fridge for up to an hour; this helps them stay together.

Brown the meatballs in the bacon fat, lard, or oil. Once they're browned, set aside.

If you browned the meatballs in a large enough pan to hold all of them, drain all but about 2 tablespoons of the fat, and keep using that pan. Otherwise, get a pot or pan large enough to hold all the meatballs, and heat 2 tablespoons of fat in it. Cook the onions in this until soft and browned at the edges, about 10 minutes. Stir from time to time. Add the garlic and cook another minute.

Add the spices, chipotles, broth, and tomato, and mix well. Nestle the meatballs into the sauce and bring to a simmer. Simmer for about 20 to 30 minutes, until the meatballs are cooked through. Eat with rice, or by themselves as an appetizer.

JAPANESE TERIYAKI MEATBALLS

Serves 4 to 6 | Prep Time: 20 minutes | Cook Time: 20 minutes

This is a traditional Japanese style of meatball called *niku dango*, and it's damn good. It's basically a teriyaki meatball, normally made with pork. Venison works fine. It's a pretty simple meatball, made "Japanese" with the addition of ginger, green onion, coarse panko breadcrumbs, and soy sauce in the mix. All by itself, it's a nice meatball.

The star of this show is the sauce, which is essentially a homemade teriyaki. Could you use store-bought teriyaki sauce? I suppose you could. But homemade is better. That's really all there is to this recipe: Easy meatballs glazed with a homemade teriyaki sauce, dusted with sesame seeds. Stick a toothpick in each meatball and you have a great party appetizer. Toss a few on top of some steamed rice and you have an easy weeknight meal. But a fair warning: Make more than you think you'll need. People seem to be unable to control themselves while eating these.

I don't like a super-sweet sauce, so I only have the 1 tablespoon of sugar in it; mirin is also sweet (it's a sweet cooking wine, fermented from rice, that you can get in most supermarkets), so that's enough for me. Feel free to double the amount of sugar if you like a typically sweet teriyaki sauce.

MEATBALLS

2 pounds finely ground venison

3 tablespoons minced green onions

1 cup panko breadcrumbs

2 tablespoons soy sauce

½ teaspoon black pepper

2 tablespoons minced fresh ginger

2 eggs

SAUCE

2 tablespoons sake

½ cup mirin, sweet Japanese cooking wine

1 tablespoon sugar

½ cup soy sauce

2 teaspoons potato or corn starch

Toasted sesame seeds, for garnish

Mix all the meatball ingredients together in a bowl. Mix all the sauce ingredients in another bowl.

Form meatballs anywhere from the size of a walnut to the size of golf ball. For best results, set the meatballs on a baking sheet and put it into the fridge for an hour to firm up. But you can cook the meatballs straight away if you'd like.

Cook the meatballs. You can deep fry them at 360°F for about 5 minutes; you can poach them in simmering water for about the same amount of time (they're ready when they float); or you can bake the meatballs at 400°F for about 20 minutes.

Glaze the meatballs. Whisk the sauce together so the starch doesn't stick to the bottom of the bowl, and pour it into a large sauté pan. Bring it to a boil and add the cooked meatballs. Roll them around in the hot sauce to glaze for 30 seconds or so. Move the meatballs to a serving plate, and sprinkle sesame seeds over them. Serve hot as an appetizer or with rice.

INDIAN KOFTA MEATBALL CURRY

Serves 4 to 6 | Prep Time: 40 minutes | Cook Time: 45 minutes

This is a Kashmiri dish called kofta, normally done with lamb or goat, that appears in one form or another throughout the Middle East and beyond, as do dolmas (see next page) and Kefta Kebabs (page 201) It's basically a meatball curry, and while the meatballs are perfectly good sauced with a store-bought Kashmiri curry in a jar—available all over the country in the "ethnic" section—I thought I'd give you a from-scratch curry in case you get adventurous. If you go the store-bought route, you'll need at least two jars of the sauce.

It can be difficult to find ground fennel seed, but whole fennel seeds are easy to find. Just mash them with mortar and pestle, or buzz them in a spice or coffee grinder.

MEATBALLS

1½ pounds finely ground venison

1 small onion, grated on a box grater

A 2-inch piece of ginger, minced and mashed into a rough puree

¼ cup chopped cilantro

1 tablespoon garam masala

2 teaspoons ground fennel seed

1 egg

1 teaspoon salt

1 cup chickpea flour (optional)

1 cup vegetable oil (optional)

If you're using store-bought curry, get it simmering gently in a pot large enough to hold all the meatballs.

If you're making your own curry, whisk the corn starch with the yogurt, and set aside at room temperature.

Now you need to turn the ginger, onion, chiles, and garlic into a paste. You can do this in several ways. Most traditional would be to pound it into submission with a mortar and pestle, which is what I do. This melds flavors and really breaks down the fibers of all the ingredients. Your other option is to put everything in a blender with just enough water to get the blades to run normally. A food processor won't do, as it won't turn the vegetables into a paste. The blender method sounds easier, but it's not, because if you put too much water into the mix, you'll wreck the next step, which is cooking the paste in butter.

When you have the vegetables mashed into a paste, fry them in the ghee over medium-low heat for 10 minutes, stirring occasionally. Don't let it brown. Mix in the tomato paste and turn the heat to medium. Fill the tomato paste can with water and stir that in. Stir in the garam masala, curry powder, and fenugreek, if using. Add enough water to make the curry into a fairly thin gravy, and bring it to a gentle simmer.

To make the meatballs, mix all the ingredients together, and form into balls the size of a walnut. You can either cook them entirely in the curry, or coat them in the chickpea flour and fry them in the oil. I prefer the latter. If you do fry them, roll the meatballs in the chickpea flour, and brown in the hot oil. Set them into the curry pot as you go.

CURRY

A 3-inch piece of ginger, minced

1 onion, minced

2 small, hot chiles, such as cayenne, chopped

5 garlic cloves, minced

¼ cup ghee (clarified butter), mustard oil, or vegetable oil

One 6-ounce can of tomato paste

2 teaspoons garam masala

2 teaspoons curry powder or turmeric

½ teaspoon ground fenugreek (optional)

½ teaspoon corn starch

½ cup plain, full-fat yogurt

When the last meatball goes into the curry, simmer everything for 10 minutes or so to make sure everything's cooked through. Turn off the heat and when the curry stops bubbling, add the yogurt by folding it in; don't stir too vigorously, otherwise it can break. If that happens, the dish will still be edible, but it won't look nice. Serve with long-grain rice.

GREEK DOLMAS

Serves 6 to 8 | Prep Time: 1 hour | Cook Time: 1 hour

Dolmas—stuffed grape leaves—are a staple appetizer all over the eastern Mediterranean, and the Greeks, Turks, Cypriots, Lebanese, and Syrians all have their own versions. Dolmas are a bit like Cajun boudin—well-spiced rice and meat bundles (page 243). Making them is a relaxing thing to do on a weekend or a day off, and, once made, the dolmas will keep in the fridge for a week or so. They are normally eaten hot, but they're fine cold, too.

Be sure to use short-grain rice, like risotto or Japanese rice, for this recipe. If you use long-grain rice, the filling won't come together correctly, and will be crumbly and taste wrong if you eat the dolmas cold. If you don't have pine nuts handy, feel free to substitute chopped dried apricots, which are also very nice.

If you are using store-bought grape leaves in brine, be sure to rinse and drain them first.

2 pounds ground venison

1 cup uncooked short-grain rice

1½ cups minced onion

½ cup chopped, toasted pine nuts (optional)

1 tablespoon chopped fresh chives
(or the green part of scallions)

2 tablespoons chopped parsley

2 to 3 tablespoons chopped fresh mint,
or 1 tablespoon dried

2 tablespoons chopped fresh dill or
fennel fronds

1 teaspoon dried oregano

1 teaspoon black pepper

2 teaspoons salt

5 tablespoons of olive oil

Juice and grated zest of 2 or 3 lemons

One 16-ounce jar of grape leaves in brine
(about 65-80 leaves), rinsed and drained

Mix the venison, rice, onion, pine nuts, fresh and dried herbs, salt, pepper, olive oil, and lemon juice together in a large bowl.

Remove the grape leaves from the jar and drain. Snip off any stems. Carefully separate the leaves, setting aside any beat-up or torn leaves to line the pot.

To fill the grape leaves, lay one down, vein side up, stem facing you. Spoon a couple of teaspoons of the filling in a little cigar shape along the stem edge of the grape leaf, where the leaf is broadest. Roll the bottom of the leaf up over the filling once or twice, then fold in the sides under the cigar you're making before rolling the leaf all the way; it's like rolling a burrito. Don't roll the dolmas too tight, because when the rice cooks, it expands and can break your dolma. Set the finished dolma on a baking sheet, seam side down. Repeat with the remaining filling and leaves.

Once all the grape leaves are rolled, line a wide, shallow pot with the beat-up or otherwise imperfect grape leaves; this prevents the dolmas from sticking. Arrange seam side down in the pot, ideally in one layer, although you can stack them if you can make sure the seam of the top dolma is resting on a dolma just below it.

Add enough water to cover the dolmas by about ½ inch. Toss in a healthy pinch of salt. Find a plate that fits in the pot to weigh down the dolmas, otherwise they will float, and bad things will happen. Bring the water to a boil, then drop it to a gentle simmer and cook for about 50 minutes.

Remove the plate, and gently move the dolmas to a serving plate. Serve warm with a drizzle of good olive oil over them and some lemon wedges.

CORNISH PASTIES

Makes about 10 6-inch pasties | **Prep Time: 3½ hours** | **Cook Time: 50 minutes**

Pasties are one of mankind's great convenience foods. Handheld, nourishing, filling, and tasty either hot or cold, they were a mainstay lunch for me when I was in graduate school at the University of Wisconsin. The pasty shop, called Myles Teddywedgers, still stands at the top of State Street, and as of 2013, twenty years after I first ate there, still makes a damn good pasty. This is my rendition of their classic.

True pasty freaks will note that I include the "Scarborough Faire" herbs of parsley, sage, rosemary, and thyme, which are not traditional. They add a lot of flavor and are still very British. If you don't like them, leave them out. If you can't get the fresh stuff, which I prefer, dried is fine—just cut the amounts in half.

Incidentally, you can also use ground venison for this recipe, although I prefer diced meat. If you do use ground meat, keep in mind that all my ground venison has fat cut into it. If yours doesn't, put a pat of butter (about two teaspoons) on top of the mixture before folding up the pasty.

And finally, if you can't find rutabagas, use turnips; if you can't find either, use all potatoes. My pastry calls for lard and butter, but you can use butter only if you'd rather. The crust is different, but still good.

A word on the vegetables. Since you are only baking the pasties for forty-five minutes, be mindful of the size of your pieces. Most good pasties have vegetables that are more sliced than chunked.

PASTRY

17½ ounces (500 grams) bread flour, about 4¼ cups

4 ounces (115 grams) lard (see above)

4 ounces (115 grams) unsalted butter (1 stick)

2 tsp salt

6 ounces cold water, about ¾ to 1 cup

Beaten egg to glaze pastry

FILLING

1 pound venison cut into small cubes

½ pound waxy potatoes (like Yukon Gold), peeled and sliced

½ pound rutabaga, peeled and sliced

1 small onion, chopped

Salt and black pepper

1 teaspoon chopped fresh sage

½ teaspoon chopped fresh rosemary

2 teaspoons chopped fresh parsley

2 teaspoons chopped fresh thyme

Mix the salt with the flour. Rub the lard and butter into the flour until it looks like breadcrumbs or wet sand. Add the water and knead until the dough comes together and becomes elastic. This will take a little longer than you might think, about 6 to 8 minutes, but you need to really knead here to make a strong dough. Cover the dough with plastic wrap and let it rest for at least 1 hour in the fridge, and up to overnight; this lets the dough relax—rolling it out immediately is virtually impossible—and allows the fats to chill.

About 15 minutes before you want to begin making the pasties, mix all the ingredients in a bowl and set aside.

Preheat the oven to 350°F. Roll out the pastry and cut into circles about 6 to 8 inches in diameter; this is a typical size for appetizer plates, which work well as a guide. If you don't have enough dough to make 10 circles, gather the excess into a ball and roll it out again.

Layer the vegetables and meat in the center of the pastry circles. Brush the outer edge with a little water. Fold the circle over to make a half-moon and press firmly to seal, taking care to push out any air pockets. Push down on the edge of the pasty and using the thumb of one hand and the thumb and forefinger of the other, twist the edge of the pastry over to form a crimp. Do this along the whole outer edge of the pasty, and tuck the end corners underneath it.

When you're done, paint the pasties with the beaten egg. Ideally, line your baking pan with a Silpat silicone baking liner or some parchment paper to prevent the pasties from sticking to the pan. Bake for about 45 to 50 minutes until golden brown.

CHINESE POTSTICKERS

Serves 6 to 8 normal people, or 4 gluttons
Prep Time: 2 hours, or about 45 minutes if you are using store-bought wrappers │ Cook Time: 20 minutes

I don't know anyone who doesn't like potstickers—even bad supermarket potstickers, which can be pretty gummy. You eat them and you say to yourself, "Damn, these are pretty gummy . . . but hey, at least they're potstickers!" It's a dumpling thing. And admittedly, most often you will make these with store-bought wrappers, which are OK but not as wonderful as handmade. I get it. Wrappers are super-easy to find in supermarkets, and they work. An upgrade would be the wrappers sold at Asian markets, which are superior to those sold in regular supermarkets; they'll be in the frozen foods section. If you have a choice, buy Shanghai-style wrappers for this recipe.

This is how I made potstickers for years, until I bought my friend Andrea Nguyen's book *Asian Dumplings*. In it, I learned how to make wrappers by hand. It is not only easier than I thought, but the result is markedly different from store-bought. So if you want to really do these right, try them with homemade wrappers sometime.

I owe a lot of this recipe to both Nguyen and Jaden Hair, another cookbook author friend of mine who runs the super-popular *Steamy Kitchen* website. I'd initially designed a good potsticker. With their help, this is a *great* potsticker.

My advice for beginners is to start with store-bought wrappers. Only after you've made a couple of batches should you bother to make your own wrappers. While making the filling is über-easy, getting the pleated fold is mildly tricky. Best not to overwhelm yourself the first time.

Serve your potstickers with a zippy soy dipping sauce, sriracha, or something else that is sweet-and-spicy. Just make more potstickers than you think you need. You'll find yourselves fighting over the last one.

Once you make these dumplings, you can freeze them on a baking sheet until solid, then fill freezer bags full of them. They will keep for a few months that way.

SAUCE

¼ cup soy sauce

3 tablespoons rice vinegar
or Chinese black vinegar

1 hot chile, minced

3 garlic cloves, minced

1 tablespoon minced ginger

1 teaspoon sugar

2 tablespoons sesame oil

FILLING

1 pound ground venison

¾ cup minced Chinese chives, green onions,
or other wild chive-like green onion

2 tablespoons grated ginger

2 tablespoons minced garlic

1 teaspoon salt

1 tablespoon chicken stock (Asian if you
have it) or water

2 tablespoons soy sauce

1 tablespoon *Shaoxing* wine or dry sherry

2 teaspoons sesame oil

WRAPPERS

Either 50 store-bought potsticker wrappers or:

2½ cups all-purpose flour (about 14 ounces)

1 cup hot water

A tortilla press or rolling pin

A dowel of wood about ½ inch thick and
6 to 10 inches long

A few tablespoons of vegetable oil
for pan-frying

Mix all the ingredients for the sauce together and let sit at room temperature while you make everything else. You can refrigerate this overnight if you want.

In a large bowl, mix all the ingredients for the filling together until well combined. Cover the dough and let it rest for at least 30 minutes, and up to overnight if you put it in the refrigerator.

Work on one dumpling at a time. Fill the wrapper with a scant tablespoon of filling. If you are using store-bought wrappers, paint the edge of the wrapper with the water and corn starch slurry (see below). Close the wrapper to form a half-moon, making sure there are no air pockets. It is probable that some of the filling will squirt out the ends as you seal them. This is normal; just drop it back into the bowl with the rest of the filling.

Pleat the edges: I usually start from the center and do 3 pleats on the left of the dumpling, then another 3 on the right of the dumpling. As you make the pleats, settle the dumpling on your work surface so it sits flat. You will need this flat surface to get a nice crispy bottom to your potsticker. Set each finished dumpling on a baking sheet lined with either parchment or a little semolina flour or corn meal.

To cook your potstickers, heat about 2 to 3 tablespoons of vegetable oil (I use peanut oil) over medium-high heat in a large, non-stick frying pan. When the oil is hot, about a minute or two, lay the potstickers down in one layer; they can touch each other. Fry like this for 1 to 2 minutes, until the bottoms are browned.

Add enough water to come up about ¼ inch. The pan will sputter and spit, so have a lid ready. Turn the heat down to medium, cover the pan, and cook for 5 minutes. After 5 minutes, move the lid partway off the pan to let steam escape. Cook 1 more minute, then remove the lid entirely. You will soon hear the cooking change from boiling to sizzling—that's your cue that they're done. Serve immediately with the dipping sauce.

TIPS ON USING STORE-BOUGHT WRAPPERS

If the wrappers are frozen, let them thaw in the fridge overnight, or sit at room temperature for an hour or two.

Once you open the package, cover the wrappers that you're not using with a damp cloth so they don't dry out.

Store-bought wrappers need a little water on their edges to properly seal; corn starch helps this even more. So have a little bowl of about ¼ cup water mixed with about a teaspoon of corn starch nearby that you can dip your finger into.

TO MAKE WRAPPERS

Put the flour in a large bowl and make a well in the center. Boil some water, turn off the heat, and pour in a healthy cup of the water into the well you've made in the flour (when I say "healthy," I mean to err on the side of more water, not less). Stir the mixture with a fork until it gets shaggy, then knead with your hands (the dough should be OK to handle) for a few minutes, until it is smooth and elastic. Put the dough in a plastic bag and let sit on the counter for at least 30 minutes and up to 2 hours.

Roll the dough into a thick snake and cut it in half, then in half again. Put the three pieces you are not using back in the plastic bag.

Roll the snake you are working with until it is about 1 inch thick. Cut it into 12 disks. Use your hands to return each disk to a nice cylinder. If the dough is tacky, dredge it lightly in a little flour.

Open your tortilla press. Put the cylinder between two pieces of plastic or wax paper (I use sheets cut from a freezer bag) and squash it with the tortilla press. Move the circle of dough to your work surface and press the next piece of dough. If you don't have a tortilla press, get one. In the meantime, use a rolling pin to roll out thin disks; this isn't easy.

Now use your little dowel to roll out the outer edges of each circle. You want to keep an area about the size of a nickel at the center thick, so hold the wrapper here while you flatten out the edges with the dowel. Do this while constantly rotating the wrapper. It does not matter if the wrapper is perfectly circular; just do your best.

Once you have your 12 wrappers, fill them and pleat as above. Continue with another 12 wrappers at a time until you finish. At first, you will be slow, and the wrappers will start to dry out. Keep a little bowl of water nearby to wet the edges, which helps them seal tightly. When you get good at this, you can knock out a dozen dumplings fast enough to not need this.

Why Bother with Handmade Wrappers?

I know, I know. We live in a busy world. Who has time to mess around with handmade pasta, or potsticker wrappers? The answer lies deep within the meaning of a dumpling. Dumplings aren't supposed to be fast food. Dumplings, made by hand, are an expression of love. They are an edible present.

What a handmade potsticker wrapper has that a store-bought one doesn't can be summed up in a word: flexibility. First, handmade dough is a lot more pliable than store-bought. And second, a handmade wrapper is not uniformly thick—which, as we will see, is vital for a good potsticker.

Cookbook author Andrea Nguyen's technique for wrapper-making requires an odd, cross-cultural bit of equipment: a tortilla press. It's a natural! The press helps you make perfect circles of dough, which you then hit with a handmade roller—a short piece of a wooden dowel about ½ to 1 inch thick. (You can buy thick dowels at your nearest home improvement store.) You can also roll them out completely by hand or use a pasta machine.

The result is really cool: The wrapper is thick where you crisp it up—the "potsticker" part—because it needs to be to not break. And the wrapper is thin where you seal it, which keeps the pleated edges dainty. Brilliant, really.

But more than that, you will know that you made something special, something downright beautiful.

KEFTA KEBABS

Serves 4 to 6 | Prep Time: 30 minutes | Cook Time: 10 minutes

This is another party snack based on street food—in this case, from North Africa. Ground meat on a stick makes an appearance all over the Mediterranean and into Persia, and every cook uses a different spice mixture. This one is inspired by Morocco and Tunisia. The herbs and spices play very well together, but if you're short on one, you can leave it out and still be fine.

It is important that you use finely ground venison and that you knead the mixture of meat, onion, and spices well so that the kebabs will actually stay on your skewers. This is not a burger just barely holding itself together. Think of this as a caseless sausage on a stick.

Serve the kebabs with roasted or grilled vegetables, crusty bread, or rice.

This recipe really works best with flat skewers. Many supermarkets sell them, but in a pinch, you can skewer the ground meat with two round bamboo skewers instead of one. That will help you flip them. Don't forget to soak the bamboo in water for an hour first, or the skewers will burn.

1 pound ground venison

1 small onion, grated or minced fine

2 tablespoons chopped parsley

2 tablespoons chopped oil-packed sun-dried tomatoes (optional)

2 teaspoons dried mint

½ to 1 teaspoon cayenne

1 teaspoon ground cumin

1 teaspoon salt

1 teaspoon black pepper

½ teaspoon ground coriander

The easy way to make these is to use finely ground venison and just mix together all the ingredients. But I find that you get a better texture and bind if you use coarsely ground venison or even stew meat, mix in everything else, and then grind everything fine. The easy way works, but if you have the time, try double-grinding it. Regardless, let the mixture sit in the fridge for 30 minutes or so to allow the flavors to meld a bit. You can keep the mix in the fridge for up to a day before the herbs start to get sad.

For the skewers, use flat metal skewers if you have them. You can use two bamboo skewers if you soak them, or, if you happen to have access to a rosemary bush, you can strip off the leaves and use a few of them as skewers—this being ground meat, the flat metal skewers are best. Be sure to soak the branches for an hour before you put them on the grill.

When you're ready to cook, build a hot fire. Charcoal is best, but gas is fine in a pinch. If you don't have a grill, you can broil the skewers. Form the meat onto the skewers into long, skinny sausages. You are looking for any length, but no more than about 3 inches thick. Grill, turning often, until the kebabs are slightly charred, about 4 to 6 minutes.

A really good sauce to accompany this dish is *tzatziki*. I have a recipe for it in page 111.

SOUTH AFRICAN BOBOTIE

Serves 6 to 8 | Prep Time: 20 minutes | Cook Time: 1 hour

This is one of the national dishes of South Africa, and has been for the better part of 400 years. It's believed to be derived from an Indonesian dish—the Dutch who settled South Africa also colonized Indonesia—and is essentially a curry meatloaf casserole with baked egg.

There are an awful lot of variations on *bobotie*, which is pronounced bo-BO-tee, but the goal is curry-like, sweet, sour, and savory. I add a little cayenne for balance, but this is not traditional. You'll note a bunch of alternatives in the ingredient list. The first listed are my preferences, followed by easier-to-find alternates.

This is a one-pot meal, although I like it served alongside rice; a salad is a good accompaniment, too. To drink, I'd go with an IPA or pale ale.

3 slices white bread

2 cups milk

2 large onions, chopped (about 3 cups)

3 tablespoons butter

2 garlic cloves, chopped

2 pounds ground venison

Salt

2 tablespoons mild curry powder

2 teaspoons garam masala (or ½ teaspoon ground clove and 1½ teaspoons ground allspice)

⅓ cup chopped cilantro or parsley (loosely packed)

Cayenne pepper to taste (I use 1 teaspoon)

2 tablespoons tamarind paste, mango chutney or peach jam

3 tablespoons golden raisins (optional)

3 citrus leaves (or bay leaves)

Juice of a lemon or lime

TOPPING

1 cup heavy cream

2 large eggs

Preheat the oven to 325°F. Soak the bread in 2 cups of milk.

Cook the onions in the butter over medium heat until they're soft, about 6 to 8 minutes. Sprinkle some salt over them as they cook. Add the garlic and the venison and brown well. Salt this as it cooks, too. Break apart the ground venison as it cooks so it looks like taco meat.

When it's pretty much browned, add the curry powder, tamarind, and all the remaining spices and herbs, as well as the raisins if using. Cover the pan, add the lemon or lime juice, and let this cook for a few minutes.

Squeeze the milk out of the bread, and mash into the mixture. Turn off the heat. Move the mix into a casserole dish and press it down well.

Beat the eggs and cream together and pour over the casserole. Bake for 45 minutes to 1 hour, until the egg mixture is set and turning golden.

FLANKS, SHANKS, AND RIBS

Flanks, shanks, and ribs are probably the most underrated cuts on a deer. People who eagerly order braised lamb shank or short ribs, or who love fajitas in restaurants, regularly toss these cuts in the grinder, feed them to their dogs, or worse, throw them out entirely. This is a sad thing. While it is true that ribs on a deer can be tricky, the shanks are every bit as easy to cook as those of lamb, veal, and beef. And enjoying venison fajitas is simply a question of slicing away silverskin with a sharp knife. You do have a sharp knife, don't you? Thought so.

I am on a shank crusade. So many hunters grind the meat off their shanks for burger or sausage, which is a shame. Shanks, being some of the hardest-working muscles on the animal, are tough and very sinewy. Grinding them is a chore, as anyone who's done it can attest; all that connective tissue gunks up the grinder, forcing you to stop and clean it repeatedly—especially if you're doing this with a giant elk or moose shank. Far better to cook those shanks whole. It will open a whole new world to you, and you will be thankful.

Flank meat and ribs are two other sorely underused cuts on a deer. Both are also often headed to the grinder, and while this is no sin, on larger deer, and especially elk and antelope, the pure cuts are far more fun to work with than just another few pounds of burger. Flank and skirt steaks, cut from the outside and inside of the belly flap, respectively, are taco meat *par excellence*. Both have a very distinct grain that makes thin slices cut across it meltingly tender. Simple grilled flank with salt, pepper, and lemon is a summertime specialty, although sometimes we'll serve it with Argentine chimichurri sauce (page 133) or marinate it for Venison Bulgogi (page 220).

Venison ribs, on the other hand, are admittedly fiddly. You can't just barbecue them like pork or beef ribs, largely because deer and their cousins are almost always older than their analog in the barnyard. A typical whitetail is two to four years old, and the largest bull elk and moose can be well over a decade old. Beef is normally about eighteen months old when slaughtered, although grass-fed animals tend to be a few months older than that. Hogs are rarely more than a year old, and most of the ribs you find in a supermarket came from pigs that were about four to six months old.

Age does two things: It makes the meat tougher, and it makes it more flavorful. To enjoy the latter, you must deal with the former. The answer is to braise or otherwise par-cook your venison ribs before finishing them in another way. Slow, moist, moderate heat gradually breaks down the connective tissue in the ribs and makes them tender enough to enjoy. On large animals, you can follow beef short rib recipes; on deer and antelope, recipes for baby back ribs.

How do you get there? The simplest way is to season your ribs and braise them in broth with some herbs and vegetables until they are tender. This takes a few hours. You can also use a pressure cooker. Cover the venison with some water or broth and cook at full pressure for about thirty minutes.

TUNISIAN BRAISED VENISON SHANKS

Serves 4 | **Prep Time: 10 minutes** | **Cook Time: 3 hours**

This is a standard North African *tagine* (a kind of stew) that features all the hallmark spices of this region's cuisine, as well as the quintessential mix of sweet-and-savory that sets Arab cooking apart—both are relics of the Medieval spice trade, which the Arabs controlled until the Renaissance.

Shanks are my favorite cut of venison to use here, but neck meat, shoulder, or even roasts cut into chunks also work.

You'll notice a lot of optional ingredients; these will allow you to tailor the dish to suit your own tastes. You wouldn't see dates and apricots in the same tagine in North Africa, but if you favor one over the other, choose that one. Similarly, if you're serving this with a big bowl of couscous or rice, you probably don't need the chickpeas—but they'll definitely add some welcome heft if you're serving this with flatbreads.

2 to 4 venison shanks

Salt

¼ cup butter or olive oil

1 large onion, chopped

4 garlic cloves, minced

1 teaspoon ground ginger

1 teaspoon ground cumin

1 teaspoon ground cinnamon

½ teaspoon turmeric

½ teaspoon cayenne pepper

Small pinch saffron (optional)

One 15-ounce can chickpeas, rinsed (optional)

½ pound peeled chestnuts, cut in half (optional)

½ cup chopped dates (optional)

½ cup chopped dried apricots (optional)

1 tablespoon honey

Cilantro or parsley, for garnish

Preheat the oven to 325°F. Salt the shanks well and set aside. Set a Dutch oven or other heavy, lidded pot over medium-low heat and slowly soften the onion in the butter, covering the pot and stirring occasionally. This will take about 10 minutes. Add the garlic and cook another 2 minutes. Add all the spices, and mix to combine. Add 3 cups of water and mix well. Bring to a simmer.

Add the shanks, cover the pot, and cook in the oven until the shanks are tender, about 2 hours. If you're using chestnuts, add them after 1½ hours.

Once the shanks are tender, add the chickpeas and any of the dried fruits you are using, and mix in the honey. Put back in the oven and cook another 15 minutes. Serve garnished with cilantro alongside couscous, rice, or flatbreads.

PORTUGUESE-STYLE SHANKS

Serves 4 | Prep Time: 15 minutes | Cook Time: 4 hours

These venison shanks are so tender you could eat them with no teeth, and the sauce is so rich you'll want to save the leftovers for pasta—it makes a great accompaniment to the agnolotti (see page 215). The basic recipe is one I've adapted from my friend David Leite's *New Portuguese Cuisine*, modified to work with venison.

4 small or 2 large venison shanks

Salt

¼ pound of bacon, thickly cut

2 yellow onions, grated on a coarse grater

1 head of garlic, cloves peeled and roughly chopped

2 cups red wine

2 cups beef stock or venison stock

1 teaspoon black peppercorns

1 teaspoon allspice berries

1 teaspoon juniper berries

8 cloves

1 cinnamon stick

1 hot dried chile

2 bay leaves

2 tablespoons molasses

Salt the shanks and set aside. In a Dutch oven or other heavy, lidded pot, cook the bacon slowly until crispy. Remove when it's done and set aside. When the bacon is done, brown the shanks on all sides except the side with the bone; this helps the shank stay together after long cooking. Take your time on this one, and do this over medium-high heat. Set the shanks aside when they're done.

Preheat the oven to 300°F.

Add the onions, and turn the heat up to high. You will notice the onions will loosen all the browned bits in the pan; scrape the bits up with a wooden spoon. Sprinkle some salt over the onions and sauté, stirring often, until the onions brown, about 5 minutes. Add the garlic and cook another minute.

Chop the bacon while the onions are cooking and add it to the pot with the garlic. Pour in the wine and bring it to a boil. Add the stock, the spices, and the shanks, bone side up. Add salt to taste. Cover the pot and cook in the oven for at least 2 hours, and likely 3 hours. You want the meat to be almost, but not quite, falling off the bone.

When the meat is ready, remove it gently so it doesn't fall apart, and tent it with foil. Fish out the bay leaves, cinnamon stick, and as many cloves, peppercorns, allspice, and juniper berries as you can; it's OK if you don't get them all. Puree the sauce in a blender, or pass it through a food mill set on a fine setting. It should be thick. If it's not, boil it down until it is. Pour over the shanks, and serve at once with mashed root veggies and something green.

AUSTRIAN BRAISED VENISON SHANKS

Serves 4 | **Prep Time: At least 1 hour, or up to overnight for the marinade**
Cook Time: 3 hours, or more for an old deer

I cooked this dish with a large shank from a big Ohio whitetail buck that my friend Joe gave me. For whatever reason, his butcher sliced the shank bones—maybe for osso buco—but not all the way through. I like the effect, because it looks cool on the platter, and it opens up the bones to the marrow, which you can easily scoop out and add to the sauerkraut mixture. Yes, it's delicious; trust me on this one. Smaller shanks work fine, too.

If you can't find squash seed oil, which is dark and tastes vaguely of roasted peanuts, use a high-quality sunflower oil or walnut oil here. You want an oil with some flavor to it, not just a bland cooking oil.

Serve this with good bread, like a German pumpernickel or a Jewish rye. And even though this is a red-meat dish, I like an Austrian white wine here. German beer is another good alternative, such as a weizenbock, or if the weather's a little warmer, the same hefeweizen you used in the pot.

1 elk shank, or up to 4 venison shanks

2 tablespoons squash seed oil or sunflower oil

1 tablespoon, plus 1 teaspoon caraway seeds

1 teaspoon garlic powder, or 2 teaspoons minced fresh garlic

Salt

4 slices bacon

1 medium onion, chopped

2 cups sauerkraut, drained

1½ cups coarsely shredded potato

1 bay leaf

1 teaspoon dried thyme

One 12- to 16-ounce bottle hefeweizen beer

1 cup stock (any kind)

Black pepper and chopped chives for garnish

Massage the venison shanks with the squash seed oil, then with the tablespoon of caraway seeds, garlic, and enough salt to season the meat well. Set this on the counter for at least 1 hour to come to room temperature; however, the seasonings will penetrate better if you leave this covered in the fridge overnight. When you are ready to cook the shank, preheat the oven to 475°F; if the shanks were refrigerated, let them come to room temperature while the oven heats. Set the shank or shanks on a rack in a roasting pan and blast them in the oven until nicely browned, about 15 minutes. Remove and set aside for now.

While the oven is heating, cook the bacon in a large pot or Dutch oven (it needs to be able to fit the shank) over medium-low heat until it's crispy. Remove, chop, and set aside.

Add the onion to the pot and sauté in the bacon fat over medium-high heat until it begins to brown on the edges, about 5 minutes. Add the sauerkraut and shredded potato and mix well. Sauté this for a minute or two, then pour in the beer and stock. Mix in the reserved bacon, the bay leaf, thyme, the teaspoon of caraway seeds, and a healthy pinch of salt. Bring this to a simmer.

When the venison is ready—out of the hot oven—nestle the shanks into the pot, cover, and cook until meltingly tender. You can do this in two ways: on the stovetop over low heat, or in a 300°F oven. Either way it should take about 3 hours, or a little longer if you are dealing with an old deer.

You can serve this in one of two ways: as a centerpiece, where everyone pulls off pieces of shank at the table; or with the meat stripped from the bones and served on top of a bed of kraut. Don't forget the marrow in the bones! Scoop it out with a spoon and stir it into the kraut for extra flavor. Add black pepper and chives right before you serve.

BRAISED VENISON SHANKS WITH GARLIC

Serves 4 | **Prep Time: 10 minutes** | **Cook Time: 2 hours**

This is a recipe specifically designed for a small shank, so you will need something like it to really appreciate the dish. I prefer to use shanks from young animals, such as yearlings or young does. Shanks from the exotic axis or fallow deer, or muntjac if you are in the United Kingdom, are perfect. If you make this with large, old animals, the flavors won't work as well.

Serve this with mashed potatoes, polenta, or something else to soak up the sauce, which is so good you'll want to save any leftovers; it's great as a pasta sauce the next day.

3 tablespoons vegetable oil or butter

4 small venison shanks

4 heads of garlic, peeled

Salt

¾ cup white wine

½ cup chicken or other light stock

1 teaspoon dried thyme

1 tablespoon chopped fresh rosemary,
    plus more for garnish

Zest of a lemon

2 tablespoons unsalted butter

Take the shanks out of the fridge, coat them in a little oil, and salt them well. Preheat the oven to 300°F.

Heat the vegetable oil or butter in a Dutch oven (or other oven-proof pan that will fit all the shanks), and brown the shanks on every side but the one with the "shin," where the bone shows clearly—if you brown this part, the shank is more likely to fall apart before you want it to. Remove the shanks as they brown, and set aside.

While the shanks are browning, peel the garlic. Think it's hard to peel 4 heads of garlic? Try this trick: Separate the cloves and put them in a metal bowl. Cover the bowl with another bowl of the same size and shake them vigorously for about 10 seconds. All the cloves will be peeled.

Put the garlic in the pot and brown just a little. Pour in the white wine, and scrape up any browned bits from the bottom of the pot with a wooden spoon. Bring this to a boil, then add the chicken stock, thyme, rosemary, and lemon zest. Bring to a simmer and add salt to taste. Return the shanks to the pot, and arrange "shin" side up with the garlic all around them. Cover the pot and cook in the oven until the meat wants to fall off the bone, anywhere from 90 minutes to 2½ hours.

Carefully remove the shanks and arrange on a baking sheet or small roasting pan. Turn the oven to 400°F. Remove about 12 of the nicest garlic cloves and set aside.

Puree the sauce in a blender, swirl in the unsalted butter, and pour the sauce into a small pot to keep warm.

Paint the shanks with some of the sauce, and put them in the oven. Paint with sauce every 5 minutes for 15 minutes, or until there is a nice glaze on the shanks. To serve, give everyone some mashed potatoes or polenta and a shank. Pour some sauce over everything, and garnish with the roasted garlic cloves and rosemary.

OSSO BUCO

Serves 4 | Prep Time: 15 minutes | Cook Time: 3 hours or so, depending on the animal.

Osso buco is an Italian classic normally done with cross sections of a calf's shank, but it's a perfect use for big shanks from huge deer, elk, or moose. The easiest way to get these cross sections is by cutting them down to the bone with a knife, then sawing them off with a hacksaw. If you have your animal processed at a butcher shop, ask the butcher to cut you cross sections about three to five inches thick.

One important tip on dealing with large shanks: Use kitchen twine to tie them tightly while cooking—this keeps them together and compact. Mostly it's for presentation, but if you skip this step you run the risk of the shanks falling apart in your sauce. Not always a bad thing.

Dried porcini mushrooms are readily available in supermarkets in little plastic packets, but any dried mushrooms will work, especially morels.

Make this dish when you have a little time, as it will always require at least two hours, and probably more. The good news is that it reheats beautifully, so you can make it on a weekend and eat it during the week. You will also have more sauce than you need—use it for pasta, or on polenta or grits for a midweek meal.

Risotto milanese is the normal accompaniment, but you could substitute polenta, or just eat some good bread with it. A salad of bitter greens is another good addition.

4 cross-cut shanks

Salt

Flour for dusting

¼ cup olive oil, butter, or bear fat

1 onion, chopped

2 carrots, chopped

2 celery stalks, chopped

½ ounce dried mushrooms (about a handful), chopped

1 cup white wine

1 cup chicken, beef, or game stock

One 28-ounce can crushed tomatoes

1 teaspoon dried thyme

1 teaspoon dried oregano

Zest of a lemon cut into large strips, white pith removed

2 bay leaves

¼ cup chopped fresh parsley, for garnish

Preheat the oven to 300°F. Heat the olive oil in a Dutch oven or other large pot set over medium-high heat. Salt the shanks well, and dust them in the flour to coat. Brown them well in the pot. Take your time and get a good browning on them, which should take a solid 10 minutes. Remove and set aside.

Add the onion, carrot, celery, and porcini mushrooms, and sauté until slightly browned around the edges, about 6 to 8 minutes. Sprinkle some salt on them as they cook.

Pour in the white wine, and use a wooden spoon to scrape up any browned bits on the bottom of the pot. When this comes to a boil, add the stock, crushed tomatoes, thyme, oregano, lemon zest, and bay leaves, and bring to a simmer. Return the shanks to the pot and turn to coat with the sauce. Cover the pot and move it to the oven. Cook until tender, between 2 and 4 hours, depending on the animal.

Serve on top of risotto or polenta, or alongside some bread, garnished with the parsley.

"Wealth arrives like a turtle,
but flees like a gazelle."

—ARABIC PROVERB

AGNOLOTTI WITH TOMATOES AND ARUGULA

Serves 6 to 8 | Prep Time: 90 minutes | Cook Time: 15 minutes

This is one of the more complicated recipes in this book, but it is very much worth learning. Pasta making is as much of a passion of mine as is sausage making, and I couldn't do a cookbook without at least one good pasta recipe. This one uses leftover venison, bitter greens, and whole canned tomatoes for a fantastic late-winter to early-spring meal.

Use leftover venison from any of the shank recipes in this chapter, from the braised whole shoulder on page 71, or from any roast—you can even use preground meat, too, so long as you cook it before you make the filling.

Agnolotti are a bit like ravioli, but they're made a little differently, and really require the use of a wheeled pasta cutter. They cost less than $10, and can easily be bought online if you don't have one. You can still make this recipe without a wheeled cutter, but the shape will be a little different. Alternatively, if you know how to make ravioli or tortellini, feel free to do that instead.

The sauce for this recipe really works well with the agnolotti, but I put this dish in this chapter specifically because the leftover sauce in most of the other shank recipes will also be a perfect accompaniment to this pasta. Either way, this is a wonderful thing to make for a date night or when you have company.

And if you are not serving eight people, you'll have pasta left over to eat in the coming weeks. To store them, freeze in one layer on a baking sheet until solid, then put into sealable freezer bags, where they can stay for a month or two before they get too brittle. To serve frozen ones, drop them frozen into salty, boiling water.

PASTA

2 cups flour, loosely packed, about 10½ ounces

3 eggs

1 teaspoon olive oil

FILLING

8 ounces leftover venison

1 tablespoon olive oil

2 green onions or 1 green garlic stalk, chopped

1 small carrot, chopped, about ½ cup

1 cup, loosely packed, chopped dandelion greens, escarole, or arugula

¼ cup grated parmesan or pecorino cheese

1 tablespoon balsamic vinegar

Salt and black pepper to taste

1 egg

SAUCE

¼ cup butter or olive oil

1 large onion, sliced root to tip

2 garlic cloves, sliced thin

8 to 12 whole peeled tomatoes, crushed in your hands

A large handful of arugula, dandelion greens, or other pungent greens, roughly torn

Salt and black pepper to taste

Mix all the ingredients for the pasta dough together in a large bowl, forming an elastic dough. If it's sticking to your fingers when you start kneading it, add a little more flour. Knead for 5 minutes, and shape the dough into a ball. Cover with plastic wrap and let the dough rest for 1 hour. Or, if you have a vacuum sealer, you can vac-seal the dough and it will be instantly hydrated, allowing you to skip the hour wait.

To make the filling, chop the meat coarsely and set in a bowl. Heat the olive oil in a small pan, and sauté the green onion and

(continued)

carrot until they soften a bit, about 5 minutes. Move the vegetables into the bowl with the meat to let cool. Once the carrot and onion have cooled a bit, add the chopped dandelion greens and mix well. Push this mixture through the fine die of a meat grinder, or buzz it into a fine, crumbly texture in a food processor.

Add the balsamic vinegar and cheese and mix well. Add salt and black pepper to taste; you can taste as you go, because everything's cooked. When the filling tastes nice, mix in the egg.

Set up your pasta making station. You will need a large, flat surface. I've made a 3-foot by 3-foot maple board for this purpose, but a clean tabletop is fine. Get a little bowl of water ready, as well as a sharp knife, a wheeled pasta cutter if you have one, as well as your pasta filling. Dust a baking sheet with semolina flour or fine cornmeal and keep it nearby.

Divide your pasta dough into six more-or-less equal pieces. Keep all but the one you are working with wrapped in the plastic. Roll your dough through your pasta machine in long strips until it is borderline translucent, which on my Atlas is the second-to-last setting, No. 8. If the sheets are more than about a foot long, slice them in half with a sharp knife. Work with one sheet at a time.

Place rough teaspoons of filling in the center of the sheet of pasta about ¾ inch apart, leaving about an inch on either end of the sheet. Carefully fold over the edge of the sheet nearest you to meet the other edge. The balls of filling will ride high like the yolk of a fresh egg, so you'll need to pat them down a bit before you seal them. Pinch the overlapping pasta down around each ball of filling with your thumb and forefinger, expelling as much air as you can. Do this along the whole length of pasta.

Using the wheeled pasta cutter, cut lengthwise along the still-attached agnolotti to form the front of each piece of pasta; If you don't have a cutter, use a knife. Do the same on each end of the sheet. Now, to make

the characteristic "pocket" shape of an agnolotti, you will need to run your pasta cutter with some force away from you, between each agnolotto: This jettisons it from the sheet. If you don't have a cutter, you can't do this, so just separate them with a knife.

Place each agnolotto on the baking sheet, and repeat this whole process until you have used all the pasta, or all the filling. This recipe will get you close to being equal, but hey, pasta making is not an exact science. Your agnolotti might be larger than mine. When they're all made, either move right to finishing the dish, or store the pasta in the fridge for a few hours. Any longer and the wet filling will destroy them, so best to freeze if you're not eating the pasta that day. To freeze, set the agnolotti in one layer on a plate or sheet and freeze solid. Then you can put them all in a freezer bag. They'll keep for a couple months before getting too brittle.

To finish the dish, get a large pot of water boiling. Salt it well. Heat the butter in a large sauté pan over medium-high heat, and sauté the onions until they brown a bit on the edges, about 5 minutes. Add the garlic and cook another minute or two. Crush each tomato in your hand over the pan so it's in a few largish chunks. Add the torn-up arugula or dandelion greens, and turn the heat to low. Cover the pan.

Boil the agnolotti until they float, then for 1 or 2 minutes longer. Add them to the sauce, turn the heat to high, and toss to coat. Serve at once.

GRILLED VENISON TACOS

Serves 4 to 6 | Prep Time: 30 minutes | Cook Time: 15 minutes

Almost everything in this recipe is variable. That's the nature of taco night. But the key is the grilling of the venison, which makes this recipe different from, say, a venison taco done with ground meat. When you use flank, as I suggest you do, trim as much silverskin off as you can, and cut it in large slabs that you can later slice very thinly across the grain of the meat. Remember, these will go into tacos, so they need to be easy to eat. Alternatively, after the meat has rested, chop it all into bite-sized pieces with a kitchen knife or cleaver. I like to use two cleavers on a cutting board in front of company, for theatrical effect.

One more note on the meat: You want it to hit the grill cold. Flank is so thin that if you let it come to room temperature, it would be overcooked by the time you got a nice char on the outside. Grilling it cold is an insurance policy against overcooking.

I also really like serving these tacos with *rajas*—roasted poblanos and onions. But if you don't like them, skip it. Hey, it's taco night. Do what makes you happy!

VENISON

2 pounds venison flank, backstrap, or leg steak, all sinew and silverskin removed

Salt

Vegetable oil to coat

Chipotle powder or chile powder

RAJAS

4 poblano, ancho, or green bell peppers

1 white or yellow onion, sliced thin

3 tablespoons olive oil

2 garlic cloves, sliced thin

Salt

EXTRAS

Corn or flour tortillas

Dry *Cotija* cheese, or shredded jack cheese

Diced tomato (plum tomatoes are best)

Sliced serrano chiles

Sliced avocado or guacamole

Cilantro

Several limes, quartered

I like to make the *rajas* first. Lay the poblano chiles on a hot grill or your stovetop burner and char the skins black; move the chiles with tongs. Put the charred chiles into a plastic or paper bag to steam for a half hour or so. Peel off the charred skin, remove the stems and seeds, and slice the poblanos into strips.

Heat the olive oil in a small frying pan over medium-high heat. Cook the sliced onions until they char a little at the edges. Add the poblanos and garlic, and cook another minute or two. Add salt to taste, turn off the heat, and set aside.

Get your grill ready. It should be very hot, and when it is you need to scrape down the grates with a wire brush. Coat the venison with some vegetable oil and salt it well. Set it on the grill and leave the grill cover open. Sear it hard without touching the venison for 2 to 4 minutes, depending on how hot your fire is and how thick your venison is. If your venison is thicker than an inch, you can get cross-hatched grill marks by picking up the meat with tongs after 2 to 4 minutes, then rotating it 45 degrees and searing it for another 2 minutes or so.

Flip the venison and sear until it's medium-rare or rare. How to tell? Use the finger test for doneness (see page 79). When the meat's ready, move it to a plate or tray and sprinkle some chipotle powder on it. Let the meat rest for 5 minutes before slicing it very thinly against the grain.

Heat the tortillas until they are flexible (read the package's instructions or make them by hand), and keep them warm by covering with a kitchen towel or putting them in a tortilla warmer, which you can find in most Latin markets or online. Serve the tortillas, venison, *rajas*, and everything else spread out on the table so everyone can mix and match while they build their own tortillas.

VENISON BULGOGI

Serves 4 to 6 | Prep Time: 24 hours, to marinate | Cook Time: 15 minutes

This is a family favorite, an Americanized version of the Korean barbecue classic that is perfect for any sort of flank or skirt steak. The key here is to marinate the meat a long time, up to two days if you have the patience, to get the flavors well-established on the meat. You also want to grill the venison over a very hot fire right from the fridge. Flank is so thin that grilling it cold helps protect the center of the meat from overcooking while you're getting those nice grill marks on the outside.

If you prefer to serve this with the something other than rice, which is traditional, it's really good sliced thin on a hoagie roll instead. Either way, you'll want some kimchi or Asian slaw to go with it.

4 green onions, minced

2 tablespoons grated ginger

4 cloves of garlic, mashed and chopped

2 tablespoons toasted sesame seeds

2 tablespoons sesame oil

3 tablespoons sugar

2 to 6 hot chiles, minced (Thai, cayenne, serrano, etc.)

1 tablespoon molasses or Asian plum sauce

¼ cup mirin, rice wine, or lemon juice

⅓ cup soy sauce

1 large venison flank steak, or 2 smaller ones

Mix all the ingredients except the venison in a bowl, or go the extra step and buzz them in a blender. Pour into a heavy-duty, sealable plastic bag and add the venison. Seal the bag, put it into a bowl or other container (in case it leaks), and set it in the refrigerator for at least 1 hour, and up to 2 days.

When you're ready to cook, remove the venison from the marinade and wipe it dry with a paper towel. Coat the meat with a little more sesame oil or vegetable oil. Bring the marinade to a boil in a small pot, and skim any froth that forms. Turn off the heat, and use this to baste the venison.

Grill over a very hot fire (charcoal if possible) with the grill cover open until the meat is medium-rare, about 3 to 5 minutes per side, depending on how thick it is. Baste the venison as it cooks. Do not let it overcook—better for the meat to be a little too rare than too well-done.

Let the venison rest for 5 minutes, then slice very thin against the grain. Serve with white rice and Asian style slaw.

ITALIAN SHORT RIBS

Serves 4 and can be scaled up | **Prep Time: 30 minutes** | **Cook Time: 3 hours**

This is an adaptation of a wonderful recipe in a wonderful book, Paul Bertolli's *Cooking by Hand*, which would be one of my "stuck on a desert island" cookbooks. It will really only work with ribs cut from a large animal: certainly elk and moose, but also the exotic red deer, nilgai, and oryx. You might be able to get away with using a great big deer, but it would have to be a lunker.

You will want the ribs cut somewhere between four and six inches long, and either in a block of ribs or as individual ribs. Trim any excess fat off the cap of the ribs, but leave some fat remaining. (If you're squeamish about venison fat, don't be. Read all about it on page 51.)

The sauce is an *agrodolce*, a sweet and sour sauce highlighted by balsamic vinegar and *saba*, which is boiled down grape must. Yeah, I know, you don't have any lying around. Only reason I do is because I grow grapes. Fortunately, you can get really close by boiling down purple grape juice by two-thirds and using that.

The celery, carrots, and onions need to be pretty fine, so I mince them in a food processor. Just make sure they don't become a paste.

3 cups purple grape juice, or 1 cup *saba*

6 ribs, each about 4 to 6 inches long

Salt and black pepper

4 slices of bacon

¼ cup olive oil

1 large celery stalk, minced

Boil down the grape juice to 1 cup in a small pot. Set aside. Take out the ribs and salt them well. Preheat the oven to 350°F.

In a large, heavy, lidded pot such as a Dutch oven, fry the bacon over medium heat until crispy. Remove, chop, and set aside.

Pat the ribs dry with a paper towel, and brown them in the bacon fat, adding olive oil if you need to. When you brown the ribs, do

(continued)

2 carrots, minced

2 large onions, minced

A big handful (or 1 standard package) dried mushrooms

¼ cup tomato paste

2 cups red wine

½ cup balsamic vinegar

10 fresh sage leaves, or 1 tablespoon dried and ground

1 sprig fresh rosemary, or 1 tablespoon dried

1 quart venison or beef broth

every side except the one with the bone showing—if you brown this side too, the bones will fall off the meat too soon. When the ribs are browned, remove them to a plate.

Add the minced vegetables and cook over medium heat until they are well browned, stirring occasionally. This should take about 8 to 10 minutes. Crumble the dried mushrooms over the vegetables, add the tomato paste, and mix well. Cook this another 3 or 4 minutes, stirring often. You want the tomato paste to darken.

At this point you'll notice that the bottom of the pot has a brown residue on it; add the red wine, and use a wooden spoon to scrape it all off. Boil the red wine down by half, then add the cooked-down grape juice and the balsamic vinegar. Mix well, and return the ribs to the pot, bone side up. Pour in any juices that have accumulated with the ribs, too. Add the herbs.

Let this cook down a few minutes, then add the venison broth and mix well. Cover the pot and put it in the oven to cook for at least 2½ hours. You want the meat to be thinking about falling off the bone, but not actually there yet. This could take as long as 4 hours with an old elk or moose.

When the meat is ready, gently remove it from the pot and set aside. Now you have a choice: You can use the braising liquid as-is, or you can make it smooth. I prefer it smooth. To do this, you can either push it through the medium plate of a food mill, use a "boat motor" stick blender, or pour everything into a blender and buzz it. I prefer the food mill option. Taste the resulting sauce. If it is to your liking, you are good to go. It might be too thin, however, in which case boil it down until it's like a barbecue sauce. Right before you serve the sauce, add some black pepper.

Coat the ribs in the hot sauce and serve with mashed potatoes or another mashed vegetable; I'm big on mashed celery root with this recipe. To drink, you'll want a big red wine like a Barolo or Bordeaux, or a big malty beer. A good Belgian beer like Chimay is a good choice.

SMOKED RIBS WITH BOURBON BBQ SAUCE

Serves 4 | Prep Time: 3 hours to par-cook the ribs | Cook Time: 2 hours in the smoker, optional 10 minutes on the grill

Contrary to what many so-called experts say, you can barbecue deer ribs. The trick is to braise them first, then get a good smoke on them. If you were to smoke them without the par-cooking stage, they'd get a nice smoke ring, but would be mummified and inedible. Once they are tender, however, you can let them rest in a smoker for a few hours, basting them to keep the meat moist until you want to serve.

What you baste your venison ribs with is your choice. Any mop of vinegar and sugar works fine, as will your favorite store-bought sauce. I happen to like the flavor of a bourbon-based barbecue sauce best with venison, making these a Kansas City-style rib, not a dry Memphis-style rib. If you want to go that route, gently press your favorite dry rub onto the meat after it's been braised, then smoke.

I prefer regular ole' deer ribs for this recipe. If you do this with elk or moose ribs, obviously they will be far larger, and you won't so much have racks as individual ribs as you would with beef. Fear not; this works fine, too.

BRAISE

4 to 6 pounds of venison ribs

5 garlic cloves, peeled and smashed

1 onion, chopped

3 bay leaves

1 teaspoon dried thyme

Salt and black pepper

1 cup red wine (optional)

Water to cover

BBQ SAUCE

¼ cup unsalted butter

1 chopped chile pepper, such as a serrano

1 medium yellow or white onion, chopped

½ cup bourbon or Tennessee whiskey

¼ cup ketchup or tomato sauce

½ cup apple cider vinegar

¼ cup molasses

3 tablespoons Worcestershire sauce

2 tablespoons brown sugar

Salt to taste

Put the ribs and all the braise ingredients in a pot and bring to a boil. Add salt to taste. Lower the heat, and simmer gently until the ribs are tender but not falling apart, usually about 2½ hours or so. Remove and let cool a bit. You can hold the ribs for a day in the fridge this way.

While the venison ribs are braising, heat the butter and oil in a small pot over medium-high heat. Cook the onion and chile until the onions turn translucent, about 4 minutes or so. Take the pan off the heat, and pour in the bourbon. Return to the stove, turn up the heat to medium-high again, and boil down the bourbon for 5 minutes.

Add the ketchup, vinegar, Worcestershire sauce, molasses, and sugar. Mix well, and simmer gently for 10 minutes. Taste it, and add more salt, brown sugar, or chiles to taste. Cook it another 10 minutes, then turn off the heat and let it cool for an hour while the venison cooks. Puree in a blender until smooth. You can make the sauce up to a week beforehand, as it keeps well in the fridge.

When you're ready, get your smoker reasonably hot, about 225°F. Lightly coat the ribs with vegetable oil or butter, and smoke them for at least 1 hour and up to 2 hours. They're already cooked—you're just adding smoke here. Paint the ribs with the BBQ sauce every 30 minutes, turning the ribs carefully halfway through.

If you want, you can finish the ribs on the grill over high heat with the cover open. Grill only for a couple minutes or so per side—the sugar in the sauce will go from caramelized to burnt quickly.

GRILLED RIBS, KOREAN STYLE

Serves 4 | **Prep Time: 3 hours to par-cook the ribs** | **Cook Time: 15 minutes on the grill**

I learned this sauce from my friend Jaden Hair, a fellow cookbook author who runs the popular website *Steamy Kitchen*. Just mix well and slather on your venison ribs and you'll see why Korean BBQ is so popular in this country.

For the braise, the star anise adds an exotic aroma to the ribs, but if you can't find it, use regular anise seeds, or even a tablespoon or two of fennel seeds. If you can't find sake, use any old white wine. For the barbecue sauce, if you can't find the Korean pepper paste—it's becoming more readily available these days—use something like sriracha, which is easily obtainable.

KOREAN BRAISE

4 to 6 pounds venison ribs

A 3-inch piece of ginger, cut into chunks and smashed

5 garlic cloves, peeled and smashed

2 star anise (optional)

¼ cup soy sauce

½ cup rice wine (sake)

Water to cover

BBQ SAUCE

¼ cup Korean fermented hot pepper paste (*gochujang*)

¼ cup sugar

¼ cup soy sauce

1 tablespoon rice wine vinegar

¼ cup sesame oil

Put the ribs and all the braise ingredients in a pot and bring to a boil, then lower the heat and simmer gently until the ribs are tender, but not falling apart, usually about 2½ hours or so. Remove and let cool a bit.

While the venison ribs are braising, mix all the BBQ sauce ingredients together until everything is smooth. This sauce keeps for a long time, so you can make it ahead and keep it in the refrigerator.

Get your grill hot. Lightly coat the ribs with vegetable or sesame oil and grill over high heat with the cover open. When you get some nice browning on the ribs, about 3 to 5 minutes, carefully turn them and paint with the BBQ sauce. Turn again and paint the other side, letting the first side caramelize. Grill only for a minute or so—the sugar in the sauce will go from caramelized to burnt quickly—then either turn over one more time or serve with the caramelized side up.

INTERLUDE: THE LEGEND OF SPORK

The morning broke clear and chilly, and the fog lay thick in California's Coastal Range valleys near King City, a little cow town in Monterey County. Phillip and I stood high above the fog on a hilltop, searching for deer.

Phillip Loughlin, who has been hunting deer for more than three decades, spotted them first: three does, munching sagebrush on a steep hillside. But then they're all steep hillsides in this part of the world. We watched the does closely, hoping their boyfriends would be near.

Deer hunting touches something visceral within all of us, whether we realize it or not. Reactions range from "you shot Bambi's mom!" to that special shine in a fellow buck hunter's eyes you see when we share stories. Few humans are ambivalent about killing deer.

This arid hillside is the southernmost range of the Columbian blacktail deer. Spot-and-stalk hunting is the rule. No tree stands in the Coastal Range, no scent attractants, grunt calls, antler rattling, or even camouflage: Wear a tan shirt or jacket and some sturdy jeans or Carhartts and you're fine. But you must have a good pair of boots, a better set of binoculars, a rifle that will shoot a long way, and the stamina to climb mountains.

Soon enough, the does' boyfriends did show up. Or, rather, boyfriend. The buck was obviously the sultan of this particular harem. He was grayer than the young does and the yearling buck who was tagging along with them. Bigger, too—about 140 pounds. Coastal Range blacktails do not grow terribly large.

Nor do Coastal Range blacktails grow gigantic antlers. This one was only a 2×3, a fork on one side, three points on the other. Not a shooter if you were some big-time TV hunter, but a decent young buck for this part of the world.

Maybe too good. The owner of this particular ranch had let me hunt blacktail deer in return for catering a big dove shoot he held on Labor Day. But I couldn't shoot just any legal deer. It seems the previous owner of the ranch had shot too many deer on it, leaving a motley assortment of bucks in charge of the place. One was a gigantic forked horn I had originally been charged with assassinating, but that plan got changed at the last minute. Phillip and I were looking for a decent buck, but one that would probably not become grand enough for a high-dollar hunt down the road.

Phillip kept glassing the Sultan. "I can shoot him now, if you want," I said. I had the buck steady in my crosshairs at a little more than 250 yards. All he was doing was grazing. Broadside shot. "I don't know," Phillip said. "He's branching," meaning the buck was developing that classic set of antlers most hunters desire.

So we let him go, and went looking for one of the Motley Crew. But none of its members showed themselves, and we drove back toward the ranch house— only to see the Sultan and his harem not forty yards above us on the hillside, still grazing. There is so little hunting pressure for blacktails on this ranch they didn't care about the vehicle. This was an all-time gimme shot. Phillip hesitated; this was just too good. But we held off. It was the first morning, and we really wanted to find an older, weirder buck to cull.

It was at lunch when Sam, one of the ranch's resident hunting guides, told us about this crazy old deer in the front of the property: It had a gnarly spike on one side of his head, and a fork on the other. A genetic oddity, as this was apparently a mature, dominant buck in the area. Phillip named him Spork, as in spike-and-fork.

Immediately, we knew we had to kill Spork. Big deer, weird antlers, hard to find; Sam had not seen the deer since it was in velvet this past spring.

That evening, we went up Bulldozer Canyon, where Spork had last been seen. It's a classic Coastal Range canyon, steep and slippery. Everything here was once the bottom of the ocean, and the white, talc-like limestone is studded with fossilized seashells. But it is weak rock that disintegrates into a slippery gravel that is extraordinarily difficult to climb on.

But climb we did, all the way to the top of the ridge into the pines. My heart was pounding like a jackhammer as we trudged up, reminding me that I am not in in the kind of shape I used to be. We picked along the ridge looking for a good spot to sit down and wait, a place where we could see the whole canyon and yet not be seen. We found a perfect spot in between an old oak and a pine tree.

When we settled down, we immediately saw the signs all around us: This was Spork's lair.

Deer scat was everywhere, including a pile still black and shiny. Cold and hard, though, which was good— it meant Spork had left, probably in the morning. (Yes, we routinely pick up deer shit. And no, we don't taste it.) How did we know it was not a doe hangout? Nearly every tree in the vicinity had been rubbed with his antlers; a sign of territoriality.

So we sat and waited. A herd of wild pigs wandered through, making lots of noise. Pigs are not deer. They're more similar to humans, in that they'll march through the wilds as if they own the place. Marching pigs sound very different from the soft touch of a deer walking, which sounds like falling leaves if you're not listening very carefully.

Waiting there, the world closed in around us. The ripples we made walking into the place receded, and we began to absorb it all. My eyes are only so-so, but my hearing is better than most. Phillip is an expert spotter of game. In this state, we hoped we would not be fooled by any movement. The sun began to fall behind the opposite ridge. "Won't be long now," Phillip said.

He was right. Out stepped a nice blacktail doe. She began eating leaves off a bush, as calm as can be. Then Spork appeared. Phillip stared at the buck through his binoculars. "That's him! That's Spork!" I got ready to shoot, my heart fluttering again. I immediately realized that the syndrome known as Buck Fever is real: I've shot many does before, but I had only shot one other buck— and that was an antelope. At this stage in my hunting career, I had never shot a buck deer before, and had to will myself to not look at the antlers.

I got my .270 ready, looked through the crosshairs, and saw him . . . sitting down, with his ass facing us, at absolutely the worst angle possible. As if he knew, the bastard. The only remotely achievable shot would be to

his neck, but I've shot deer in the neck before and it can be iffy.

"Relax, he'll get up and follow his lady friend soon enough," Phillip said. So we waited. And waited. And waited. The doe got more than 100 yards away from Spork, but he still just sat there. Light was fading fast. He was not going to stand up before shooting light ended. Shit.

"OK, ready now," Phillip said. I readied. He called out his best impression of a bleating doe. "Beeap!" Spork looked at us, but did not move. Phillip did it again. This time Spork did not even bother looking in our direction. Light was almost gone. Phillip stood up. Spork looked, but stayed in his semi-recumbent position.

Finally, Phillip started waving his arms around and twirling his hat in the air. At last, Spork took an interest. But in a bad way. I had him in my crosshairs at one instant, but in another he had leapt up the hillside and trotted away. No shot. At the same moment, I was thinking that if Spork were a mule deer, he'd stop and look back at us; he did. Broadside.

Time slowed. In less than a second, I got Spork back in my crosshairs, put them on his heart, felt my own heart pound, pulled the trigger—and realized I could see brush between Spork and my scope. CRACK! It was done, a copper bullet was in the air, and I knew before it hit him that I had done Spork a grave injustice.

He jumped and dashed over the edge of the ridge and into a thicket of pin oaks, juniper, and thornbushes.

"I don't feel good about that shot," I said.

We rushed over to where I thought I hit Spork, looking for blood. Its color would help us figure out exactly where I'd hit him. Lurid red blood is a heart shot. That same color with little flecks of foam is a lung shot. Liver blood is darker, as is muscle blood. I looked around the zone while Phillip followed Spork's tracks.

No blood. Not a drop. Anywhere. We could not hear Spork in the brush. Light was fading. "Go down that hillside and see if you see him laid up under a bush or something. And keep your rifle ready in case he pops out in front of you. I'll swing around and meet you at the bottom of the ridge," Phillip said.

Down I went. Fell is more like it. The hillside was so steep it was all I could do not to fall ass-over-tea kettle on the slippery gravel. I tried as best I could to stay semi-quiet, but I definitely made a racket. About twenty yards down, my stomach began churning: This is very thick brush, it's dark. *We are not going to find this deer. Oh my God.*

I passed a spot that looked like Spork had run into, and crept into the bush. I squatted, stock still, and listened. Nothing. I remembered that spot and continued down the hill, hoping to see Phillip at the bottom.

What I saw was a fence. I was in a corner of a fence, with nothing but more rocky gravel in front of me for a quarter mile. Now it was truly dark. I shouldered my rifle and realized I needed to get out of here before I got lost. But after another heart-hammering climb up the gravel I realized: *I am lost.* Phillip was nowhere. There was no way I was going back up that Hill of Death, but I figured I could find the road and walk back from there.

The trail turned, and I found myself in a place I did not recognize. The stars were the only light. It was at that moment it struck me that I could be spending the night here. Wandering around in the pitch dark is a terrible idea, especially in a place you can turn your ankle easily. I did have my day pack with me, which had water and several of the fig cakes I bring with me on trips like this. But no flashlight. Stupid.

After a few minutes, however, the panic response ended and I realized that I knew where I could find the road, even if I needed to bushwhack my way to it. So I turned around and eventually found my way back. I can honestly say I was scared, for at least a little while. But as Phillip said later, every true deer hunter has gotten lost, if only for a short time like I'd done. It's a rite of passage.

That night we replayed the shot over and over, and the total lack of blood made us wonder if I'd even hit Spork at all. Phillip said he'd looked hit, but he'd never seen a hit deer not drop any blood. Was it the copper ammo? Was it the brush I'd hit, which deflected the bullet? Either way, we needed to go back to that spot and search in the morning.

When we reached the ridge in the morning, it was confirmed: no blood. We began to think we'd see Spork looking at us on the ridge. For two hours, we blanketed that area, looking for sign. As the sun began to warm, we finally headed up the Hill of Death. This hill is so steep and so slippery, we had to grab onto the fence with one hand—avoiding the strands of barbed wire—and haul ourselves upward.

At last we came to the spot I'd thought Spork had gone down. Phillip picked up his tracks and crept into the bush. For twenty minutes he followed sign, moving slowly, looking for blood. "I think Spork is off running around somewhere," Phillip said. "Meet me at the top of the hill."

I had not gone ten steps when he called out, "Wait! I found him."

Spork was dead. And my first reaction had been right. I shot him in the gut, and he had bled to death internally overnight. It would have been a grim death, and I began to feel nauseous again about how it all had happened. But competing with that emotion was the elation that we had indeed found him. Bad shot or no, we had closure. We had done our job and had not just left him in the bush and gone off and shot another deer, perhaps the Sultan.

Now we had to haul Spork, which Phillip estimated at four years old and about 140 pounds, up the Hill of Death. It almost killed me, but I suppose I deserve even harsher penance for doing Spork the injustice of a slow death.

When we cut him open, much of the meat was tainted. My heart sank even lower. Spork had lain on his left side when he died, so all that meat was ruined. Writing this now, it sounds more tragic than I felt at the time. At that moment, I was still just happy we'd found him—and been able to save half the meat. I am still confronted by such a mix of emotions about this hunt that they've all crashed into themselves, leaving a dull uncertainty.

I am no longer a virgin buck hunter. Thanks to Phillip, I learned so much on this hunt, and finally understand why buck hunters feel such a strong urge to head into the woods every year. Bucks are far harder to kill than does, and to hunt a particular buck is even tougher still. There is definitely an element of a duel that develops, and it is not just a testosterone-soaked, manly-man thing. On my way home, I stopped at a convenience store for some water. I moved Spork's head (I intend to save the skull) from the bed of my pickup to the back seat, not wanting to force everyone who passes by to see a dead deer.

A young woman of about twenty saw me do it: "Hey, is that a deer head?"

Oh no. "Uh, yeah. It is."

"Can I see it?"

Huh? "You bet. It's a weird deer. Old, with only a fork and a spike on it."

She admired it. "That buck's got a lot of character. I've been chasing a 4×4 on our property for five years. He always slips me. But I'm hoping to get him this year."

I smiled. She smiled. I said, "Go get him! And good luck to you."

"Thanks! Can't wait to get out there this weekend!"

As I drove off, I understood.

THE WOBBLY BITS

Heart, liver, kidneys. Tongue, heads, brains, even tripe and the euphemistically named "lights," which are lungs. Collectively, all this is known as the "fifth quarter" of an animal—those parts the English have tabbed "the wobbly bits," and which you will see in markets labeled less euphonically as "variety meats." I am talking about offal, the inner parts and extremities of animals in general, and cervids specifically, a collection of meats that, for the most part, I love dearly.

Why, when I have access to backstraps galore, lovely roasts, and the holy tenderloin, do I enjoy these so much? Because making these cuts taste wonderful is a true act of cooking. It's the culinary equivalent of alchemy. Sometimes it is as simple as properly cooked liver smothered in onions and studded with chopped crispy bacon. Sometimes it's long-simmered tongue, or fire-grilled slices of heart. Rarely do you need any technical skill to make the wobbly bits taste nice. But you do need some information first. Walk with me as I show you how.

I used to think that no one else but me loved the "fifth quarter" on a deer. Having no preconceived notions about what is and is not good to eat on a deer, I worked my way through the liver, heart,

kidneys, tongue, and even marrow bones as though I were a kid opening up presents on Christmas morning. Each offered something new and exciting, a new texture, a new flavor, a new challenge in the kitchen.

Then I began reading other venison cookbooks and talking to other deer hunters, and soon learned that eating venison offal wasn't as universal as I'd thought. For a time, I really did think I was something of an anomaly in the hunting world.

But after my first book was published and I began to drive across the country, talking to folks all the way, I was overjoyed to learn that, far from being loathed, many of these bits and bobbles within what's unceremoniously called "the gutpile" are treasured symbols of a successful hunt: liver and onions on the evening of the hunt; heart pot roast at deer camp; grilled heart on toast for breakfast. The reason I'd not heard so much about eating venison offal was because it is most often eaten simply, and soon after the deer has hit the ground.

To honor that, I do have a few dead-simple recipes in this chapter for deer camp, and I'd be remiss to not include my version of liver and onions (Deer Camp Liver and Onions, page 239). But the reason I was so jazzed about eating venison offal remains as strong today as it was when I shot my first deer almost two decades ago: Hearts, livers, kidneys and the like all offer something different from the ocean of red meat on the rest of the animal. Cooking them often requires patience, and sometimes legitimate cooking skill. But when it comes together, I feel I've created something grand from something that many consider inedible.

What follows are my favorite recipes for the wobbly bits from deer, antelope, elk, moose, and the like. Virtually all of them work with any of these animals, although I vastly prefer the dainty little kidneys on deer to the monstrous kidneys on moose and elk, although they are both perfectly edible. Conversely, extracting marrow from the femur of deer is fiddly, but is child's play with elk and moose.

But before we get to the recipes, you'll need to know a few tips and techniques to get the most out of your wobbly bits.

WHAT, EXACTLY, ARE WE TALKING ABOUT?

When I refer to offal (and all its euphemisms), I am specifically talking about the following:

- Heart
- Liver
- Kidneys
- Tongue
- Marrow
- Caul fat (the lacy membranous skein of fat that encircles all the lower organs)
- Stomach (tripe)
- Head/brains

The fascinating thing about all of these bits is that they are all edible—and all have historic recipes associated with them, if not for venison per se, then for their kitchen cousins the sheep and the cow. In England, the whole lot is known as umbles, and if this has a familiar ring to it, that's because "to eat humble pie" refers to a real pie made from the innards of deer; the rest of the animal was reserved for the lords. As it happens, umble pie can be very, very good; its echo today is British steak and kidney pie.

I have recipes in this book for all of these parts except the brains. I am not a fan of brains, and with chronic wasting disease so prevalent in many parts of the country, eating deer brains may well be dangerous.

ARE THESE PARTS SAFE?

In a word, yes—with a few caveats. Deer tend not to be heavily parasitized, but it can happen. Livers are one location for potential wee beasties, so look over the liver before saving it. If it has weird striations, whitish flecks, or wormy looking things in it, toss the liver. Most liver parasites are visible.

If you feel like working with the stomachs of deer to make haggis or tripe, understand that ruminants use bacteria to help them digest. Most of these bacteria are not harmful (although many are stinky), but still you don't want to mess around if you are making tripe. I use a dilute solution of hydrogen peroxide to cleanse my deer tripe (see page 33).

Of most concern in terms of food safety is the issue of chronic wasting disease. There's a full examination of CWD as it pertains to cooking venison on page 16, but for this chapter our particular focus is the marrow and head of the animal. If you live in an area with CWD, don't eat these parts. While there's no evidence linking CWD to humans, if it were to jump species—which can happen with this sort of ailment—it would most likely be from people eating brains, spinal tissue, or marrow. Fortunately, CWD doesn't exist in most of the West, nor does it exist among caribou.

IN THE FIELD

In the field, you need to be ready to collect your wobbly bits before you put an animal on the ground. Offal is very perishable, and it tends to get dirtier than the rest of the meat. Be prepared and you'll be better off. I always bring a few items in my pack for this job:

- **Several sealable plastic bags.** I keep each bit in a separate bag.

- **Paper towels.** Wiping off excess blood is important. It can give the organ an off taste if left on too long. I also like to rest the innards on paper towels on the grass to cool off before I put them into bags.

- **Water.** In addition to carrying water for drinking, it's important in the field to have water to rinse off the bloody innards. I'd avoid rinsing in a stream because of the possibility of the meat picking up giardia or other waterborne disease; many organs are best served lightly cooked, and you want to be careful. Snow is fine to use, too.

- **A cooler with ice if it's above freezing out.** I keep this in the truck, but it's important to chill down the innards as fast as possible. They need to get cold faster than the rest of the animal.

AT HOME

When you get home, you need to do some prep work before you can store your various bits. Rinse everything well under cold water and carefully pick off anything that might have attached itself to the organs; caul fat especially seems to pick up debris. For hearts, try to wash out any blood clots in the arteries before you vacuum seal them.

Once they're all rinsed, you can vacuum seal tongues and hearts straight away.

For the liver, trim off any membranes and connective tissue and discard, then slice the liver into portions you might eat at one sitting before sealing and freezing. My advice is to take one further step: After cutting into pieces you intend to serve, soak them in milk overnight, or in a weak brine of three tablespoons kosher salt to one quart water. Either will pull out some of the blood and tame the often gnarly smell of deer liver. This step will go a long way toward making skeptics believe that deer liver is tasty.

Kidneys come encased in hard fat. I rarely eat this fat, as it's very waxy in deer. But it can be rendered to use as waterproofing if you want (see page 53). Keep the kidneys whole for storage.

All the best marrow is in the femur on the hind legs. If you have access to a bandsaw, you can cut the bones canoe-style (lengthwise), which exposes a lot of marrow and is easier to cook. If you don't have one, use a hacksaw to cut off both ends of the femur to leave the shaft. Cut into three- or four-inch cylinders. For regular deer, which are too small to really do the marrow bone cylinders, saw off the ends of the femur and use a chopstick or dowel to push out the marrow. Soak the marrow in the same weak brine as you would soak the liver for twenty-four hours in the fridge; this draws out blood. Use this marrow for the German Marrow Dumplings (page 255). If you are not serving it straight away, seal and freeze.

If you've saved the caul fat, rinse well, gently fold it into smallish squares, and vacuum seal it.

Heads don't store well, so if you are going to use one, my advice is to use it fresh. I like to make head cheese—*coppa di testa, fromage de tête, presskopf*, etc.—from does sometimes. If you do, keep the tongue in the head and use any recipe for pork head cheese. Another route would be to roast it whole the way they do in Scotland, Morocco, and Mexico.

PREPPING HEARTS

The easiest way to prep a deer heart is to slice off the top, which consists mostly of veins and arteries, hollow it out, stuff something nice inside, and bake. But to me, that's not a very good way to eat a heart. Better to unroll it like a scroll and cook it that way.

To do this, start by trimming off any visible fat on the outside of the heart. Now look at the top of the heart. See all the gaps and holes? Use them as a guide to slice the heart into several thick cutlets. You'll get one really nice cutlet, then two slightly thicker ones.

Carefully cut away all the vein-y bits from the inside of the heart; they look like cobwebs sticking to its inner walls. You should now have two to four nice, clean hunks of meat. If you are dealing with an elk or moose heart, note that they will be quite large—close to four pounds in moose.

From here you can either pound the heart flat to make Jägerschnitzel (page 87), or Grilled Deer Heart with Peppers (page 234). Or you can cut it into small chunks for Peruvian Anticuchos de Corazón (page 237).

"These are the animals you may eat: the ox, the sheep, the goat, the deer, the gazelle, the roe deer, the wild goat, the ibex, the antelope and the mountain sheep. You may eat any animal that has a split hoof divided in two and that chews the cud."

—DEUTERONOMY 14:4-6

PREPPING LIVERS FOR COOKING

Many people recoil at deer or elk liver because it, well, stinks. But there's an easy way to prep a venison liver so it will be almost as mild as calf's liver. I am assuming you've brined your liver as I mention on page 231. Of course, if you like your liver straight up, skip this.

After the brining, rinse off the liver and soak it in milk (I normally use 2% milk, but I don't think it matters) for up to two days in the refrigerator. This also seems to pull out blood, and the resulting liver, which I rinse once more before cooking further, is *much, much* milder in flavor.

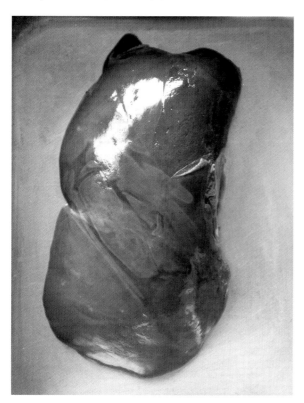

PREPPING KIDNEYS

Kidneys can be cooked whole, but most people like them better cleaned and sliced in half or chunked.

The first thing you need to do is pinch the gossamer membrane on the outside of the kidney and slip it off. It's so thin you might not think it's there, but it's so strong that when it contracts on hitting the heat, it will disfigure your kidney. Well, not *your* kidney, the deer's.

Now slice the kidney lengthwise, to preserve its shape. You'll see a lot of white stuff in the center. I like to snip this out with kitchen shears as best I can. You can slice it out with a knife, but kidneys are slippery things, and the shears seem to work better.

Finally, most people prefer to soak kidneys in milk, buttermilk, or a dilute vinegar solution to remove some of the , well, "aroma." My favorite is straight-up milk, which seems to tame the kidney's wildness a touch. Soak for up to two days if you want.

GRILLED DEER HEART WITH PEPPERS

Serves 2 to 6, depending on the heart | **Prep Time: 30 minutes, plus up to a day for marinating**
Cook Time: 15 minutes

As much as I love a classic jägerschnitzel done with a deer heart, this is my hands-down favorite way to cook them. Marinated and then grilled over very high heat just long enough for the center to warm, then sliced thin with some grilled peppers and onions—man oh man, you've got to try it.

With a typical deer heart from a whitetail deer, a blacktail, or a muley, one heart will feed two people. Maybe. A big deer will definitely feed two, an antelope only one. An elk heart or a moose heart will feed up to six.

My final piece of advice: Undercook the hearts just a little. For whatever reason, hearts tend to go from pretty pink to icky gray faster than other cuts. And an overcooked heart is a sad thing. Best to undercook a bit, then let the meat rest for a good ten minutes.

If all goes well, you will be rewarded. Grilled hearts have a smoky, charred flavor on the outside, a tang from your marinade, and a dense, firm texture somewhere between ribeye and flank steak. Slice thin and enjoy. Oh, and if you're serving people who might get all squinchy about eating deer heart, don't tell them until after they've demolished their plate.

A tip on the peppers and onions: Cut them into large pieces so they don't fall through your grill grates. For the onions, make sure you keep the stem end attached, which keeps them together on the grill. And cook the skin side of the peppers first—if you get any parts that blacken, the skin peels right off. You actually want significant blackening here, so keep your grill ragingly hot.

1 or 2 deer hearts, or 1 elk or moose heart

4 tablespoons olive oil, divided

1 tablespoon sherry or red wine vinegar

1 tablespoon Worcestershire sauce

1 teaspoon salt

1 teaspoon dried oregano

1 teaspoon dried thyme

1 teaspoon ground black pepper

3 or 4 colored bell peppers, cut into 2 to 3 pieces each

1 large onion, cut into large wedges

Trim the hearts as discussed above. In a large bowl, mix 2 tablespoons of olive oil with the vinegar, Worcestershire sauce, salt, oregano, thyme, and black pepper. Massage the marinade into the meat, put everything into a container that can just about hold everything, and marinate for as little as 30 minutes, or as much as 2 days.

When you are ready to cook, get your grill hot. Coat the peppers and onion in the rest of the olive oil and salt well. Put the veggies on the grill—skin side down for the peppers—and leave them alone with the grill cover open for 8 minutes. Flip everything and put the hearts on the grill. Cook, uncovered, for 5 more minutes. Remove the vegetables and put them in some foil to steam.

Turn the pieces of heart. Keep an eye on them, as small hearts might only need 2 or 3 more minutes, and very large ones might need a few more. If you're using a thermometer, you want to get the meat off the grill when it is 130°F in the center. You can also use the finger test for doneness (page 79).

Tent the hearts loosely with foil and let rest for 5 minutes. Sprinkle with black pepper and good sea salt and slice thin. Serve with the vegetables and some crusty bread.

PERUVIAN ANTICUCHOS DE CORAZÓN

Serves 4 as a snack or appetizer | **Prep Time: 1 hour or longer, to marinate** | **Cook Time: 10 minutes**

This is an ancient dish, dating back before European contact with the Inca in the early 1500s. Originally done with llama or whitetail deer (yes, there are whitetails in the Andes), *anticuchos* (ahn-ti-koo-cho-ss) are basically marinated kebabs done with heart.

The main ingredient of the marinade is a Peruvian chile paste called *ají panca*. You can find it in good Latin markets or online. But my recipe uses Mexican chipotles, which are way easier to find. Bottom line is you want a thick puree of mildly hot chiles—don't blow your head off with heat here. You can get close with some chipotles in adobo buzzed in a blender with a few preserved red bell peppers.

Normally, anticuchos are just a snack or appetizer, not a main meal. But if you have lots of deer hearts, go for it. And yes, you can make these with other parts of the deer.

You should always cook these skewers over charcoal or other open flame, and they are traditionally served with potatoes (also native to the Andes), corn, and hot sauce.

A word on prepping the heart. After cutting it into pieces as described on page 232, you will want to tenderize it. Mostly I do this with a Jaccard meat tenderizer, which is a nifty handheld device with a handle and lots of sharp, pointy blades. You put the meat on the cutting board and bounce the Jaccard all over the meat, making hundreds of little cuts in it. Works very well with any tough piece of meat, hearts especially. A Jaccard is cheap, too, costing about $18 in any good supermarket or online.

Your other option is to score the heart meat with many thinly spaced, crosshatched cuts from a knife. I don't love this method for anticuchos, but it will work in a pinch. You can also pound the heart into flat cutlets and thread them on the skewers.

---

3 roasted red peppers, chopped

1 to 4 chipotles in adobo, depending on how hot you want things to be

1 tablespoon minced garlic

¼ cup red wine vinegar

1 tablespoon dried oregano

½ cup vegetable oil

Salt

1 teaspoon ground cumin

2 to 4 venison hearts, trimmed and cut into 3-inch pieces

Skewers

Mix all the marinade ingredients together and buzz them into a puree in a food processor or blender. Submerge the heart pieces in the marinade for at least 1 hour, and up to a day.

Thread the heart pieces on the skewers—this helps you flip them more easily and helps them cook more evenly. Grill over very high heat with the grill cover open until you get a nice char on the outside, about 3 minutes per side. Baste with the marinade as the skewers cook.

SICHUAN SPICY HEART STIR-FRY

Serves 4 | Prep Time: 20 minutes | Cook Time: 15 minutes

Heart meat works really well with Chinese stir-fries because it's dense enough to slice into uniform, small pieces, and it cooks up quickly. In this case, you're shredding the meat after trimming and tenderizing the heart. Any heart will work here, as will any good piece of venison, so long as it's free of fat and connective tissue.

Most of the ingredients here are easy to find; the bamboo shoots and chile bean paste will be in the Asian or "ethnic" section of your supermarket. I've found them even in many small town markets.

One word of caution: Don't double this recipe. Stir fries need really high heat to work, and you kill that if you overload the pan. If you want to make a double batch, set out the ingredients for both batches and do them one after another. That's how they do it in Chinese restaurants.

SAUCE

2 teaspoons sugar

2 tablespoons *Shaoxing* wine or dry sherry

1 tablespoon Chinese black vinegar or malt vinegar

1 tablespoon soy sauce

¼ cup beef broth

2 teaspoons cornstarch

2 teaspoons sesame oil

FOR THE HEART

1 pound venison heart

2 tablespoons chile bean paste

2 teaspoons minced fresh ginger

2 cloves garlic, sliced thin

One 8-ounce can bamboo shoots, sliced into matchsticks

4 green onions, sliced into thin discs

4 to 5 small hot chiles, sliced

Start by prepping the heart. Slice off any fat and any vein-y looking bits of the heart first. Now slice off large pieces using the chambers of the heart as a guide. Trim any connective tissue; there's often weblike tissue on the interior of the chambers. Now you are left with pure meat. You will likely have more than the pound you need. Use this for another dish, or make a second batch of this one.

Slice the big pieces crosswise into thin slices—this is pretty easy to do because heart meat is so dense—then tenderize them. Put the heart slabs between two pieces of plastic wrap and pound with a meat mallet or an empty wine bottle, or pierce them all over with a jaccard meat tenderizer. Once the slabs have been tenderized, cut them into thin slivers of about ¼ inch wide. If you've ever had Chinese "shredded" dishes—usually pork, beef or chicken—this is what you're going for.

To make the dish, mix all the ingredients for the sauce except for the sesame oil in a bowl. Set aside. Put 2 tablespoons of peanut oil (or some other vegetable oil) in a wok and turn the heat to high. When the oil starts smoking, take the wok off the heat and add the chile bean paste and minced ginger to the oil. Put it back on the heat and cook for 30 seconds.

Add the heart, garlic, green onions, chiles, and bamboo shoots and stir fry 2 minutes. Pour in the sauce and boil furiously for 2 minutes. Turn off the heat, add the sesame oil, and serve with rice.

DEER CAMP LIVER AND ONIONS

Serves 4 | **Prep Time: 10 minutes** | **Cook Time: 30 minutes**

You pretty much can't do a venison cookbook without liver and onions. To many, this is the first meal after a successful hunt, either that night or for breakfast the following morning. There are a zillion variations on this recipe, but this is the one I like best.

You caramelize the onions, which form a sweet and savory bed for thin slices of liver—I cut them about ¼ to ½ inch thick. Sometimes I dust the liver in flour, sometimes not. Then you fry bacon, and sear the liver in the fat. Remember that liver is best cooked medium or even rare. Fully cooked liver, which is gray inside, is nasty, at least to me. Scallions, chives, or some other sort of green onion balances things out, and a little splash of lemon juice brightens things up.

All of the ingredients are easy to have on hand in deer camp. Honey never goes bad, and lemons will keep for more than a month in the fridge. Onions will also last for more than a month in the pantry.

You'll want either hash browns or good bread to go along with this.

¼ pound thick cut bacon

2 onions, sliced root to tip

2 tablespoons butter

Salt

1 teaspoon fresh or dried thyme

1 tablespoon honey or brown sugar (optional)

8 thin slices of deer liver, prepped (see page 231)

Flour for dusting

4 green onions or ¼ cup chives, chopped

Black pepper

Zest and juice of a lemon (optional)

Fry the bacon in a large frying pan until crispy, then remove it and chop roughly.

Remove all but about 2 tablespoons of bacon fat from the pan (but save it) and turn the heat to high. When the bacon fat is hot, add the onions. Toss to combine. Salt the onions, cover the pan, and turn the heat to medium-low. Let the onions cook this way, stirring occasionally, for 20 minutes. Add the butter, thyme, and optional honey, stir to combine, and cook another 5 to 10 minutes. If too much liquid forms in the pan, uncover it and it will cook away. Remove the onions from the pan and set aside. Wipe out the pan.

Add another 2 tablespoons of bacon fat. Get the pan very hot. Turn on your stovetop fan, as things will start to smoke. Dust the liver slices with flour and sear them in the bacon fat for no more than 90 seconds per side—I prefer 1 minute per side, which leaves the interior of the liver nice and pink.

Remove the liver and let it rest while you reheat the onions and bacon. Add the green onions or chives, toss to combine, and just heat through, about 2 minutes. Give everyone some of the onions and top with the liver slices. Grind some black pepper over everything and garnish with the lemon zest and juice.

LIVER DUMPLINGS

Serves 4 to 6 | Prep Time: 20 minutes | Cook Time: 20 minutes

This is a recipe for the liver-phobic. It incorporates the liver seamlessly into a rich, meaty dumpling you eat with sauerkraut and onions, or, as I like it, in a dark, clear meat broth. It has none of that tacky-chalky mouthfeel of liver that many of us, including me, detest.

Pretty much every nation from Germany to Poland to Russia and the rest of Eastern Europe does a liver dumpling, and this one is an amalgam of them all.

Note that it is very important to get as much blood out of the liver as possible before making these dumplings, or they will taste and smell very strong. First, I slice the liver into several large pieces. Then I brine the liver overnight in a solution of ¼ cup kosher salt to one quart of water. Then I discard the brine and replace it with milk, and let the liver soak for up to two days. When you're ready to cook, discard the milk and proceed.

¼ cup minced or grated onion

1 tablespoon bacon fat, butter, or vegetable oil

Salt

1 pound liver

1 teaspoon salt

1 teaspoon ground black pepper

½ teaspoon dried marjoram (optional)

A pinch of celery seed (optional)

1 tablespoon minced fresh parsley

1 beaten egg

3 tablespoons breadcrumbs

3 tablespoons rye flour or all-purpose flour

1 quart of Dark Venison Broth (page 66)

Chopped parsley, chives, chervil, or lovage for garnish

In a small frying pan, cook the onion in the bacon fat over medium-low heat until soft and translucent. Don't brown it. Let it come to room temperature before proceeding.

While the onions are cooling, trim off any connective tissue from the liver. Now you need to mince it. You can use a meat grinder, but I find that whaling on it with a chef's knife does the same thing without the extra clean-up. I shoot for an almost puree, but some people like their dumplings chunkier.

Scrape the liver into a bowl and add the remaining ingredients. The celery seed and marjoram are excellent in these dumplings, but if you don't have them handy you can skip. Ditto for the rye flour, which I find adds a layer of flavor that works well with the liver. Regular flour works fine.

The mixture will be wet, so form it into dumplings with two spoons. If you are serving the dumplings with sauerkraut and onions, use tablespoons. If you are serving them in soup, use teaspoons. You will want to cook the dumplings in water before putting them in the broth; if you cook them directly in the broth, the broth will get cloudy. So bring a large pot of salty water to a boil and drop the dumplings in gently. Simmer the dumplings gently until they float, then 2 minutes more. Remove them and set on a plate until you are ready to serve.

To serve, heat up the broth. Place a few dumplings in everyone's bowl and pour the broth over them. Garnish with parsley or chives.

FAGGOTS (BRITISH MEATBALLS)

Serves 4 to 6 | Prep Time: 25 minutes | Cook Time: 50 minutes

This is a British classic, available all over the island in various forms. Incidentally, the odd name comes from a Middle English term for a bundle of something (usually sticks); in this case, it's meat wrapped in caul fat. In some places these are also called "savoury ducks," which is even weirder.

If you're in a hurry, you can indeed start with ground pork or venison—something meat processors really love to give you a lot of if you don't butcher your own deer. You must make sure that the ground meat has some fat in it, otherwise your meatballs will be dry and sad.

The caul fat really matters here. Your meatballs will be far better with it than with the thin bacon, but they'll still work with the bacon. Most butchers will have it frozen, and even some larger supermarkets, like Whole Foods, should be able to order it for you. Caul fat can be frozen and thawed several times with few ill effects, so you can keep some on hand for whenever you want to make this or its French cousin, *crepinettes*.

Serve this with the traditional mashed potatoes (or rutabagas) and peas. Gravy is a must.

1 pound venison

½ pound bacon ends (or regular bacon)

½ pound venison liver

1 cup oats or breadcrumbs

1 cup minced onion

1 teaspoon salt

2 teaspoon dried thyme

1 tablespoon fresh sage, minced

½ teaspoon nutmeg

3 tablespoons chopped fresh parsley

2 cups venison broth or beef broth

Caul fat or very thin bacon

Take the caul fat out if you are using it and soak it in tepid water with a little salt tossed in, maybe a teaspoon. This will help it loosen.

Cut the venison, bacon, and liver into 1-inch chunks and freeze for 30 minutes to an hour, until they are about half-frozen. Grind the oats in a food processor or spice grinder into a coarse meal like coarse corn meal. Or, just use breadcrumbs.

When the meat is ready, mix it with the onions and grind on a medium die, 6 mm if you have one, or the "coarse" on a KitchenAid grinder. Put the meat in a bowl and mix with the oats and all the herbs and spices. Preheat the oven to 375°F.

Gently unravel the caul fat into one layer and lay it on a clean work surface. Form balls with the meat mixture a little smaller than a baseball or the size of a small orange. You want them big. Place the ball on the caul fat and slice enough of the caul around it to wrap the ball completely. Arrange seam side down in a baking dish. If you can't find caul fat and are using thin bacon, wrap the balls in bacon strips until you have them covered. Repeat until all the meat is used.

Bake uncovered in an oven for 40 to 50 minutes, basting every 10 to 15 minutes with the stock. Serve with mashed potatoes and peas.

CAJUN BOUDIN BALLS

Serves 6 to 8 | Prep Time: 20 minutes, to get to the boudin stage. Another 30 minutes to make and bread the balls
Cook Time: 2 hours for the boudin, 30 minutes to fry the balls

Quite possibly the greatest fast food on Planet Earth. I first had *boudin* balls (boo-dan) at a place called the Best Stop, in Scott, Louisiana, which is that state's western frontier. Hot, fried balls of sausage, seasoning and rice? Oh my God, so good! I bought a dozen, and ate them all the way to Austin, Texas, 372 miles away. This is my version of both the boudin needed to make the balls, and the balls themselves. Traditional boudin is with pork and pork liver, but venison and venison liver work great, too.

Keep in mind that you can stuff the boudin into hog casings and smoke it if you want.

Once made, you can eat these cold as a snack, or take them out of the fridge, let them come to room temperature, and refry them for a couple minutes to crisp up. Or you can reheat them in a 400°F oven on a baking sheet. If you have lots of leftovers, freeze them on a plate, then put the frozen boudin balls in a freezer bag, where they will keep for several months.

Cajun Remoulade

This is a fantastic all-purpose sauce for fried anything. Serve this with the Boudin Balls as a start.

1¼ cups mayonnaise

¼ cup mustard (Creole mustard if possible)

1 tablespoon sweet paprika

1 to 2 teaspoons Cajun or Creole seasoning

2 teaspoons prepared horseradish

1 teaspoon pickle juice (dill or sweet, your preference)

1 teaspoon hot sauce (preferably Tabasco)

1 large clove garlic, minced and smashed

Mix everything together and serve cold.

BOUDIN

⅔ pound venison

¾ pound fatty pork shoulder or "country ribs"

1 pound venison liver

1 onion, chopped (about 1 cup)

3 garlic cloves, minced

1 green bell pepper, chopped

3 celery stalks, chopped

1½ tablespoons Cajun seasoning

1 tablespoon ground black pepper

1 tablespoon paprika

1 teaspoon cayenne

½ cup minced parsley

½ cup chopped green onions

5 cups cooked short- or medium-grain rice

BALLS

1 cup flour

2 cups breadcrumbs

3 eggs

½ cup milk

Vegetable oil, for deep-frying

Cut the venison, pork, and liver into chunks that will fit into a grinder. Put the meats and enough water to cover by about an inch into a pot and bring to a boil. Skim off any scum that floats to the top. Reduce to a simmer and add the onions, garlic, bell peppers and celery, plus about 1 tablespoon Cajun seasoning. Simmer for 90 minutes, or until the meats are tender. Drain most of the liquid from the pot (reserving its contents), but keep about 2 cups of the broth. Let the meats cool a bit before proceeding.

Add ½ cup of the parsley and ½ cup of the green onions to the meats and vegetables and grind everything through a coarse die, ideally 8 to 10 mm. Alternatively, you can just chop everything by hand. Put the mixture into a mixing bowl. Stir in the rice, Cajun seasoning, and other spices, and the rest of the parsley and green onions. Add the broth, ½ cup at a time, and mix thoroughly into a paste. You now have boudin, and you can put this in a casing if you'd like and smoke it. Or make these balls.

To do that, set up a breading station. Put the flour into one large, shallow bowl. You can add a little Cajun seasoning to it if you want, but be careful, as the pre-made seasoning mixes tend to be very salty. Beat the eggs with the milk and put that in another large, shallow bowl. Finally, put the breadcrumbs in a third bowl.

Form the boudin into little balls—I like them a little larger than a walnut—and dredge in the flour, then the egg wash, then the breadcrumbs. Set them on a baking sheet. If you have time, let them chill in the fridge for up to a few hours before frying them; this helps them hold their shape.

Fry the boudin balls in 350°F oil until golden brown, about 3 to 5 minutes. Do this in batches and keep the balls warm in a 200°F oven while you do the rest. Serve with hot sauce, Cajun remoulade, mustard, or whatever you please.

BRAISED VENISON TONGUE

Serves 4 to 6 as an appetizer | Prep Time: 15 minutes | Cook Time: 3 hours

I came up with this dish when I was serving several dozen people but only had one little venison tongue to go around. (Yes, I served lots of other things, too.) Tongues need slow cooking to make them tender, plus you need to peel the skin off to get at the savory, dense meat underneath.

It's a super-easy dish. Drop the tongue in some broth with a couple bay leaves, a few juniper berries if you have them, and one dried chile. Let this simmer for several hours, peel, and put back in the broth until you are ready to serve.

Slice thin, coat with a little olive oil, then serve atop some homemade horseradish cream on a cracker. Simple and delicious—so good, even tongue-haters will like it.

1 or 2 deer tongues

1 quart beef or venison stock

6 to 10 juniper berries

1 dried chile, broken in half

2 or 3 bay leaves

HORSERADISH SAUCE

3 tablespoons prepared horseradish, or a
4-inch piece of horseradish grated into a
bowl with 1 tablespoon vinegar, 1 teaspoon
water, and a large pinch of salt.

½ cup sour cream

2 tablespoons Dijon or brown mustard

2 tablespoons chopped chives

Salt

Olive oil

Crackers

Put the broth, juniper, bay, chile, and the tongue into a pot and simmer gently for 2 hours.

Meanwhile, make the horseradish sauce. Mix the horseradish, mustard, sour cream, and chives together well. Taste for salt and add some if needed. If you want it more horseradish-y, add more. Set aside in the fridge until the tongue is ready.

After about 2 hours, take the tongue out and let it cool a few minutes. Peel the skin off with your fingers or a paring knife and put the tongue back into the stock. Simmer for another hour, or until the tongue is easily pierced with the point of a knife.

Take the tongue out and slice it thin. While it is still warm, coat the slices with olive oil and set aside to cool.

When it's cool, spoon a dab of the horseradish sauce on a cracker and top with a slice of tongue. Serve cool or at room temperature.

A LOVELY TONGUE SANDWICH

Serves 4 | Prep Time: 3 to 5 days, for brining the tongue | Cook Time: 3 to 4 hours, to braise the tongue

This sandwich is kind of a big deal (sort of like Ron Burgundy of "Anchorman" fame). It actually takes three days to make, so you have to know you want to eat it. I can assure you, you want to eat this sandwich. All that time is spent with the tongues brining in the fridge, anyway, so it's not as big a commitment as you might think.

Basically, you corn the tongue like you would any other cut of meat (Corned Venison, page 263), simmer it in a broth for a few hours, peel it, slice, sear, and stuff in a sandwich. So OK, it's not something you mindlessly make in the morning before hitting the deer stand. It's a dinner sandwich, or one for a nice weekend lunch.

I use deer tongues here, but the chef whose recipe I am indebted to, April Bloomfield of The Spotted Pig in New York City, uses beef tongue—and beef tongue is not so different from a bison, moose, or elk tongue, although beef tongue does need a bit longer to brine. Oh, and I use a bit of curing salt in my brine because I love that red color and "hammy" flavor you get from it. You can skip it if you want, but the meat will be gray and not red.

The condiments and accompaniments to this sandwich are just what I happen to like. Feel free to play around as you want.

4 deer tongues or 1 elk, moose,
    or bison tongue

BRINE

¼ cup kosher salt

1 quart water

1 tablespoon black peppercorns, cracked

5 to 8 cloves

3 bay leaves

½ teaspoon Instacure No. 1 (optional)

TO COOK THE TONGUES

1 carrot, chopped

2 celery stalks, chopped

½ onion, chopped

2 bay leaves

Bring the brine ingredients to a boil, then let cool to room temperature; this infuses the flavors into the brine. Submerge the tongues in the brine and refrigerate for 3 days (5 days if you are using moose, elk, or bison tongues). Once brined, you can remove the tongues from the brine and keep in the fridge a few days before you cook them.

Put the tongues, the vegetables, and the herbs in a pot that just about fits them. Cover with water by one inch and bring to a boil. Drop the heat to a gentle simmer and cook, covered, until the point of a thin, sharp knife easily pierces the thickest part, about 3 to 5 hours.

Remove the tongues (save the broth) and set them on a cutting board to cool. As soon as they are cool enough to work with— about 10 minutes—peel off the skin around the tongues. It should come off easily. Discard. Return the peeled tongues to the broth and allow to come to room temperature on the stove. At this point, you have corned tongue, which you can keep in the broth in the refrigerator for up to a week.

To make the sandwich, slice the rolls almost all the way through to the other side and dig out a trench on both sides of the bread to accommodate the fillings. You can toast it if you want.

HORSERADISH MAYO

4 tablespoons mayonnaise

1 tablespoon prepared horseradish, or to taste

1 teaspoon Dijon mustard

1 teaspoon lemon juice

Salt and black pepper to taste

FOR THE SANDWICH

Sandwich rolls

Grilled, caramelized, or raw onions

Zippy greens like arugula, cress or
dandelion greens

Cut the tongues into ¼-inch slices on the diagonal if you can. Lay down about 2 tablespoons of oil, lard, or bacon fat (bacon fat is best) in a large frying pan and set it over medium-high heat. When the oil is hot, sear the tongue slices. They will want to stick a little, so use a metal spatula to flip them. They'll need only about 2 minutes per side to crisp. Set them aside.

Mix all the ingredients for the horseradish mayo together and when it tastes the way you like it, slather it on both sides of the roll.

Add some onions if you like, lots of tongue slices, and the greens. The greens are important because they help cut the richness of the tongue and the mayo. Slice the roll in half and have at it!

TACOS DE LENGUA

Serves 6 to 8　|　Prep Time: 15 minutes　|　Cook Time: 3 hours

This is a taco truck standard where I live in Northern California. Typically, it's braised beef tongue chunked and seared on the flat-top, then added to corn tortillas with some salsa and lime. Super simple.

I like my tongue sliced thin or shredded, not in big chunks, but it's up to you. I also like a bit more in the way of toppings, and I especially think a fiery salsa verde or roasted chile salsa, plus some fresh avocado, is a perfect balance with the rich, tender tongue meat.

This is beer food. Mexican beer or German lagers, or hell, Budweiser or Miller are just fine here.

An elk, moose, or bison tongue,
　　or 4 to 6 deer tongues

1 large onion, chopped

5 garlic cloves, peeled and crushed

5 bay leaves

1 tablespoon black peppercorns

2 tablespoons salt

3 tablespoons lard or vegetable oil

Corn tortillas

Salsa (canned or homemade)

Diced avocado (optional)

Cilantro

Quick pickled red onion (page 128)

Put the tongue in a large pot and cover it with water by 2 inches. Bring to a boil and skim any froth that forms on the water's surface. When it's all gone, drop the heat to a simmer and add the onion, garlic, bay, black peppercorns, and salt. Simmer the tongue until the sharp point of a thin knife will pierce it easily, about 2 to 3 hours.

When the tongue is tender, set it on a cutting board to cool somewhat. When it's just barely cool enough to handle, peel off the skin and discard. You can do all this up to a week ahead if you want. Just cool the peeled tongue and wrap in plastic wrap. It'll keep in the refrigerator a week.

When you're ready to make the tacos, slice the tongue on the diagonal into ¼-inch slices. Sear them in the lard until they're nicely browned, then chop roughly. Serve on warm corn tortillas with the salsa, avocado, cilantro, and pickled red onions.

"Those who hunt deer sometimes find tigers."

—INDIAN PROVERB

GRILLED VENISON KIDNEYS

Serves 2 as an appetizer | **Prep Time: 24 hours** | **Cook Time: 10 minutes**

Kidneys can be challenging. If you don't soak them long enough, they can be bitter and, well, smell and taste a little like pee. That should not deter you from keeping the kidneys from the deer you shoot. Properly soaked, venison kidneys are delicious and not at all off-putting.

The key is to prep the kidneys first and then soak them in milk for several days in the fridge. I know it seems like a lot for a little piece of meat—the kidneys from a normal-sized deer will only serve two people as an appetizer. Just give it a go. Directions for prepping the kidneys are above.

Grill, or sear the kidneys in a ripping hot pan, and serve them simply. I like them with just lemon and a high-quality salt, but a good country mustard is also nice.

2 venison kidneys

1 cup milk

Kosher salt

2 tablespoons olive oil

Juice of a lemon

Coarse finishing salt like fleur de sel

Carefully peel the membranes off the kidneys. Slice them in half lengthwise so you preserve the kidney shape. Cut out the hard, white centers of the kidneys with kitchen shears or a paring knife. Soak the kidneys in the milk in the refrigerator for a day. If the milk turns that disturbingly pink color of Strawberry Quik, change it.

Rinse off the kidneys and pat them dry with a paper towel. Coat with olive oil and sprinkle some kosher salt on them.

Place the kidneys cut side down on a very hot grill. They will want to curl up, so gently press down on them with a spatula. Sear like this for 2 to 3 minutes. Turn the kidneys over and sear in the same way for another minute or two. Keep the grill cover open the whole time. Kidneys should be served when they're still a little pink in the middle.

Take the kidneys off the grill and allow to rest on a cutting board for 3 minutes. Sprinkle some lemon juice over them. Serve finished with some really good olive oil and a bit of coarse salt.

DEVILED KIDNEYS

Serves 2 as a snack, and 1 as a meal | **Prep Time: 10 minutes** | **Cook Time: 10 minutes**

Deviled kidney is an old British standby, and my version of it owes a lot to one of my culinary inspirations: the great Chef Fergus Henderson of St. John in London. A rendition of this recipe done with lamb appears in his excellent book *The Whole Beast: Nose to Tail Eating*. If only I could cook for Fergus someday.

Most people don't have lots of venison kidneys lying around, so this recipe reflects that. But if you do have, say, eight to ten kidneys, just scale up this recipe.

I like to soak my kidneys in milk for a day before doing this recipe, as it makes them taste milder. But you can skip this if you want.

I am a big fan of mushrooms with kidneys—it's a texture thing. I prefer the mighty porcini mushroom here, but any good, fresh mushroom will do.

Serve your kidneys on excellent toast. A pale ale or even a porter would be perfect with this, as would a nice red wine.

½ pound fresh mushrooms, cut into large-ish pieces (optional)

2 to 4 deer kidneys

¼ cup flour

1 teaspoon cayenne

1½ teaspoons dry mustard (Colman's if you can get it)

1 teaspoon salt

1 teaspoon ground black pepper

6 tablespoons unsalted butter, divided

Worcestershire sauce

3 tablespoons chicken, venison or beef stock

Clean and trim the kidneys as shown on page 233. Cut each half into 3 or 4 pieces. If you're using the mushrooms, sear them in a hot pan with 3 tablespoons of unsalted butter until nicely browned on their edges. Remove them and set aside for the moment.

Mix the flour with the cayenne, mustard, salt, and black pepper, and dust the kidneys with it.

Get the pan very hot, then add 3 more tablespoons of butter. Brown the kidneys in the butter. You may need to press them down with a spatula, as they will want to arch upwards. Turn and cook another minute or two. Remove them and cut into pieces you'd like to eat.

Return the kidneys and the mushrooms to the pan, add a big splash of Worcestershire sauce and the stock, and shake the pan to meld everything together. Let this cook for a minute or two.

Remove the kidneys and mushrooms and set them on top of your toast. Boil down the sauce for a few minutes—don't let it boil completely away—then pour it over everything and serve.

VENISON TRIPE NEAPOLITAN STYLE

Serves 2 | Prep Time: 1 hour | Cook Time: 2 hours

Simmered in a spicy Italian red sauce is how I first ate tripe as a kid in the Italian restaurants of New Jersey and Long Island. It's a pretty innocuous way to eat tripe, which essentially takes the role of pasta in a zippy tomato sauce.

Usually, you will see this done with honeycomb tripe from beef, but the corresponding section of a deer's stomach is tiny, so you will most often use the rumen, which is sold commercially as "blanket tripe"; it's the large, first stomach. If you feel like cleaning out the honeycomb (for example, the second stomach) of an elk or moose, go for it.

By the time you've cleaned and simmered the tripe, the usable portion from a small doe or buck will feed two people, so keep that in mind. This recipe can be scaled up easily, though.

The odd inclusion of vanilla extract in the initial simmering process is a tip I learned from Chef Mario Batali's cookbook *Babbo*. The addition removes most of that barnyard odor people hate about tripe.

You need to serve this with good, crusty bread and a light red wine like a Chianti, pinot noir, or grenache. If you are a beer person, lean hoppy, not malty here.

TRIPE

Cleaned tripe from 1 deer (see page 33)

¼ cup white or cider vinegar

1 teaspoon vanilla extract

A healthy pinch of salt

SAUCE

¼ cup olive oil

½ cup carrot, roughly chopped

½ cup celery stalk, roughly chopped

½ cup onion, roughly chopped

3 garlic cloves, minced

1 to 2 teaspoons hot chile flakes

1 tablespoon tomato paste

1 cup white wine

1 can (28 to 32 ounces) crushed tomatoes

1 or 2 bay leaves

4 to 6 sage leaves, minced

Salt and black pepper

2 tablespoons chopped parsley or basil

Grated Parmesan or pecorino cheese

Set the tripe in a heavy pot and cover with water by 1 inch. Add the vinegar and vanilla extract. Boil and skim off any foam that forms on the surface. Simmer gently for 1 hour until reasonably tender.

After an hour, remove the tripe and set on a baking sheet to cool. If you notice any unsightly brownish-gray bits on the smooth side of the tripe—the one without the terrycloth texture—scrape them off with a knife. If you're in a hurry, slice the tripe into strips about 2 inches long by ½ inch wide. Or chill the tripe in the fridge overnight and then slice, which makes things easier.

To finish the dish, buzz the carrot, celery, and onion in a food processor until finely chopped. Cook this in a heavy, lidded pot with the olive oil over medium heat until the vegetables are soft but not browned, about 5 minutes. Add the garlic and chile flakes and cook another minute.

Mix in the tomato paste. Cook until everything just begins to stick to the bottom of the pot, then add the white wine. Scrape up any browned bits on the bottom of the pot with a wooden spoon, and let the wine boil for a minute.

Add the crushed tomatoes, bay leaves, sage, and salt. Add the cut-up tripe to the pot and simmer gently until the tripe has the texture of al dente pasta. To serve, add black pepper to taste along with the chopped parsley. Top with the grated cheese and serve with good, crusty bread.

GERMAN MARROW DUMPLINGS

Serves 4 | **Prep Time: 30 minutes** | **Cook Time: 15 minutes**

These are easy to make, thrifty, and wonderful to eat. What's not to love? I prefer to make these with marrow from deer (as opposed to elk or moose) because usually the amount of marrow you get from a typical deer's femurs is just about right for this recipe. But of course any marrow will do.

If you haven't already done so, first soak your marrow to remove blood (instructions on page 231). If you make this with store-bought marrow, you need not do this.

Know that these are dense dumplings that require a fair amount of cooking to lighten up. Don't worry, they won't fall apart.

Serve as a soup course in a larger meal, or as a simple weeknight meal with some vegetables and, if you're feeling flush, a simply roasted or grilled piece of meat.

---

2 ounces bone marrow, chopped fine

2 ounces flour, about ½ cup

½ teaspoon baking powder

¾ cup fine breadcrumbs

2 teaspoons finely chopped shallot or onion

1 tablespoon finely chopped parsley

½ teaspoon salt

½ teaspoon black pepper

1 egg

Get a pot of salted water or broth boiling. Mix all the ingredients together in a large bowl and form into balls about the size of a large hazelnut or small walnut. Move each marrow dumpling into the water or broth, and let them cook until they float. When they do, cover the pot and let the dumpling simmer gently over medium-low heat for 7 to 10 minutes. You might need to do this in two batches so you don't overload the pot.

Serve these dumplings in a clear venison or other broth. The Dark Venison Broth on page 66 is a good choice. Garnish with shredded leeks, carrots, or chopped chives or parsley.

CURING VENISON AND MAKING SAUSAGE

When it comes to culinary artistry, it's hard to top the beauty of a properly cured ham, or the fermented twang of smoked salami, or even that pop—Germans call it *knacken*—of a well-made sausage hot off the grill. Most often called by its French name *charcuterie*, the art and craft of curing meat is something every deer hunter should consider learning. Yes, there are processors out there who do a good job, sometimes even a great job. But mastering this skill allows you to craft everything to your own tastes. The control you have once you know how to make sausage or cure ham is, frankly, empowering. And let's face it, the look on people's faces when you tell them you made that salami or snack stick or ham is so worth it.

Curing venison and making venison sausages and salami is similar to doing the same thing with pork, but not exactly alike. For starters, venison tends to be lean. Whitetails living around alfalfa fields in the Midwest often have a thick layer of fat, but it's less common to find a fat mule deer or California blacktail. That said, any deer can put on fat, especially in a good acorn year. And in moderation, that fat can be useful, too (see page 51).

SAUSAGES

Sausages are a mainstay in venison cookery. And let me tell you, if you know how to make your own sausages, you will never buy them again. Controlling the seasoning, the fat content, the grind, the size, and the level of smoke in your links is an act of true creation. It's kind of a rush when it all comes together.

The recipe for Venison Sausages with Sage and Juniper (page 270) is a master recipe. Use that for all the detailed instructions on grinding, mixing, and making links. Beyond that will be recipes that will increase in difficulty, until you get to salami: Salami, or dry-cured sausages, are the pinnacle of the sausage-maker's craft.

SPECIAL EQUIPMENT NEEDED

You will need some special equipment to make sausages. You can hand-chop or grind meat in a food processor, and stuff by hand with a funnel, but unless you are an expert, this results in an inferior sausage and is far more work. At a minimum, you'll need a meat grinder. I use a dedicated grinder from Weston Products.

If you're serious about making sausages, you'll want some extra gear. Here's my set-up:

- Hog, sheep, and beef casings, available at butcher shops or online
- A dedicated sausage stuffer; avoid both the KitchenAid attachment and those cornucopia-shaped stuffers.
- A wooden rack to hang sausages to dry

When you are just beginning, start by making sausage patties, not links. Remember, you can also wrap your sausage meat in blanched cabbage or chard leaves, roll it in bulgur wheat and make Lebanese *kibbeh*, wrap it in caul fat (available from good butchers, although you might need to order ahead), or stuff it in grape leaves.

If you do plan to stuff your sausages, hog casings are the easiest to buy. Nearly every good butcher has them, and they're inexpensive. Most come heavily salted in plastic tubs and must be soaked in warm water for a half hour or more to reconstitute them. You can also use narrow sheep casings or very wide beef casings, but you may need to special order them from your butcher, or buy them online from dealers such as Weston, The Sausage Maker, or Butcher & Packer. You can buy artificial casings made from edible collagen, but I only use them for Slim Jim-like snack sticks, and only then because they are even narrower than sheep casings.

VENISON SAUSAGE BASICS

Venison's leanness can be a problem when you decide to make sausages. If you have a fat deer, you can use its fat to grind with sausages, but that fat is different from pork fat—it can coat your mouth if you use too much (see sidebar, page 51). A good rule of thumb is to include no more than 50 percent deer fat with your sausage grind: For a five-pound batch of sausages, I typically include half a pound of deer

Why I Measure Salt in Grams

In a word, control. Old style, traditional recipes use teaspoons and tablespoons for ingredients, and honestly that's perfectly fine for seasonings like pepper and herbs and garlic. But for salt, it just won't work—and it is more than just a flavor issue; it is one of safety.

Salts are not equally ground. A tablespoon of, say, Morton's kosher salt will not be the same weight of salt that you'd get in a tablespoon of Diamond Crystal salt, and definitely won't even be close to a tablespoon of table salt. (For the record, I use Diamond Crystal kosher salt.)

I can tell you that the difference between thirty-four grams of salt and thirty-eight grams of salt in a five-pound batch of sausage is very noticeable—despite the fact that, depending on which brand of salt you use, each could be a couple tablespoons. What's more, when you are curing meats, you need a set percentage of salt to be safe; normally it's about 2.5 percent to 3 percent, including the curing salt. You can't get there accurately with tablespoons.

In terms of the salts used for curing, sodium nitrite and sodium nitrate, you generally want them to be one-quarter of one percent (0.25%) of the weight of the meat and fat. So in my five-pound batches, my standard is 6 grams. Hard to reach this precision just scooping out teaspoons. Incidentally, if you put too much nitrite in your meat it can cause dehydration, nausea, vomiting, and shortness of breath. So get the scale, OK?

fat and a shade more than half a pound of pork fat along with the lean venison.

Pork fat is the primo fat for making any sausage or salami. You can use beef fat, but I don't much like it. Pork fat is softer than beef fat and far more neutral-tasting. Add beef fat to a venison sausage and it still tastes like beef. Add pork fat to a venison sausage and it tastes like venison. Good pork fat can be had in any decent supermarket and in all butcher shops. It's usually really cheap, too. Your first choice should be back fat, which is easier to cut and slightly harder than the fat in the shoulder, which is the next best thing. Pork bellies are OK, but there is enough meat in them to influence the flavor of your sausage—not necessarily a bad thing, but you should be aware of it before you toss some bellies into the grinder.

Sausage is traditionally made with the random trim and wobbly bits of an animal. The idea of grinding up a nice roast or, God forbid, the backstrap of an animal, would make an old-school butcher vomit. And while it is true that sausage-making with these luxury cuts is easier—you have far less silverskin and gristly parts to contend with—if you take your time and remove as much silverskin as you can by hand, you can make excellent sausages with the sketchier pieces from the critter. Alternatively, if you plan on triple-grinding your meat fine, and you have a burly grinder, you can pretty much ignore the silverskin.

And most venison sausages and salami *should* be ground twice, or even three times. When you butcher, you will be faced again and again with the choice of either discarding some good chunk of meat that's loaded with connective tissue, or of putting it through the grinder anyway. Put it through the grinder. Start with the coarsest setting, like 10 mm or even a 12 mm, which is really wide. Then go with something like 7 mm or 6 mm, and then, if you want, the fine 4.5 mm or even 3 mm die. Silverskin will gunk up your grinder if you go right to the narrow die, sometimes quickly. You'll know this is

happening when the meat and fat that comes out of the grinder begins to smear together instead of coming out looking like meaty spaghetti.

Make sure your venison and fat are *very* cold when you do this. Ideal temperature is around freezing, about 32ºF or thereabouts; the salt with the meat will prevent it from freezing solid. Put the meat and fat in the freezer for an hour or so between grindings to be sure. This helps prevent smear, where the fat breaks down and coats the meat. If this happens you will never get a good bind on the sausage, and it'll be crumbly, like bad cat food.

While you mix the meat, you still want to see individual little pieces of fat, like those little marshmallows in a kid's breakfast cereal. I often mix by hand now, and I know by feel when the mix has bound: Your achingly numb hands will feel the mass as one thing, rather than lots of bits of meat. You can pick up an entire five-pound batch and it will hang together.

Use natural casings to make your sausages; I don't like synthetic casings, except for "snack sticks." Thread a whole casing on your sausage stuffer, then make one big coil of sausage at once. After you have big coils, *then* link them. For fresh sausages, I pinch off six- to eight-inch links with my fingers, then roll them in opposite ways. I roll the first link away from me, the next link toward me. That helps the links keep their shape while you dry them.

Drying links helps the sausages tighten up in their skins, which improves the texture. I use a wooden clothes-drying rack to hang my sausages, and it works like a charm. Hang your links for a couple of hours at room temperature and then let them sit overnight, uncovered, in the fridge, surrounded by paper towels to soak up any stray moisture. Even better is to let them hang at around 33ºF to 40ºF overnight. Can you eat them the first day? You bet, but the texture and flavor will improve the second day.

All of this work applies equally to salami, which are just dry-cured sausages. You do need to use a different curing salt, in this case Instacure No. 2, and it's best to get a bacterial starter culture from a place like The Sausage Maker or Butcher & Packer. Why? You need the good bugs in the starter culture to properly ferment the salami—and yes, salami is a fermented meat product. That's why it's tangy; it's the lactic acid you're tasting. More on this later.

ADVANCED SAUSAGE-MAKING TIPS

Once you have several batches of sausages under your belt, you can start thinking more about perfecting your craft. Here are a few advanced tricks and tips I've learned over the years.

When making fresh sausages, use fresh ingredients if possible: fresh herbs, fresh garlic, etc. You will notice the difference.

When you do use dried spices (seeds like black pepper, fennel, and coriander, for example), toast them in a dry pan first. It makes them taste stronger, even weeks later. Don't toast dried herbs, though, or you'll burn them.

Stuff your sausage rather loosely when making the initial coil. This gives you more wiggle room to make links. If your initial coil is too taut, you won't be able to twist them enough to keep the whole coil from unraveling. They can (and do) burst when this happens.

Vary the length of your sausage links depending on how rich they are. This is, of course, a matter of opinion, but I think leaner links ought to be long and skinny, and fatty ones shorter and plumper.

The liquid you use to moisten your links matters a lot. The exact same sausage recipe made with red wine will taste different with white wine. Vinegar will change it again, as will water or fruit juice or liqueur; I've added ouzo in a few of my recipes. Put some thought into not only what kind of liquid you want to use, but also the quality of it. If you won't drink it, don't use it.

The most important thing to learn is balance. Make enough sausages, and after a while you will develop an eye for how much spices or herbs would overpower the meat, how long to make links, etc. A good sausage has all its flavor elements in harmony. Savory is easy; so is salty. Sour can come from vinegar, sweet from any number of sources. Herbs need to play well with one another, as do spices.

My final bit of advice: Write everything down. If you don't keep accurate notes, you will never be able to tinker with your recipes, and, most importantly, you will never be able to recapture those moments of perfection.

SALAMI, METTWURST, SAUCISSON

Dry-cured sausages are the most technically advanced level of sausage making. You'll need extra equipment to make these sausages, and what's more, you'll need patience. None of these recipes can be made in less than two days, and all require long drying times in a special environment.

Whole books have been written about making salami, and I highly recommend *The Art of Making Fermented Sausages* by Stanley and Adam Marianski, *Cooking by Hand* by Paul Bertolli, and *Salumi* by Michael Ruhlman and Brian Polcyn. These books will give you an excellent overall grounding in the ins and outs of making dry-cured salami. What follows is a primer.

CURES AND BACTERIA

While salami *can* be made without nitrates or starter bacteria, only experts can make such salami safely. Nitrate, which you will find commercially as Instacure or Prague Powder No. 2, and scientifically as sodium nitrate (although the various No. 2 cures

also include some pure nitrite, too), are important safeguards against botulism and food poisoning. These additives also help the meat bind to itself and give it a pretty red color.

And for those who may recoil at the thought of nitrates in their food, know that the commercial products are extremely safe, and are used in precise measurements. Many so-called uncured charcuterie products available in the markets are selling a lie: They *all* include celery juice or celery extract, which is nothing more than nitrate; it's just "natural" nitrate. In fact, you will ingest more nitrates by eating a plate of celery with blue cheese than you would by gorging yourself on salami and sausages.

Specialized bacterial starters are not strictly needed so long as you make salami in the right conditions, but again, unless you are an experienced salami-maker, I *highly* recommend using them. These starters inoculate your salami with good bacteria, and these bacteria crowd out and kill any toxic bacteria. They are also vital to getting that distinctive tangy flavor of a good salame: The lactic acid the good bacteria give off is what makes the meat tangy.

You can buy Instacure No. 2 at most decent butcher's shops, and you can order it online. Bacterial starters are available online through outlets such as Butcher & Packer and Sausagemaker.com.

Curing Chamber

You will need to hang your dry cured sausages in a curing chamber. That chamber needs to be between 50°F and 60°F, with an ideal of 55°F, along with a humidity of 60 percent to 85 percent. If you are blessed with a basement that meets these criteria, you're good to go. Most of us are not, however. So you need to build a chamber.

Many people start with a wine fridge. This is great if you already have one, as they allow you to control temperature and, to some extent, humidity.

But if you don't own one already, you can set up what I use. My curing rig is the following:

- An old fridge bought on Craigslist

- A temperature regulator bought from my local brew shop. The regulator goes into the wall, the refrigerator plugs into the regulator, and a probe goes into the fridge itself. You set the temperature with a dial gauge.

- A small humidifier that sits inside the fridge. I live in California, where humidity levels can drop to 10 percent. This will destroy salami in a day, so I need extra humidity. To control it, I use a humidity regulator, which I bought online. It works the same as a temperature regulator.

- Or, for a little more money you can get a combination regulator that covers both temperature and humidity. Auber Instruments makes one for about $130.

- A spray bottle with water. Even with the humidifier, I tend to spritz my salami every day or two. This won't be necessary in humid places.

The whole shebang cost me less than $200, and I can control both temperature and humidity with precision.

Vac Vacay

Once you've finished hanging your cured meats, consider giving them a vacation in a vacuum bag for a week or more. Sealing a salami or cured loin or ham in a vac-bag and storing it in the fridge will help the moisture in the meat equalize, which reduces or even eliminates any case hardening, which is that dark ring around the outside edge of a dry-cured sausage. Case hardening is caused by the meat drying too fast, so the outside dries harder than the center. If it gets too severe, case hardening can destroy your sausage: The dried outer ring forms a barrier to the center, preventing the core of the sausage from drying properly. It then rots from within. This is why we cure meat at high humidities.

"... just as a deer herd lives in mortal fear of its wolves, so does a mountain live in mortal fear of its deer."

—ALDO LEOPOLD, *Thinking Like a Mountain*

CORNED VENISON

Makes one 2- to 4-pound roast | **Prep Time: 5 days or so** | **Cook Time: 3 hours**

Corning venison at home is so good that every deer hunter out there really ought to learn this technique—you will get far more enjoyment out of the leg roasts from your venison. I typically use whole-muscle roasts from the hind leg to do this: big sirloin roasts, rump roasts, the "football roast," and such. But any big hunk of venison will work. The advantage of the whole-muscle roasts is that they have less sinew and connective tissue, which take hours to break down. I suppose you could use the backstrap, but then you'd have venison Canadian bacon.

The technique is simple: Brine your meat, then simmer it into tenderness. It takes several days, but it isn't labor-intensive at all. Corned venison is great hot or cold, with root vegetables, cabbage, cold in sandwiches (how I eat most of my corned venison), or chopped into hash.

Once made, you can keep corned venison in the fridge for a couple weeks, or freeze it for a year.

One final tip: When you're done with the corned venison, leave it in the cooking broth. Store that in the fridge. Why? The broth keeps the venison moist. If you leave it out of the brine, the meat can get very dry, even crumbly.

½ gallon water

Heaping ½ cup kosher salt

⅓ cup sugar

½ ounce Instacure No. 1 (sodium nitrite)

1 tablespoon cracked black pepper

1 tablespoon toasted coriander seeds

6 bay leaves, crushed

1 tablespoon mustard seeds

1 tablespoon dried thyme

1 teaspoon caraway seeds

1 cinnamon stick

6 cloves

5 chopped garlic cloves

A 2- to 4-pound venison roast

Add everything but the roast to a pot and bring it to a boil. Turn off the heat and cover, then let it cool to room temperature while covered. This will take a few hours. Meanwhile, trim off any silverskin you find on the roast. Leave the fat. Once the brine is cool, find a container just about large enough to hold the roast, place the meat inside, and cover with the brine. You might have extra, which you can discard.

Make sure the roast is completely submerged in the brine; I use a clean stone to weigh the meat down. You can also just flip the meat every day. Cover and put in the fridge for 5 to 7 days, depending on the roast's size. A 2-pound roast might only need 4 days. The longer you soak, the saltier it will get—but you want the salt and nitrite to work its way to the center of the roast, and that takes time, which is typically 2 days per pound of meat. Err on the side of extra days, not fewer days.

After the allotted time has passed, you have corned venison. To cook and eat, rinse off the meat, then put the roast in a pot just large enough to hold it and cover with fresh water. You don't want too large a pot or the fresh water will leach out too much flavor from the meat—it's an osmosis thing. Partially cover the pot and simmer very gently—don't boil—for at least 3 hours and up to 5 hours. The meat itself will be cooked in an hour or less, but you want the sinews and connective tissue in the roast to soften, and that takes time.

Eat hot or cold. It is absolutely fantastic with good mustard and some sauerkraut on a sandwich.

VENISON PASTRAMI

Makes a little less than 2 pounds | **Prep Time: 3 days, curing and drying time** | **Cook Time: 4 hours smoking time**

I highly recommend that you use a single-muscle roast, ideally from the hind leg or even backstrap for this recipe, as this is a lean, smoked meat that you'll end up slicing thin and serving in a sandwich. If you have silverskin or connective tissue in your roast, it will not soften and then get stuck in your teeth when you eat it. You have been warned.

A word on the Instacure. The three grams I call for will actually be enough to cure up to about three pounds of venison. A general rule is about 1¼ grams of Instacure per pound, but you do need a few grams initially to get things started. Do not use more than I call for, though.

Keep an eye on your venison's internal temperature when you're smoking it. A piece of backstrap can be ready in ninety minutes in a hot smoker, which to my mind isn't enough time on the smoke. Try to keep your smoker at 200°F or cooler; I like to keep it at 160°F, which lets me smoke the meat for a solid three to four hours.

What wood? Your choice. I prefer oak, maple, or hickory for this, followed by walnut, pecan, or cherry.

Once you make your pastrami, it will need to be eaten within a week or two, or you'll need to vacuum seal and freeze it.

A 2-pound piece of venison, a hind leg roast or backstrap

Kosher salt (see recipe notes)

3 grams Instacure No. 1 (good for up to 3 pounds of meat)

½ teaspoon dried thyme

¼ teaspoon celery seed

¼ teaspoon caraway seed

1 teaspoon sugar

¼ teaspoon crushed juniper (optional)

1 teaspoon plus 3 tablespoons ground black pepper

¼ cup brandy, red wine, vinegar or water

3 tablespoons coarsely ground coriander

Weigh your venison. For every pound of meat, you'll need 22 grams of kosher salt, which is about 1 ½ tablespoons. Mix the salt, curing salt and sugar, as well as the thyme, celery seed, caraway, juniper, and the teaspoon of black pepper, and grind them all together in a spice grinder. Pack the venison with this mixture, massaging it into the meat. Put the meat into a Ziploc bag or closed container and set it in the fridge for 3 to 5 days. The longer it sits, the saltier it will be. A general rule is to leave the backstrap of a deer for 3 days, that of an elk or moose for 5 days. A deer roast will need about 5 days; a big moose or elk roast might need as much as a week to 8 days. If you're unsure, leave the meat in one more day than you think you need to. Again, the general rule is 2 days per pound of meat.

Rinse the cure off the venison and pat it dry. It's fine if you have a little bit of the cure stuck to the meat, but you don't want too much. Put the venison on a rack in the fridge and let it dry uncovered for a day.

Dip the meat into the brandy—or really any other liquid you want—and then coat thoroughly in the remaining black pepper and ground coriander seed. I like to grind this myself so the texture is a little coarse, a little fine.

Smoke the venison at about 160°F to 200°F until the interior hits 145°F, which takes me about 3 hours. Let the pastrami cool and eat as lunch meat, or on crackers or whatever.

JERKY

Jerky, the ultimate road food. Meat snack. Beef leather. Chewy, savory, spicy, sweet, it's been my favorite thing to gnaw on ever since I ate biltong, the Mother of All Jerkies, in Zimbabwe twenty years ago. Making your own jerky at home is a snap: Slice, brine, dry, eat. But making good jerky, I mean really good jerky, is harder than that.

I've made jerky a lot in recent years, and I've come to learn that nuances matter. How thick do you slice the meat? Across the grain or with it? What do you marinate it in? Or do you do a dry cure instead? How long is enough? How long is too long? Dry in an oven or dehydrator? Again, how long? There is also the realm of ground meat jerky, which we'll get to later.

Slice thickness determines whether you will have chewy jerky or the really brittle stuff you need to moisten with your saliva before you can even begin to eat it; this latter stuff will last forever at room temperature.

Across the grain makes it easier to tear with your teeth, but the shorter strands are a little less satisfying as you gnaw them. Slicing with the grain can make for a challenging chew, but the fun lasts longer this way.

Brining, marinating, or dry curing is virtually freestyle. So long as you have ample salt (or something salty, like soy sauce or Worcestershire sauce), you're in business. I'm not normally a fan of marinating meats, because marinades penetrate only about ⅛ inch into the meat (see page 58). But considering that I prefer to slice my meat for jerky about ¼ inch anyway, marinating works in this case. How long? Longer than you think you might need. Seasonings in jerky tend to fade a lot with the drying process, so you really want it to get in there.

As for the drying process, a dehydrator beats an oven hands down. (Weston and Excalibur make excellent dehydrators.) Even a low oven cooks the meat a bit too much, leaving it crispy. Of course, if you like crispy, go for it.

Through a fair bit of trial and error, I've come up with several satisfying recipes for venison jerky. They're not complicated, which is a bonus, and they really pack a lot of flavor into the meat.

Jerky Variations

Follow the same directions for the Chipotle Jerky (right), but use these alternate marinades.

TERIYAKI JERKY

1¼ cup soy sauce

⅔ cup sugar

1 cup sake or other rice wine

½ cup mirin (optional)

¼ cup rice vinegar

2 cloves garlic, peeled and roughly chopped

1 teaspoon Instacure No. 1

SRIRACHA HONEY LIME JERKY

½ cup soy sauce

1 cup sriracha hot sauce

⅔ cup honey

½ cup lime juice

1 teaspoon Instacure No. 1

1 tablespoon kosher salt

MEXICAN MACHACA

3 tablespoons kosher salt

¼ cup lime juice

1 teaspoon Instacure No. 1 (optional)

1 tablespoon Mexican oregano

2 tablespoons guajillo chile powder, or 2 teaspoons cayenne

Note: For this recipe, you will want to slice the meat with the grain, not against it. And marinate it for only 24 hours.

CHIPOTLE JERKY

Makes *a lot* | **Prep Time: 48 to 72 hours, for a good long marinating time** | **Cook Time: 5 hours in the dehydrator**

The key to this recipe is the chipotle in adobo. Don't worry—it sounds more esoteric than it really is. It's basically smoked jalapeños canned in a rich, spicy adobo sauce. There are several makers of this magical stuff, and the little cans are widely available in Latin markets and most supermarkets that have a Hispanic food section. If all else fails, you can buy chipotles in adobo online.

You do need some curing salt to make sure this jerky completely safe. I use Instacure No. 1, which protects the meat as it slowly cooks in the dehydrator. You don't need this if you use an oven, but since I dehydrate at a relatively cool 145°F to 155°F, I use the nitrite.

The end result is a chewy, slightly thick jerky loaded with an almost "spicy BBQ" flavor. It's an addicting flavor—I ate three pieces one after the other, unconsciously, as I was trying to evaluate the flavor. That instinctive taking-another-bite is always a good sign.

5 to 6 pounds venison roast

1 cup soy sauce

⅔ cup sugar

1 cup chopped onion

1 head garlic, peeled and roughly chopped

One 7-ounce can of chipotles in adobo

Juice of 2 limes

1 teaspoon Instacure No. 1

2 tablespoons salt

Put the soy, sugar, onion, garlic, chipotles, lime juice, curing salt, and enough water to fill the can of chipotles into the blender and blend until smooth. Taste and add salt if you need it—the marinade should taste pretty salty.

Cut the venison roast against the grain into roughly ¼-inch slices. Mix the marinade into the meat well. The slices are going to want to stick to each other, so use your hands (wear gloves if you're sensitive to chiles) to make sure each side of every slice gets well coated. It's enough for up to 6 pounds of meat. Pack the mixture into a non-reactive (plastic, ceramic, or stainless steel) container, cover, and refrigerate for 24 to 72 hours. How long depends on your personal salt tolerance and on whether you plan on storing the finished jerky for months or not; I go three days.

When you're ready, lay the meat on dehydrator trays in one layer. Don't let the slices of meat touch. Set the dehydrator to 160°F for 2 hours, then drop it down to 145°F until the jerky is ready. When it's ready, the jerky will still be pliable, but will fracture and crack a little when you bend it. All told, the jerky should be ready in about 6 hours. If you're planning to store this at room temperature for a long time, dry the meat until it is brittle.

If you're using an oven, set the oven as low as it will go and use something to prop open the door to let air circulate inside the oven. If you have a convection oven, use it.

Store it in the fridge for up to a month. Or freeze it until the Second Coming. I vacuum seal jerky and take it on road trips.

PEMMICAN-STYLE GROUND MEAT JERKY

Makes about ¾ pound of jerky, and can be scaled up | **Prep Time: 24 to 48 hours**
Cook Time: 4 to 8 hours, depending on your dehydrator

Not all jerky needs to be made from intact pieces of meat. True, this is traditional jerky, but you can also make an excellent jerky-like product using ground venison. The very best of these is the Tanka Bar, a pemmican-like meat bar made by the Oglala Sioux Indians in South Dakota that's available online. This recipe is a hat tip to the Tanka Bar.

You do need a special piece of equipment to really do this right, however. You need a jerky gun. It's basically a caulking gun modified for food use. Several companies make them, but the one I use is made by Weston.

I like to grind the meat and fat for this right before making the jerky, but any ground venison will do. You will want at least a little fat in the grind, however, because otherwise the jerky will be pretty crumbly and dry.

If you don't use bacon, you'll want to increase the salt to twenty-five grams. And if you have smoked salt, you'll want to use it.

1¾ pounds venison

¼ pound bacon

1 cup dried cranberries or other berries

18 grams salt, about 2 tablespoons

3 grams Instacure No. 1, about ½ teaspoon

2 teaspoons ground black pepper

½ teaspoon ground mace or nutmeg

1 tablespoon onion powder

1 tablespoon of paprika, smoked if possible

2 to 3 tablespoons sugar

¼ cup water

Grind the venison, bacon, and dried cranberries through the fine die of your grinder. If you're using pre-ground venison, chop the dried cranberries well and add them to the ground meat. Put the meat and cranberries in a large bowl and add all the remaining ingredients. Mix well with your (very clean) hands until everything comes together and starts to stick to itself.

If you have a vacuum sealer, seal the mixture and set in the fridge for 24 to 48 hours. If you don't, pack the meat mixture into a lidded container and press some plastic wrap directly onto the surface and let it sit that way.

The next day, separate the mixture into two or three chunks, depending on how big your jerky gun is. Pack it in and squeeze out lengths of jerky onto your dehydrator trays. Make sure they are separated from each other. Dehydrate at 150°F until the meat is mostly dry, but still chewy.

This sort of jerky doesn't keep as long as traditional jerky because of the fat content. But it will keep for several weeks in the fridge, and it freezes well.

VENISON SAUSAGE WITH SAGE AND JUNIPER

Makes 5 pounds, about 20 to 22 links

This is a sausage I was inspired to make after I returned from a deer hunting trip to Catalina Island, which is off the coast of Los Angeles, believe it or not. I'm a firm believer in the cooking adage "what lives together in life can live together on the plate," and we found lots of native sages and juniper bushes on the island.

The two main players here are sage and juniper, boosted by the juniper-herbiness of gin. It makes this sausage taste the way the hillsides of California smell on a warm summer's day. I add a touch of celery seed, too, which seems to punch up the taste of the venison.

How to cook these sausages? Grill slowly, or brown in a pan, then pan roast at 325°F for twenty minutes. You can also use these links in a stew, or in a sausage, peppers, and onions sandwich.

4 pounds venison

1 pound pork fat

33 grams Kosher salt (about 2 tablespoons)

3 grams Instacure No. 1 (optional)

15 grams ground juniper berries
(about a tablespoon)

25 grams fresh chopped sage
(about 2 tablespoons)

1 tablespoon ground black pepper

3 grams celery seed (about ½ teaspoon)

¼ cup gin

¼ cup cold water

Hog casings

Chop the venison and pork fat into 1-inch chunks, or however big you need to fit into your grinder. (Expert step: Mix the salt and curing salt with just the meat—not the fat or any other ingredients—and refrigerate overnight. This helps develop myosin, which helps bind the sausage better later.)

Get out about 10 to 15 feet of hog casings and soak them in warm water. If you don't trust your source, run water through them to check for punctures or weak spots.

If you haven't already done so, combine the salt, curing salt, herbs, and spices with the meat, and mix well. Chill the meat and fat until it's almost frozen by putting it in the freezer for an hour or two.

Grind through your meat grinder using the coarse die; I use an 8 mm or a 10 mm die for this. If your room is warmer than 69°F, set the bowl for the ground meat into another bowl of ice to keep it cold. If the mixture is still below 38°F, you can grind a second time through the fine die; I use a 4.5 mm for this. If the meat mixture has warmed too much, put it into the freezer to chill and put the removable grinder parts (blade, die, hopper, etc.) into the fridge to stay cool. Clean the rest of the grinder and put into the freezer. Grind when the meat is very cold, about 32°F.

Add the gin and cold water and mix thoroughly using either a KitchenAid or other stand mixer on low for 60 to 90 seconds or with your (very clean) hands; I use my hands, which ache with cold as I do this (yours should too).

Stuff the sausage into the casings. Twist off links by pinching a link and twisting it, first in one direction, and then, with the next link, the other direction. Or you could tie them off with kitchen string.

Now look at the links, which will probably have air pockets in them. Use a sterile needle or sausage pricker (set it aglow in your stovetop flame) to puncture the casing over all the air pockets. Gently compress the links together to squeeze out the air pockets and rotate the links a bit more to tighten; this takes practice.

Hang the sausages in a cool place. At normal room temperatures, hang for 2 hours. But if you have a place where the temperatures are between 33°F and 40°F, hang for up to a day. Once the links have dried a bit, put them in the fridge until needed. They will keep for a week. You can also smoke these sausages to an internal temperature of 150°F, and they'll keep for about 10 days. They also freeze well.

BRITISH BANGERS

Makes about 5 pounds' worth
Prep Time: 90 minutes, if you have made sausages before. Longer if you're a newbie

I can't remember the first time I had bangers and mash, but if I had to guess, it would have been at Lily Flanagan's, an Irish pub in Islip on Long Island, back in the early 1990s. I just remember it as generic "sausage," with nice mashed potatoes and peas. Later, in 1995, on a thirty-six-hour layover in London, I had the real deal. Still pretty generic, but definitely better: It was a softish link, with warm spices and an interesting bind that made it comforting to eat.

I later learned that the unusual mouthfeel of the banger is caused by the inclusion of some sort of grain in the link: breadcrumbs, oats, barley, or some such. I've heard various theories on why British charcuterie does this—virtually no other sausage-making nation does, with the exception of the famous Swedish potato sausage—ranging from scarcity during the World Wars to, well, it just tastes good. I used to think it was some sort of scandalous cheapening of a good sausage, but I've recently come around. The addition of a grain in the mix can and does add something positive. Texture, sure, but also flavor. I'm partial to barley or oats coarsely ground in a coffee grinder.

There is no One True Banger, just as there is no one recipe for Italian sausage or Polish kielbasa. My version is adapted from a recipe for a Gloucester-style sausage I found in a charming little book called *British Charcuterie*.

Once you make these, the obvious thing to do with them is to make bangers and mash, with peas. Just pull a page from your Thanksgiving playbook and make mashed potatoes, gravy, and peas in butter. That's it. You can also put these in a bun and serve with mustard and kraut, or with pickled onions.

4 pounds venison, cut into chunks

1 pound pork fat, or ½ pound pork fat and
   ½ pound venison fat, cut into chunks

36 grams kosher salt, about 2 tablespoons plus
   a teaspoon

2 teaspoons fresh or dried thyme

2 teaspoons white pepper

1 teaspoon minced fresh sage

1 teaspoon porcini powder (optional)

1 teaspoon onion powder

½ teaspoon mace

½ teaspoon nutmeg

8 ounces coarsely ground oats, barley, or,
   alternately, breadcrumbs

¾ cup malty beer

Hog casings

Get out about 10 to 15 feet of hog casings and soak them in warm water. If you don't trust your source, run water through them to check for punctures or weak spots.

Make sure all your equipment is cold by freezing the grinding plate, blades, and the bowl you will put the meat into for 30 minutes to an hour. Do the same for the meat and fat. When everything's nice and cold, mix the meat and fat with all the spices (leave out the oats and beer for the moment).

Grind through your meat grinder using the coarse die; I use an 8 mm or a 10 mm die for this. If your room is warmer than 69°F, set the bowl for the ground meat into another bowl of ice to keep it cold. If the mixture is still below 38°F, you can grind a second time through the fine die; I use a 4.5 mm for this. If the meat mixture has warmed too much, put it into the freezer to chill and put the removable grinder parts (blade, die, hopper, etc.) into the fridge to stay cool. Clean the rest of the grinder and put into the freezer. Grind when the meat is very cold, about 32°F.

Once the sausage has been ground twice, test the temperature again to make sure it's 35°F or colder. I prefer to chill the mix down to 28°F to 32°F for this next stage. Chill the mix, and when it's cold enough, take it out and add the oats and beer. Now, mix and knead this all up in a big bin or bowl with your (very clean) hands for a solid 2 minutes—your hands will ache with cold, which is good. You want everything to almost emulsify.

Stuff the sausage into hog casings rather loosely. I like bangers to be about 6 to 8 inches long, but it's your choice. To twist them into links, tie off one end of the coil you just made. Pinch off links with your two hands and roll the link between them forward a couple times. Move down the coil and repeat, only this time roll backwards a few times. Repeat until you do the whole coil.

Now look at the links, which will probably have air pockets in them. Use a sterile needle or sausage pricker (set it aglow in your stovetop flame) to puncture the casing over all the air pockets. Gently compress the links together to squeeze out the air pockets and rotate the links a bit more to tighten; this takes practice.

Hang your links for at least 1 hour if your room is warm, and up to a day if you can hang them in a place that's 40°F or cooler. Let the sausages dry uncovered in the fridge overnight before you seal them up and freeze. Bangers will keep a week in the fridge and a year in the freezer.

WISCONSIN RED BRATS

Makes about 5 pounds of sausage | **Prep Time: Overnight, plus about 2 hours**
Cook Time: 2 to 4 hours in the smoker

On Wisconsin! I'm a proud graduate of the University of Wisconsin, where I spent many an evening drinking beer, watching the Badgers, and eating red brats from State Street Brats in Madison. Red brats are smoky and addictive. Learn to make this link and you'll find yourself rooting for my Badgers, at least a little.

For the mustard seed, just grind whole seeds a bit in a spice grinder to crack them up.

3 pounds venison

2 pounds very fatty pork shoulder or pork belly

35 grams kosher salt

5 grams Instacure No. 1

1 tablespoon sugar

25 grams powdered milk

3 tablespoons minced garlic

1 tablespoon freshly ground black pepper

2 teaspoons coarsely ground mustard seed

1½ teaspoons ground mace or nutmeg

1½ teaspoons dried sage

¾ cup cold lager beer

Hog casings

Get out about 10 to 15 feet of hog casings and soak them in warm water. If you don't trust your source, run water through them to check for punctures or weak spots.

Cut the venison and pork into chunks that will fit into your grinder. Mix with the salt, sugar, and curing salt (Instacure No. 1) and refrigerate overnight. Doing this helps the sausage bind to itself later. You can skip the overnight rest, but your sausage will not be as firm in the casing.

When you're ready to make the sausage, freeze your grinder's grinding plate and blades, and the bowl you will put the meat into, for 30 minutes to an hour. Do the same for the meat and fat. When everything's nice and cold—no warmer than 38°F—mix the meat and fat with the powdered milk and all the spices.

Grind it all through a coarse plate; I use a 10 mm plate. Test the temperature of the mixture, and if it's 35°F or colder, go ahead and grind *half* the mixture again through a fine die, like a 4.5 mm. Set it back with the rest of the ground meat mixture. If it's warmer than 35°F, put the mix back into the freezer to chill. This might take an hour or so if you've let the meat warm up too much. Use the time to clean up.

Once the sausage has been ground twice, test the temperature again to make sure it's 35°F or colder. I prefer to chill the mix down to 28°F to 32°F for this next stage. Chill the mix, and when it's cold enough, take it out and add the beer. Now, mix, and knead this all up in a big bin or bowl with your (very clean) hands for a solid 2 minutes—your hands will ache with cold, which is good. You want everything to almost emulsify.

Stuff the sausage into hog casings rather loosely. Do this in a coil before you make the links. I like this sausage in links of about 6 to 8 inches long, but it's your choice. To twist them into individual sausages, tie off one end of the coil you just made. Pinch off links with your two hands and roll the link between them forward a few times. Move down the coil and repeat, only this time roll backwards a few times. Repeat until you do the whole coil.

Now look at the links, which will probably have air pockets in them. Use a sterile needle or sausage pricker (set it aglow in your stovetop flame) to puncture the casing over all the air pockets. Gently compress the links together to squeeze out the air pockets and rotate the links a bit more to tighten; this takes practice.

Dry your links in a cool place for at least 24 hours and up to 3 days. I hang mine in a curing fridge set to 55°F, with about 75 percent humidity. The curing salt will protect them during this time. If you haven't used curing salt, dry the sausage uncovered in the fridge for a day.

To smoke the links, hang in a cool smoker and let the heat come up slowly until it hits about 200°F. Smoke the links until their internal temperature hits 155°F. This may take less than 4 hours, but internal temperature is more important. As soon as the sausages are cooked, submerge them in an ice water bath until cool. Pat dry and store in the fridge.

"Of all the wonders of nature, a tree in summer is perhaps the most remarkable; with the possible exception of a moose singing 'Embraceable You' in spats."

—WOODY ALLEN

ROMANIAN VENISON SAUSAGE

Makes about 5 pounds of sausage | Prep Time: Overnight, plus about 2 hours | Cook Time: 4 hours in the smoker

This is historically a Jewish sausage from Romania, and traditionally uses lamb or beef. So making this as an all-venison sausage makes sense. If you don't have or don't want to use venison fat, use pork or beef fat instead.

This is a rich, finely ground, smoked link that gets a lot of flavor from mustard seeds in the grind. I find that using wide hog casings, like 38-42 mm casings, linked to only about four or five inches, makes a nice contrast with most other sausages on a plate, which normally rely on narrower hog casings and longer links. But don't beat yourself up if you can't find the wide casings. The sausage will be just fine.

You can, of course, make this sausage without the curing salt, and eat it unsmoked. Unsmoked, they will keep a week in the fridge. Smoked, they'll last ten days to two weeks. Frozen, they'll last more than a year if vacuum sealed.

---

5 pounds of fatty venison, or 4 pounds venison and 1 pound pork or beef fat

33 grams kosher salt

5 grams Instacure No. 1

1 tablespoon minced garlic

1 tablespoon freshly ground black pepper

1 tablespoon sugar

2 teaspoons ground coriander

1 teaspoon mustard powder

½ teaspoon ground allspice

½ teaspoon ground cloves

½ teaspoon ground bay leaf

2 tablespoons whole mustard seeds

¾ cup cold water

Hog casings, preferably 38-42mm

Get out about 15 to 20 feet of hog casings and soak them in warm water. If you don't trust your source, run water through them to check for punctures or weak spots.

Cut the venison into chunks that will fit into your grinder. Mix with the salt and curing salt (Instacure No. 1) and refrigerate overnight. Doing this helps the sausage bind to itself later. You can skip the overnight rest, but your sausage will not be as firm in the casing.

When you're ready to make the sausage, freeze your grinder's grinding plate and blades, and the bowl you will put the meat into, for 30 minutes to an hour. Do the same for the meat and fat. When everything's nice and cold—no warmer than 38°F—mix the meat and fat with all the spices (leave out the mustard seeds and water for the moment).

Grind it all through a coarse plate; I use a 10 mm plate. Test the temperature of the mixture, and if it's 35°F or colder, go ahead and grind it all again through a fine die, like a 4.5 mm. If it's warmer than 35°F, put the mix back into the freezer to chill. This might take an hour or so if you've let the meat warm up too much. Use the time to clean up.

Once the sausage has been ground twice, test the temperature again to make sure it's 35°F or colder. I prefer to chill the mix down to 28°F to 32°F for this next stage. Chill the mix, and when

(continued)

it's cold enough, take it out and add the mustard seeds and water. Now, mix and knead this all up in a big bin or bowl with your (very clean) hands for a solid 2 minutes—your hands will ache with cold, which is good. You want everything to almost emulsify.

Stuff the sausage into hog casings rather loosely. Do this in a coil before you make the links. I like this sausage in links of about 4 to 6 inches long, but it's your choice. To twist them into individual sausages, tie off one end of the coil you just made. Pinch off links with your two hands and roll the link between them forward a few times. Move down the coil and repeat, only this time roll backwards a few times. Repeat until you do the whole coil.

Now look at the links, which will probably have air pockets in them. Use a sterile needle or sausage pricker (set it aglow in your stovetop flame) to puncture the casing over all the air pockets. Gently compress the links together to squeeze out the air pockets and rotate the links a bit more to tighten; this takes practice.

Dry your links in a cold place for at least 24 hours and up to 3 days. I hang mine in a curing fridge set to 55°F, with about 75 percent humidity. The curing salt will protect them during this time. If you haven't used curing salt, dry the sausage uncovered in the fridge for a day.

To smoke the links, hang in a cool smoker and let the heat come up slowly until it hits about 200°F. Smoke the links until their internal temperature hits 155°F. This might take less than 4 hours, but internal temperature is more important. As soon as the sausages are cooked, submerge them in an ice water bath until cool. Pat dry and store in the fridge.

MEXICAN-STYLE CHORIZO

Makes about 5 pounds

Mexican chorizo is very different from its Spanish cousin. Mexican chorizo is softer, spicier, and more floral than Spanish chorizo. Making an authentic one is tricky if you don't have some of the ingredients, but even if you leave some out, it'll still be good.

If you can't find all of the ingredients, know that only a few are critical to a good Mexican chorizo. One such is achiote paste, which is available at any Mexican market, or you can buy it online. Mexican oregano is different from Mediterranean oregano, but either works. Chipotle powder rocks, but is not completely necessary. You do need cayenne and some other chile powder, but these are easily available in Latin markets—or you can grind dried chiles yourself, which is what I do.

4 pounds venison

1 pound pork fat

34 grams kosher salt, about 3 tablespoons

15 grams sugar, about 1 tablespoon

6 garlic cloves, minced

6 grams oregano, about 2 tablespoons

5 grams ground cumin, about 2 teaspoons

3 grams chipotle powder, about 1 heaping teaspoon

5 grams cayenne, 1 tablespoon

28 grams pasilla, ancho or mulato chile powder, about 3 tablespoons (optional)

2 tablespoons achiote paste

¼ cup tequila (the cheap stuff)

¼ cup red wine vinegar or lime juice

Hog casings

Cut the meat and fat into chunks that will fit into your meat grinder. Combine the salt, sugar, and all the dry spices (not the achiote paste) with the meat and fat, mix well with your hands, and chill it until it's almost frozen by putting it in the freezer for an hour or so.

Get out about 10 to 15 feet of hog casings and soak them in warm water. If you don't trust your source, run water through them to check for punctures or weak spots.

Mix the tequila and vinegar with the achiote paste and chill it in the fridge.

Grind the meat mixture through your meat grinder using a medium die—about 6.5 mm. If your room is warm, set the bowl for the ground meat into another bowl of ice to keep it cold. Make sure the meat mixture is very cold before moving on to the next step—you want it between 28°F and 35°F.

Add the tequila-achiote mixture and mix thoroughly either using a KitchenAid or other stand mixer on low for 60 to 90 seconds, or with your (very clean) hands. This is important to get the sausage to bind properly. Once it's mixed well, put it back in the fridge and clean up.

Stuff the sausage into the casings all at once. To twist them into individual sausages, tie off one end of the coil you just made. Pinch off links with your two hands and roll the link between

(continued)

them forward a few times. Move down the coil and repeat, only this time roll backwards a few times. Repeat until you do the whole coil. Or you could tie them off with butcher's string.

Now look at the links, which will probably have air pockets in them. Use a sterile needle or sausage pricker (set it aglow in your stovetop flame) to puncture the casing over all the air pockets. Gently compress the links together to squeeze out the air pockets and rotate the links a bit more to tighten; this takes practice.

Hang the sausages in a cool place for up to 4 hours (the colder it is, the longer you can hang them). If it's warm out, hang for just one hour. Once they've dried a bit, put in the fridge until needed. They will keep for at least a week in the fridge. If you're freezing the sausages, wait a day before doing so. This will tighten up the sausages and help them keep their shape in the deep-freeze.

KABANOSY, THE WORLD'S GREATEST MEAT STICK

Makes about 10 long links | **Prep Time: 4 hours** | **Cook Time: 4 hours, plus hanging time afterward**

Kabanosy, pronounced Kah-bah-NOSH-ee, is what a Slim Jim dreams about becoming when it grows up. It is lightly spiced with garlic, nutmeg, black pepper, and a hint of caraway, smoked over cherry, apple, or beech wood, then hung for a few days to dry.

It is an unusual sausage because even though it's air dried, you don't use starter cultures or Instacure No. 2, which is the sodium nitrate you normally use for dry-cured sausages. The drying process is too short for that. Traditionally, this is a pork sausage, but venison works well with it. Once made, they will keep in the fridge for a couple of weeks or so; after you vacuum seal them or wrap them tightly, they will freeze for up to a year without loss of quality.

To make a proper kabanosy, you will need sheep casings. Many butcher shops have them, but they are harder to find than the regular hog casings. You can also buy sheep casings online. In addition, you will need to smoke these links, preferably over cherry, apple, or beech wood. If you don't have any of these, oak, maple, or hickory would be fine.

2½ pounds pork, venison, wild boar, bear, or other meat

10 ounces pork fat

25 grams kosher salt, about 3 tablespoons

3 grams Instacure No. 1, about ½ teaspoon

4 grams sugar, about a heaping teaspoon

4 garlic cloves, minced

4 grams crushed black pepper, about 2 teaspoons

2 grams nutmeg, about 1 heaping teaspoon

2 grams caraway seed, 2 teaspoons

1 gram celery seed, about ¼ teaspoon

⅓ cup ice water

Cut the meat and fat into pieces that will fit in your grinder. Mix all the salts and spices with the meat and fat. Put everything in the freezer for 1 hour to chill. Meanwhile, take out about 20 feet of sheep casings and soak them in tepid water.

Grind the mixture in the fine die of your grinder, making sure everything stays cold. If the meat warms beyond 40°F, stop and freeze everything for 30 minutes to cool it down. Put the ground meat into the fridge while you clean up.

Using a KitchenAid or other stand mixer, or your (very clean) hands, add the ice water and mix the meat and fat—use the lowest setting on a stand mixer—until it binds, about 1 to 2 minutes. Again, put the meat into the fridge while you clean up.

Flush the sheep casings with warm water and set aside.

Put the meat mixture into your sausage stuffer and stuff into the sheep casings. Remember that sheep casings are weaker than hog casings, so you do not want to overstuff them. As you're stuffing, fill up a link between 12 inches and 24 inches, leaving plenty of extra casing on either end. Cut the casing and continue to make these large links until you've used all the meat.

(continued)

Use a sterilized needle to pierce the casings wherever there are air pockets. Gently squeeze the meat in the casings to tighten. You may break some until you get the hang of it. If you do, put the meat back into the stuffer and make another link. Once all the links are firm in their casings, tie the ends together in a double or triple knot. Trim any excess casing.

Hang the links to dry in a cool place for several hours, depending on how warm it is. If the temperature is 70°F or above, hang for only an hour.

Move the links to a smoker and smoke until the interior of the meat hits 150°, keeping your smoker cool enough so that this takes about 2 to 4 hours. You want the links to get lots of smoke time.

Let the links cool, then move to a place to hang them. Ideally, this place is between 35°F and 60°F and dark. Hang the links for 3 to 5 days to let them dry out a bit. They are now reasonably shelf stable, but I keep them in the fridge. If for some reason you plan on keeping them more than a month or so, wrap tightly (or vacuum seal) and freeze.

BASIC VENISON SALAMI

Makes about 5 pounds | **Prep Time: 3 hours to make the sausages, then at least 1 month to cure and dry**

With the possible exception of a whole dry-aged ham, to my mind, salami is the highest form of the butcher's art. The careful crafting of raw meat, salt, spices, and time create something very different from a fresh sausage. It's not crazy to call it alchemy. But making salami is no joke. It takes time, attention to detail (and sanitation), plus a careful eye to troubleshoot problems. Doing this at home is not for beginners. Make fresh sausages until you are comfortable with the process before moving to this recipe.

When you do pluck up enough courage to make your own salami at home, this is the recipe you should start with. It is the classic, the "little black dress" of salami, flavored only with salt, black pepper, and a bit of garlic. The meat is the star here, not the spices. Every salami-making culture makes a version of this sausage, and recipes are similar whether you look to Spain or France or Italy or Hungary or Germany—although these last two nations tend to smoke their salami, too.

If you've never made fresh sausages before, come back when you've made a dozen or so batches. You need to be comfortable with the basic sausage-making process before you take the step of curing them. You also need some special equipment. Don't try to shortcut salami making. You'll pay for it eventually.

First, you need a good grinder; I use a Weston grinder. You need a sausage stuffer, too. Lots of companies make good ones. Can you hand-cut the meat and fat? Yes, but it requires a sharp knife and an awful lot of patience.

To hang your sausages for the few days it takes to ferment them, I use a simple wooden clothes-drying rack. I also buy "S" hooks from the local hardware store to hang the links. You'll also need a humidifier both for the fermentation process and while your links are drying. Finally, you must have a curing chamber; I use an old fridge (see page 261).

The salami-making process is this: You make sausage, only with added sodium nitrate (Instacure No. 2) and a starter culture, then ferment the sausages at room temperature for a few days to let the good bacteria in the starter beat back any bad bugs within the meat. Do you need these two ingredients? Absolutely. Yeah, I hear you: "But can't salami be made without them?" Yes. But *you* can't. The people who can pull it off work in places where they've made salami for decades or even centuries, and the ambient air already has the good bacteria; it's like a sourdough. For you and me, adding nitrate and starter culture is our insurance policy against botulism and listeria.

The last stage is to hang the links to dry out slowly in the chamber or in a basement. The key to successful drying is to let the sausages dry slowly, little by little. Why? This does two things: First, it prevents the dreaded "case hardening," where the outside of the salami dries too fast and prevents the interior from drying properly. And second, the longer you cure your salami, the better it will taste.

Truly great salami has a distinct funk to it, like cheese. I've made a lot of decent salami, some mediocre and a few crappy ones. Only once in a while does everything work perfectly. It's part of the learning process, which never ends.

Follow this recipe, get decent equipment, and you should be fine. But remember: Sausage making is a sprint; salami making is a marathon. You must be careful and sanitary at the start—we're dealing with raw meat here—and you cannot forget about your salami while it cures or you may be very, very sad. Still, this ain't rocket science. You can make salami at home, and when you do, it's one of the most satisfying things you can make with your own two hands.

4 pounds venison

1 pound pork fatback

51 grams salt

6 grams Instacure No. 2

1 tablespoon coarsely ground black pepper

2 tablespoons minced fresh garlic

1 tablespoon minced fresh rosemary

⅓ cup red wine

¼ cup distilled water

20 grams FRM-52 starter culture,
    or T-SPX culture

Hog casings, preferably 38-42 mm wide

Start by setting out ½ to ⅔ pound of the venison and dicing it fine. Do the same for ¼ pound of the fat. I like doing this because it varies the grind within the sausage from very fine to chunky. To me, this is more interesting. You can run it all through the grinder if you prefer, or if you think someone will get all crazy if they see big pieces of fat in their salami. Cut the remaining fat and meat into chunks that will fit into your grinder. Trim as much sinew and silverskin as you can.

Put both the diced and chunked fat into separate containers in the fridge. Mix the salt and curing salt with just the meat and put it into the fridge overnight, keeping the diced and chunked pieces separate. This overnight rest helps develop myosin, which will give you a tighter bind when you stuff the links later.

The next day, put the fat and your grinding equipment—blade, coarse and fine die, etc.—in the freezer. Mix the garlic, rosemary, and half the black pepper into the meat you plan on grinding. Put that in the freezer, too. Let everything chill down until the meat hits about 30°F or so. It won't freeze solid because of the salt. Normally, this takes about 90 minutes. While you're waiting, soak about 15 feet of hog casings in a bowl of warm water, and put the red wine in the fridge.

When the meat and fat are cold, take them out and mix together, but keep the diced meat and fat separate for now. Grind ½ to ⅔ of the mixture through the coarse die of the grinder, about 8 to 10 mm. Grind the rest through the fine die, about 4.5 mm. I do this to vary my grind, which makes for a better texture in my opinion. Sometimes I do ¾ fine and ¼ coarse, depending on my mood. The key is variability.

Put the meat and fatback into the freezer while you clean up. Dissolve the starter culture with the distilled water.

When the meat mixture is back below 35°F, you can mix it. I put the mixture into a big plastic bin with the diced fat and meat, the remaining black pepper, the red wine and the starter culture mixture, and mix it by hand for about 2 minutes. If you do this, you'll know the mixture's cold enough if your hands ache from the chill. Or, you can put everything into a big stand mixer and mix on low for 90 seconds to 2 minutes. I prefer to mix by hand.

Put the sausage into the fridge while you clean up. Run some clean water through your casings to flush them and to see if you have any leaks. Cut lengths of casing of about two feet long and set all but one back in the water. Thread one onto your sausage stuffer.

Pack the sausage into your stuffer and get ready to make the salami. Leave 4 to 6 inches of casing hanging from the edge of the stuffer as a "tail"; you'll use this to tie off the salami in a bit. Start working the meat into the casing, using your fingers to flush any air out of the casing and to regulate the flow. I prefer straight links about a foot long or so. Remove the link from the stuffer and repeat with the remaining casings and sausage.

Now gently compress the meat within each casing, watching for air bubbles. Heat a needle or a sausage pricker in the flames of your stove to sterilize it, and prick the links to let any trapped air out. Tie off both ends of the link in a double or triple knot (you don't need a specialized butterfly knot with hog casings), and then tie a loop of kitchen twine to one end, making sure the twine knot is underneath the casing knot you just made: This will prevent the twine from slipping off. Hang your sausages from "S" hooks or somesuch on a wooden rack.

To ferment your links, you will need to keep them warm and moist. I do this by putting a humidifier under the hanging sausages and then tenting the whole shebang with big garbage bags that I've sliced open on one end. I also use a water sprayer to spritz my sausages a couple of times a day. Doing this prevents the casings from hardening. Keep your sausages hanging at room temperature (65 to 80°F) in about 85 percent humidity for two to three days.

Now you need to dry your sausages and turn them into salami. Hang them in a place that is about 50°F to 60°F with about 80 to 90 percent humidity. In most cases, you will need to put a humidifier under your links. I also spritz them with water once a day for the first 2 weeks. After the first week of hanging, drop the humidity to 70 to 80 percent. On the third week, drop it again to 65 to 70 percent and hold it there until 4 to 10 weeks have elapsed since the salami went into the chamber.

You now have salami. To store long-term, vacuum seal them individually and keep in the fridge. They will last indefinitely this way, and the vacuum sealing will keep them from becoming rock hard. You can also freeze them.

The Many Colors of Mold

When you cure meats, mold happens. Mold comes in many colors, each representing a different variety. In general, it's no big deal, especially since many people just peel off the casing of their salami when they intend to eat it, even though the casing is perfectly edible. A general rule of thumb says that tight white mold is fine, really fuzzy white mold is OK, green mold not great but not a disaster, and black mold is bad. If you should start getting green or black mold, wipe down your links with vinegar; you may need to scrub a bit to get all the mold off. Smoked salami tend not to develop mold, incidentally. One more note: If you have mold on your salami and you do the vac vacay I mention on page 262, the exterior of the links will get slimy when you take them out. In that case you really want to peel off the casing.

BOERENMETWORST

Makes about 5 pounds | Prep Time: 3 hours to make the sausages, then at least 1 month to cure and dry
Cook Time: 2 to 4 hours cold smoking

This is a Dutch sausage that is dried and smoked. Literally, it means "farmer's dry sausage," and it's a proper summer sausage from the Old Country. You make the links, let them ferment for a few days, then smoke them very gently—you don't want them to cook. Then you hang them to dry for a few weeks before eating.

There is a distinctive flavor to Dutch (and Afrikaner) sausages that comes from the liberal use of coriander, ginger, cloves, and black pepper. Allspice is another common addition, and if you want to add some, you can mix in a ½ teaspoon.

Note that if you want an Upper Midwest style summer sausage, let the links hang for only two or three weeks, so they are still a little soft.

3½ pounds venison

1 pound fatty pork shoulder

½ pound pork fatback

51 grams salt

6 grams Instacure No. 2

10 grams dextrose (granulated sugar if you can't get it)

1 tablespoon cracked black pepper

1 tablespoon coarsely ground coriander seed

2 teaspoons coarsely ground mustard seed

1 teaspoon powdered ginger

½ teaspoon ground cloves

¼ cup malt vinegar

⅓ cup distilled water

10 grams F-LC or FRM-52 starter culture

Hog casings, preferably 38-42 mm wide

Cut the meat and fat into chunks that will fit into your grinder. Trim as much sinew and silverskin as you can. Put the fat into a container in the fridge. Mix the dextrose, salt, and curing salt with the meats and put it into the fridge overnight. This helps develop myosin, which will give you a tighter bind when you stuff the links later.

The next day, put your grinding equipment—blade, coarse and fine die, etc.—into the freezer. Mix the ginger, cloves, and half of the remaining spices with the meat and fat. Put the mixture into the freezer and let everything chill down until it hits about 30°F or so. Because of the salt, it won't freeze solid. Normally, this takes about 90 minutes. While you're waiting, soak about 15 feet of hog casings in a bowl of warm water, and put the malt vinegar in the fridge.

When the meat and fat are cold, take them out and grind through the coarse die of the grinder; I use a 10 mm plate. Test the temperature of the mixture, and if it's 35°F or colder, go ahead and grind it all again through a fine die, like a 4.5 mm. If it's warmer than 35°F, put the mix back into the freezer to chill. This might take an hour or so if you've let the meat warm up too much. Use the time to clean up, and to dissolve your starter culture in the distilled water.

Once the sausage has been ground twice, test the temperature again to make sure it's 35°F or colder. I prefer to chill the mix down to 28°F to 32°F for this next stage. Chill the mix, and when it's cold enough, take it out and add the remaining spices, the vinegar, and the water-starter culture mixture. Now, mix and knead this all up in a big bin or bowl with your (very clean) hands for a solid 2 minutes—your hands will ache with cold, which is good. You want everything to almost emulsify.

Stuff the sausage into hog casings rather loosely. For this sausage, you want long rings—you'll tie the ends together eventually. First make long links of about 2 feet long, with plenty of extra casing on either side. Do this with all the sausage before moving on.

When you're ready, gently compress the long links to fill the casing. Keep an eye out for air pockets. Use a sterile needle or sausage pricker (set it aglow in your stovetop flame) to puncture the casing over all the air pockets. Gently compress the links together to squeeze out the air pockets; this takes practice. Tie the ends of the casing together in a double or triple knot.

Hang the links from a clothes rack or somesuch. I use "S" rings you buy from the hardware store to hang them from the clothes rack rods. Now you need to ferment your links, keeping them warm and moist. I do this by putting a humidifier under the hanging sausages and then tenting the whole shebang with big garbage bags that I've sliced open on one end. I also use a water sprayer to spritz my sausages a couple of times a day. Doing this prevents the casings from hardening. Keep your sausages hanging at room temperature (65 to 80°F) at about 85 percent humidity for three days.

Move the sausages to your smoker and smoke them over very low heat for up to 4 hours of continuous smoke. It is vitally important that you do not cook your links here, so put ice in the water tray of the smoker, and smoke on a cold day or in the early morning. Do not let the smoker rise above 100°F. If it gets too hot, open the door of the smoker, or just take the links out.

Now you need to dry your sausages and turn them into salami. Hang them in a place that is about 50°F to 60°F with about 80 to 90 percent humidity. In most cases, you will need to put a humidifier under your links. I also spritz them with water once a day for the first 2 weeks. After the first week of hanging, drop the humidity to 70 to 80 percent. On the third week drop it again to 65 to 70 percent and hold it there until a total of 4 to 8 weeks has elapsed since the salami went into the chamber.

You now have *boerenmetworst*. To store long-term, vacuum seal them individually and keep in the fridge. They will last indefinitely this way, and the vacuum sealing will keep them from becoming rock hard. You can also freeze them.

SPANISH CHORIZO

Makes about 5 pounds | **Prep Time: 3 hours to make the sausages, then at least 1 month to cure and dry**

Chorizo is normally made with pork—except when it's made with "retired" bulls from the ring. But chorizo works great with venison, especially old bull moose or elk, or rutty bucks.

Try to get Spanish smoked paprika for this recipe. Yes, you can use regular paprika, but it will not be nearly the same. If you want, you can add up to one tablespoon of hot paprika in place of one of the tablespoons of smoked paprika.

A word on the casings. This recipe calls for the widest hog casings available, easily obtainable online from Weston, The Sausage Maker, or Butcher & Packer (see Special Equipment Needed, page 256). If you can only get standard hog casings, dry the salami for only three weeks.

4 pounds venison

1 pound pork fatback

51 grams salt

6 grams Instacure No. 2

12 grams dextrose (sugar if you can't get it)

1 tablespoon cracked black pepper

3 tablespoons smoked paprika

1 teaspoon dried oregano

⅓ cup sherry or white wine

¼ cup distilled water

10 grams T-SPX or FRM-52 starter culture

Hog casings, preferably 38-42 mm wide

Cut the meat and fat into chunks that will fit into your grinder. Trim as much sinew and silverskin as you can. Put the fat into a container in the fridge. Mix the dextrose, salt, and curing salt with the meats and put it into the fridge overnight. This helps develop myosin, which will give you a tighter bind when you stuff the links later.

The next day, put your grinding equipment—blade, coarse and fine die, etc.—into the freezer. Mix the spices with the meat and fat. Put the mixture into the freezer and let everything chill down until it hits about 30°F or so. It won't freeze solid because of the salt. Normally, this takes about 90 minutes. While you're waiting, soak about 15 feet of hog casings in a bowl of warm water, and put the sherry in the fridge.

When the meat and fat are cold, take them out and grind through the coarse die of the grinder; I use a 10 mm plate. Test the temperature of the mixture, and if it's 35°F or colder, go ahead and grind *half* the mixture again through a fine die, like a 4.5 mm or something similar. If it's warmer than 35°F, put the mix back in the freezer to chill. This might take an hour or so if you've let the meat warm up too much. Use the time to clean up, and to dissolve your starter culture in the distilled water.

Once the sausage has been ground, test the temperature again to make sure it's 35°F or colder. I prefer to chill the mix down to 28°F to 32°F for this next stage. Chill the mix, and when it's cold enough, take it out and add the sherry and the water-starter culture mixture. Now, mix and knead this all up in a big bin or bowl with your (very clean) hands for a solid 2 minutes—your hands will ache with cold, which is good. You want everything to almost emulsify.

Stuff the sausage into hog casings rather loosely. For this sausage, you want long rings—you'll tie the ends together eventually. First make long links of about 2 feet long, with plenty of extra casing on either side. Do this with all the sausage before moving on.

When you're ready, gently compress the long links to fill the casing. Keep an eye out for air pockets. Use a sterile needle or sausage pricker (set it aglow in your stovetop flame) to puncture the casing over all the air pockets. Gently compress the links together to squeeze out the air pockets; this takes practice. Tie the ends of the casing together in a double or triple knot.

Hang the links from a clothes rack or something similiar. I use "S" rings you buy from the hardware store to hang them from the clothes rack rods. Now you need to ferment your links, keeping them warm and moist. I do this by putting a humidifier under the hanging sausages and then tenting the whole shebang with big garbage bags that I've sliced open on one end. I also use a water sprayer to spritz my sausages a couple of times a day. Doing this prevents the casings from hardening. Keep your sausages hanging at room temperature (65 to 80°F) for two days.

Now you need to dry your sausages and turn them into salami. Hang them in a place that is about 50°F to 60°F with about 80 to 90 percent humidity. In most cases, you will need to put a humidifier under your links. I also spritz them with water once a day for the first 2 weeks. After the first week of hanging, drop the humidity to 70 to 80 percent. On the third week drop it again to 65 to 70 percent and hold it there until a total of 4 to 8 weeks has elapsed since the salami went into the chamber.

You now have Spanish chorizo. To store long-term, vacuum seal them individually and keep in the fridge. They will last indefinitely this way, and the vacuum sealing will keep them from becoming rock hard. You can also freeze them.

ICELANDIC VENISON "GRAVLAX"

Serves 4 to 8 as an appetizer | **Prep Time: 3 days**

Made with lamb instead of venison, this is a traditional starter or snack in Iceland. It tastes somewhere between the totally raw and the cured, like the Deer Ham, Alpine Style recipe on page 295. Herbs are a major player here, and the meat is surprisingly substantial for being pounded so thin. It's truly a unique preparation, and well worth the few days it takes to cure.

Serve with pickles, mustard, or a drizzle of vinegar—something acidic. Preserved mushrooms are excellent with it, as are the very un-Icelandic preserved artichoke hearts. A little coarse sea salt is a good touch, too. Once made, venison gravlax will keep for a week or more in the fridge, and a year in the freezer if you vacuum seal it.

½ to ¾ pound piece of venison backstrap
  or eye round

1 cup kosher salt, about 6 ounces

½ cup sugar, about 3 ounces

2 tablespoons dried thyme,
  or 4 tablespoons fresh

1 tablespoon minced fresh chives

1 tablespoon minced fresh rosemary

1 tablespoon freshly ground black pepper

Start by removing every little bit of silverskin and fat from the meat. Once the venison is trimmed, mix the salt and sugar in a non-reactive, lidded container (I use a plastic one), and bury the venison in the mixture. Refrigerate overnight.

The next day, rinse off the cure and pat the venison dry. Mix the herbs and pepper together and roll the meat in it. Do this several times, really pressing the herbs in. If you have a vacuum sealer, seal the venison now and refrigerate it for at least 24 hours, and up to a week. If you don't have a vac sealer, wrap the meat tightly in two layers of plastic wrap and refrigerate.

To serve, cut off pieces about ¼ inch thick—the texture of the meat is such that you won't be able to slice it super thin—and place each piece between two pieces of plastic wrap. Pound them thin with a meat mallet, rubber mallet, or an empty wine bottle. Lay each slice on a plate and serve with the accompaniments mentioned in the head notes.

POTTED HOUGH

Serves 8 to 12 as an appetizer | Prep Time: 10 minutes | Cook Time: 3 hours

Potted hough is a Scottish snack that's a lot like a French rillette—in other words, a really rough pâté you can spread on toast or crackers. How exactly it's pronounced depends on whom you ask: It ranges from "hoe" to "huff." Regardless, it's an ingenious way to make a lunch meat, and a fantastic use of deer shanks or neck meat. You can use other parts of the deer, too, but you really want something with lots of connective tissue.

Hough means "shin" in Scots dialect, so do try to use the shank if you can. I find that one good-sized deer shank is perfect for this dish. You'll also need a pig's foot, or at least half a calf's foot. Why? Collagen. There's a decent amount in a deer shank, but you want this to set up in the fridge, so you need the boost. Any butcher will be able to get you either a trotter or a calf's foot, as will any Latin or Asian market. Usually they come sliced in half.

Other than that, this is a pretty straightforward recipe. Make this in big batches, and store them in ramekins or small containers. A little goes a long way. Potted hough will keep for two weeks in the fridge or a year in the freezer.

Serve it with something acidic, like pickles or mustard, on toast or crackers.

2 pounds venison shank or neck meat (bone-in)

1 pig's foot, sliced in half

1 large carrot, chopped

1 large onion, chopped

3 bay leaves

Salt

1 teaspoon dried thyme

½ teaspoon mace or nutmeg

½ teaspoon ginger powder

1 tablespoon Worcestershire sauce

3 tablespoons Scotch or other whiskey

Salt and black pepper to taste

Put the shank and pig's foot into a large pot and cover with water. Bring it to a boil and skim off any scum that floats to the surface. When the frothing subsides, add the carrot, onion, bay leaves, and a healthy pinch of salt, and drop the heat to a simmer. Simmer until the meat falls off the bone—about 3 hours.

Fish out everything and discard the bones and bay leaves. Reserve the cooking liquid. Roughly chop the meat and all of the pig's foot that's not bone, and add some of the vegetables if you want. Refrigerate overnight. Boil the cooking liquid down by half and refrigerate that, too.

The next day, the meats will be a gelled block. Run this through a grinder with a coarse plate. If you don't have a grinder, take a little of the mixture out at a time and chop it fine. The collagen will start to melt at room temperature, which is why you need to chop in batches if you don't have the grinder.

Put the ground meats into a large bowl and add all the remaining ingredients except the salt and pepper. Heat up the cooking liquid, which should have gelled overnight. Add about ¼ cup to the meats and mix vigorously. Add salt to taste, making the mixture a bit on the salty side—when it's chilled it won't taste as salty. Chill and serve.

For longer storage, melt duck fat, butter, or lard over the top of the potted hough. This will help it keep for up to a month in the fridge.

Variation: SPICY SPANISH-STYLE RILLETTES

Serves 4 to 6 | Prep Time: 24 to 48 hours | Cook Time: 6 to 8 hours

THE MEAT

2 pounds venison shoulder, neck, or shank

1 pig's foot (optional)

1 onion, chopped

2 bay leaves

A sprig of rosemary

A sprig of thyme

Stems from 1 bunch parsley

A handful of black peppercorns, cracked

Salt to taste

TO FINISH

2 tablespoons sweet paprika

2 tablespoons Tabasco or other hot sauce

2 teaspoons smoked paprika

4 garlic cloves, minced

Salt and black pepper to taste

2 to 3 tablespoons sherry

Butter, duck fat, or lard (for longer storage)

Put the meat into a pot and cover with water. Bring to a boil and skim any froth that collects on the surface. When you've taken care of that, drop the heat to a bare simmer and add all the remaining ingredients for the meat. Let this simmer gently until the meat is falling off the bones, or, if it's boneless, when the meat begins to fall apart.

Remove the meat and let it cool enough to handle. Shred it and chop it roughly. You don't want the fibers of the meat to be too long, or the rillettes will be stringy. Strain the cooking liquid and use it as stock for something else (it'll keep in the fridge a week, and can be frozen).

Put the shredded meat into a large bowl and add the paprika, hot sauce, garlic, and sherry. Mix well and add salt and black pepper to taste. Now you will want to beat in as much duck fat, lard, or butter as you want. The fat needs to be solid, but not cold. How much fat? Rillettes are a very rough spread, remember, so you want this mixture to be spreadable on toast. I usually use at least ½ cup of duck fat, but if I'm feeling luxurious, I'll use a full cup.

Once you have added all the fat in you want, you'll likely need to tinker with the salt, the sherry—which should be detectable in the final rillette—as well as the heat. Remember, you want this to be a little too salty because when you eventually serve it cold, that saltiness will be tamed; humans don't perceive saltiness as much in cold foods.

Pack the rillettes into ramekins or small containers and let them set up in the fridge. For long term storage, melt some lard or butter and pour a ¼-inch layer on top of the rillettes. Kept this way, they will keep in the fridge for several weeks. Once the protective layer of fat has hardened, you can also vacuum seal the whole ramekin and freeze it for months.

DEER HAM, ALPINE STYLE

Makes 2 hams | **Prep Time: About 120 days**

Venison hams present a problem: They are always skinned, and they rarely have much fat on them. Fortunately, there is a tradition of curing such a piece of meat in the Italian Alps. They cure legs of wild ibex and call the result *mocetta* (MOE-chet-uh).

Here in North America, think about doing this with antelope legs, or legs from small whitetail or blacktail deer like does or young bucks; coues deer or Sitka blacktail would be ideal. Axis deer are a good choice, too.

Skinless hams cure easily but are tougher to age well because they can dry out fast. You'll need to watch your humidity wherever you hang this thing. Start with about 90 percent humidity. As the meat ages, the humidity needs to drop week by week until you hit 60 percent humidity. Then you can let it rest for months. You're looking at a total of about five months for this project, tops. You can get away with hanging it less, but I wouldn't. There's something about long-aged meat that's special.

2 young deer hind legs

10 grams Instacure No. 2

2 cups Kosher salt

1 cup white sugar

25 grams garlic powder

10 grams juniper berries

12 grams black pepper

5 grams dried thyme

12 grams fresh rosemary

15 bay leaves

Grind the juniper berries, black pepper, thyme, and bay leaves together until fine. Mince the rosemary. Combine all the spices with the salts and mix well. Divide this mixture in half. Put one part of the cure away in a sealed container.

Carefully rub half the mixture into the venison legs, making sure to get lots into the ball joint that had connected the leg to the pelvis; this is where leg cuts often spoil. Massage the spices and salts into the meat.

Put the legs into a large container and refrigerate for 2 to 3 weeks. Drain off any liquid that seeps out of the meat. You will know it's about done when the meat has firmed up quite a bit.

Rinse off the cure and pat the legs dry. Repeat Step 3 with the second half of the cure.

Let the legs cure in the fridge for another 10 days or so. The longer you go, the saltier the meat will be—and the longer it will last without spoiling.

When you're ready, rinse off the cure again and soak the legs in fresh water for an hour. This relieves a little of the saltiness and results in a moister cure—you needed to cure with so much salt for so long to make sure it penetrated all the way through to the bone. The water soak removes some of that salt so it won't be overpowering when you ultimately serve the *mocetta*.

Hang for 3 to 5 months. You want a temperature between 50°F and 60°F (colder at the beginning, and warmer near the end), and a humidity starting at about 90 percent and slowly decreasing— say, 5 percent a week) until you're at about 60 percent humidity.

Once it's ready, you can cut the meat from the bone and slice thin, or slice bone-in. Serve at room temperature with cheese and a husky red wine. Wrap closely and store in the fridge, or seal it and freeze it. The bones, when you're done, make fantastic stock.

CODA: THE GAME AND THE FEAST

It wasn't easy to finish this book. As I wrote the manuscript, tested more recipes, and learned more about our human relationship with the antlered (and horned) creatures of six continents, I kept wanting to add more and more and more. But all things must end, including this book.

I finally realized that there can be no One True Venison Cookbook, as much as I want this book to fill that role. Deer and their cousins are just too ingrained in our lives to be able to say, "This is everything you need to know." This book comes as close as I can to that, but even as we put the finishing touches on it, I learned of new ways the people of the world cook and preserve their own local variety of venison. And for every knockout recipe I have in this book, there are a dozen I chose not to include.

All this said, I hope this book launches you on your own journey with whatever variety of deer-like animal you choose to bring home. I wrote *Buck, Buck, Moose* to open up to North American readers humankind's global heritage with venison, to give you insight not only into recipes from far-off lands, but also to just how much you can do with the body of a deer, or elk, or antelope. Nearly every part of a deer is edible and celebrated somewhere in this world. Hopefully, this book has given you a glimpse into that culinary party.

Make no mistake: I'm neither scolding nor wagging my proverbial finger at you for not eating every single part of the animals you bring home. Hell, even I don't do that. What I am doing is urging you to give *some* of those unfamiliar parts, or those seemingly exotic preparations that you may not be familiar with, the ole' college try. I know I have been pleasantly surprised over the years by oddities like deviled deer kidneys and venison marrow, and I'm hoping you will be, too. There is more to life than bacon, backstraps, and cream of mushroom soup.

Most of all, I want this book to begin a conversation—a conversation between you and your own preconceived notions, and between you and your family, friends, and hunting buddies. And a conversation between you and me. The readers of *Hunter Angler Gardener Cook* (honest-food.net) have helped me make this book better, and I want to keep that interchange alive in the years that follow the publication of this book. So if you have a question, or want to share a success—or failure—drop me a line. I'm easy to find.

Until then, shoot straight, explore, eat well, and, most of all, enjoy your role in autumn's eternal dance between deer and hunter.

—HANK SHAW
Orangevale, California

ACKNOWLEDGMENTS

I probably put more work into *Buck, Buck, Moose* than into both my previous books combined. Not only was there the extensive research, the days spent afield, and the many hours cooking and experimenting in the kitchen, there was also the multitude of tasks associated with producing a professional quality cookbook in-house. That said, this is also the book for which I have the greatest number of people to thank. Without you, this book would not exist.

First and foremost, I thank the 1,356 backers of the Kickstarter campaign that funded this book. You truly made this possible. Among this legion of awesomeness are a few people who deserve a special shout out: My mom and dad, my brother Fred and my sister Lizz; Tori Avey; Alan Davis; Jeremy Baumann; Brian Brenton; Wally Burton; Marty Cutler; Paul Czarkowski; Dawn and Andy French; Benjamin and Brandi Gatewood; Dan, Alison, and Abigail Hess; Cam Barnes; Tom Kise; Rob, Lisa, and Tucker Knox; Jack Kuechler; Peter Lescoe; The Midtown Hunting Crew; Gil Roberts; Shadowtrekker Adventures; Kate and Christian Spinillo; Casey, Regina, Cade, and Quinn Stafford; Capt. Ryan Steptoe; Jonathon Stranger; Michael Neal Timmons; Peter Tira; Chris Tocatlian; Paul Trojano; Philip Wick; Tama Matsuoka Wong; Evan Vos; and Dr. Renee and J.R. Young.

I'd also like to thank both Weston Products and the California Deer Association for their generous support of this project. Their contributions have made this a better book.

As I am merely a passable deer hunter, I want to thank Phillip Loughlin, Joe Navari, Matt Greene, Tim Huber, Randy King, Steve Rinella, Tad Stout, and Ian Shaul for taking me out and showing me new things about chasing antlered critters. I hope to share the field with you all again someday soon.

I'd especially like to thank my friends David Leite, Elise Bauer, Jaden Hair, and Rosetta Costantino for encouraging me to publish this book in this way. It's been scary, but hey, we've gotten this far, eh?

I need to thank everyone who worked on this project. First, to all those who tested recipes for this book; there are lots of you, and I know who you are. Without you, these recipes would not be as good as they turned out to be. A hat tip to Gregory Berger, who designed our shirts and hoodies. To Alex Mayer and Richard Feit, who did the heavy-lifting on the editing for this beast. To Kelly Cox and Lucas Longacre, who shot our video. And a huge huzzah to sister Laura for not only designing this gorgeous book that you're holding, but also for holding my hand through an often byzantine printing and production process.

Finally, I want to thank Holly Heyser, my best friend, live-in photographer, and general partner in crimes, misdemeanors, and other assorted adventures. Not only did she take most of the photos in this book and serve as guinea pig for experimental recipes, she also had my back during some particularly tough times in the book's production. Thanks, Holl. You're the best.

SELECTED READING

Consider this collection to be an explorer's guide to the topic rather than a comprehensive bibliography. These are some of my favorite books about the arcana of charcuterie, butchery, and game cookery, and for delving into the relationship between hunting and our humanity.

CHARCUTERIE, BUTCHERY, AND GAME COOKERY

Cameron, Angus, and Judith Jones. *The L.L. Bean Game & Fish Cookbook*. New York: Random House, 1983.

Clarke, Eileen. *The Venison Cookbook*. Stillwater, MN: Voyageur Press, 1996.

De Gouy, L.P. *The Derrydale Game Cookbook*. Lanham, MD: Derrydale Press, 2000.

Fearnley-Whittingstall, Hugh. *The River Cottage Meat Book*. London: Hodder and Stoughton, 2004.

Fromm, Eric, and Al Cambronne. *Gut it, Cut it, Cook it: The Deer Hunter's Guide to Processing & Preparing Venison*. Iola, WI: Krause Publications, 2009.

Griffiths, Jesse. *Afield: A Chef's Guide to Preparing and Cooking Wild Game and Fish*. New York: Welcome Books, 2012.

Gutenbrunner, Kurt. *Neue Cuisine: The Elegant Tastes of Vienna: Recipes from Café Sabarsky, Wallse, and Blau Gans*. New York: Rizzoli, 2011.

Hasheider, Philip. *The Complete Book of Butchering, Smoking, Curing, and Sausage Making: How to Harvest your Livestick and Wild Game*. Minneapolis: Voyageur Press, 2010.

Kutas, Rytek. *Great Sausage Making and Meat Curing*. Buffalo, NY: The Sausage Maker, 2008.

Landers, Jackson. *The Beginner's Guide to Hunting Deer for Food*. North Adams, MA: Storey Publishing, 2011.

Leite, David. *The New Portuguese Table: Exciting Flavors from Europe's Western Coast*. New York: Clarkson Potter, 2009.

Leysath, Scott. *The Sporting Chef's Better Venison Cookbook*. Iola, WI: Krause Publications, 2012.

Livingston, A.D. *Venison Cookbook*. Mechanicsburg, PA: Stackpole Books, 1993.

Marianski, Stanley, and Adam Marianski. *The Art of Making Fermented Sausages*. Parker, CO: Outskirts Press, 2008

———. *Home Production of Quality Meats and Sausages*. Seminole, FL: Bookmagic, 2010.

McGee, Harold. *On Food and Cooking: The Science and Lore of the Kitchen*. New York: Scribner, 2004.

McLagan, Jennifer. *Odd Bits: How to Cook the Rest of the Animal*. Berkeley, CA: Ten Speed Press, 2011.

McGrail, Joie, and Bill McGrail. *The Catch and the Feast*. New York: Weybright and Talley, 1969.

Mettler, John J., Jr. *Basic Butchering of Livestock & Game*. North Adams, MA: Storey Publishing, 2003.

Nilsson, Magnus. *The Nordic Cookbook*. New York: Phaidon Press, 2015.

Nolen, Jeremy, and Jessica Nolen. *New German Cooking: Recipes for Classics Revisited*. San Francisco: Chronicle Books, 2014.

Rinella, Steven. *The Complete Guide to Hunting, Butchering, and Cooking Wild Game: Volume 1: Big Game*. New York: Speigel & Grau, 2015.

Ruhlman, Michael, and Brian Polcyn. *Charcuterie: The Craft of Salting, Smoking, and Curing.* New York: W. W. Norton, 2005.

Schwabe, Calvin W. *Unmentionable Cuisine.* Charlottesville, VA: University of Virginia Press, 1999.

Shaw, Hank. *Hunt, Gather, Cook.* Emmaus, PA: Rodale, 2011.

Sheraton, Mimi. *The German Cookbook: A Complete Guide to Mastering Authentic German Cooking.* New York: Random House, 1993.

Strybel, Robert, and Maria Strybel. *Polish Heritage Cookery, rev. and exp. ed.* New York: Hippocrene Books, 2005.

Webster, Harold W., Jr. *The Complete Venison Cookbook.* Brandon, MS: Quail Ridge Press, 1996.

Wright, Clarissa Dickson, and Johnny Scott. *The Game Cookbook.* Lanham, MD: Kyle Books, 2005.

HUNTING AND HUMANITY

Bulliet, Richard. *Hunters, Herders, and Hamburgers: The Past and Future of Human-Animal Relationships.* New York: Columbia University Press, 2005.

Cambronne, Al. *Deerland: America's Hunt for Ecological Balance and the Essence of Wilderness.* New York: Lyons Press, 2013.

Fletcher, John. *Deer.* London: Reaktion Books, 2014.

Nelson, Richard. *Heart and Blood.* New York: Vintage Books, 1997.

Pickering, Travis Rayne. *Rough and Tumble: Aggression, Hunting, and Human Evolution.* Berkeley, CA: University of California Press, 2013.

Stanford, Craig B. *The Hunting Apes: Meat Eating and the Origins of the Human Behavior.* Princeton, NJ: Princeton University Press, 1999.

Tattersall, Ian. *Masters of the Planet: The Search for our Human Origins.* New York: Palgrave Macmillan, 2012.

RESOURCES

Many organizations work hard to expand, maintain, and restore habitat for deer, elk, and other big game animals here in North America. Consider joining them and becoming an active conservationist-hunter—and in the process, get a leg up on how to hunt and how to get access to hunting grounds for these animals. Here is a sample of what's out there:

Arizona Deer Association (azdeer.org): P.O. Box 21868, Mesa, AZ 85277, info@azdeer.org

California Deer Association (caldeer.org): info@caldeer.org

Minnesota Deer Hunters Association (mndeerhunters.com): 460 Peterson Road, Grand Rapids, MN 55744, (800) 450-3337

Mule Deer Foundation (muledeer.org): 1939 South 4130 West, Ste. H Salt Lake City, UT 84104, askmdf@muledeer.org

Rocky Mountain Elk Foundation (rmef.org): PO Box 8249 Missoula, MT 59807, (406) 523-4500

INDEX

Boldface page references
indicate photographs.

A

Age and toughness, 13, 50
Aging. *See* Hanging and aging
Agnolotti with Tomatoes and
    Arugula, 215, **216,** 217
Agrodolce, 221
Albóndigas al Chipotle, **188,**
    189
Antelope
    age and toughness, 13
    pronghorn, flavor, 13
    Austrian Braised Venison
        Shanks, 209, **209,** 210

B

Backcountry essentials, 60
Backstrap
    choice of cut, 81
    chops, 81
    Country Fried Venison
        Steak, 88–89, **89**
    deer, cooking, 12
    elk or moose, cooking, 12
    Grilled Venison Tacos, 218,
        218, 219
    Icelandic Venison with
        Blueberry Sauce, **102,**
        103–104
    Jägerschnitzel, **86,** 87
    medallions, 81
    medallions, marinating, 59
    Souvlaki, 109, **110,** 111, **111**
    Steak Diane, **84,** 84–85
    Thai Venison Satay Skewers,
        90
    Venison Stroganoff, **117,**
        117–118
    Venison with Caramelized
        Onions and Mushrooms,
        105, 105–106
    Venison with Cumberland
        Sauce, **82,** 83
    Venison with Morel Sauce,
        96, 97
    Venison with Spring
        Vegetables, **98,** 99

Vietnamese Shaking
    Venison, **107,** 107–108
Whole Grilled Backstrap, 74
Backstraps, loins, and
    tenderloins, 79–118
Bangers, British Bangers, 272–
    273, **273**
Barbacoa, **126,** 127
*Basic Butchering of Livestock
    & Game* (Mettler), 30
Basic Roast Venison, 121–122
Basic Venison Burger, A, **172,**
    173–174, **174**
Basic Venison Salami, 283–
    285, **284**
Basic Venison Stir-Fry, **92,** 93
BBQ sauce
    Bourbon BBQ Sauce, 223
    South Carolina BBQ Sauce,
        131
Beef, comparisons with, 14
Beer and wine, 61
Bergmann's Rule, 70
Bison, 13
Blade roast, 42
Blood, 24
Blueberry Sauce, **102,** 103
Bobotie, **202,** 203
Boerenmetworst, 286–287,
    287
Bolognese Sauce, **184,** 185
Bones
    Basic Venison Broth, 65
    Dark Venison Broth, 66
    Venison Glace de Viande, 67
Borscht, **150,** 151
Brain, prep, 230, 231
Braised Shoulder of Venison,
    71
Braised Venison Shanks with
    Garlic, 211, **211,** 212
Braised Venison Tongue, 245
Bratwurst, 274–275
British Bangers, 272–273, **273**
Broken Arrow Ranch, 18–19
Broth, 62, **64,** 65
    Basic Venison Broth, **64,** 65
    Dark Venison Broth, 66
    substitutes, 62
Browning meats, 155

Bulgogi, 220
Burgers, 46, 169–170
    Basic Venison Burger, A,
        172, 173–174, **174**
    and fat, 170
    Mushroom Burgers, 177
    Venison Smashburgers, 175
Burgoo, 154, **155**
Butchering, 28–46, 50
    backstraps, 37, **38**
    backstraps, fine work,
        42–43, **43**
    brisket or breast, 39, **39**
    burgers, 46
    fine work, 41–46
    flanks, 40, **40**
    front legs, fine work, 42
    hind legs, 44, **45,** 46
    legs, 34, **34, 35**
    leg steak, 30
    neck, 38, **38**
    offal, 32, **32**
    pleasure of, 29–30
    primal cuts, 34
    ribs, 40
    sausage, 46
    shanks, 41
    tenderloin, 36
    tools, 30–32
    tripe, 33
Butchers, professional, 26,
    29, 30
Buying venison, 18–19

C

Cajun Boudin Balls, 243, **243,**
    244
Cajun Remoulade, 243
Cajun Sauce Piquante, 143
Calories in venison, 14
Canning, 48
Caramelized Onions and
    Mushrooms, **105,** 105–106
Carbonnade, **152,** 153
Caribou
    age and toughness, 13
    diet, 12
Carryover heat, 70
    and cooking low and slow,
        70

Caul fat, 22
    Faggots (British Meatballs),
        241, **241,** 242, **242**
    prep, 230–231
Centers for Disease Control
    and Prevention, 17–18
Chamber sealers, 47
Cherry tomatoes, **100,** 101
Chest freezer, 47
Chili, 178, **178,** 179
Chilindrón, **160,** 161
Chimichurri, 133
Chinese Potstickers, 197, **197,**
    198–199
Chinese Tangerine Venison,
    94–95
Chipotle Jerky, 267
Chorizo
    Mexican-Style Chorizo, 279,
        279, 280
    Spanish Chorizo, 288–289,
        289
Colcannon, 103, 104
*Complete Book of Butchering,
    Smoking, Cooking and
    Sausage Making, The,*
    (Hasheider), 30
*Complete Guide to Hunting,
    Butchering and Cooking
    Wild Game, Vol. I, The,*
    (Rinella), 30
Confit, 129
Cooking by Hand (Bertolli),
    221
Cooling meat, 26–27
Corned Venison, 263, **263,** 264
Cornish Pasties, 195, **195,** 196
Country Fried Venison Steak,
    88–89, **89**
Cumberland Sauce, **82,** 83
Curing, 256, 261–262
    chamber, 261–262
    Corned Venison, 263, **263,**
        264
    Icelandic Venison "Gravlax,"
        290, 291
    nitrates, 261
    salts, 257
    sausages, 261–262
    vacuum bag, 262
    Venison Pastrami, 265

Curing and making sausage, 256–296
Curry, 156, **156,** 157, 192–193

D

D'Artagnan Foods, 19
Deer
    backstrap, 12
    basics, 11–19
    blacktail deer, age and
        toughness, 13
    camp essentials, 60
    diet, 12
    fallow deer, flavor, 13
    farmed deer, 18
    fat, 51–53
    mule deer, diet, 12
    red deer, flavor, 12
    whitetail deer, 12
    whitetail deer, age and
        toughness, 13
Deer Camp Liver and Onions,
    239
Deer Ham, Alpine Style, 295,
    295, 296
Deviled Kidneys, **250,** 251
Diet, and flavor, 12, 50
Doneness test, 79–80
Dumplings, 165
    Bavarian Dumplings, 75, 77
    German Marrow Dumplings,
        254, 255
Dzik de Venado (Yucatán
    Venison: Barbacoa
    Variation), 128, **128**

E

Elk
    age and toughness, 13
    backstrap, 12
    diet, 12
Environmental impact, 15
Ethiopian Spiced Butter, 113,
    113
Ethiopian Tibs, 112
Eye round, 44

F

Faggots (British Meatballs),
    241, **241,** 242, **242**
Fallow deer, flavor, 13

Farmed deer and elk, 18
Fat, 14
    and burgers, 170, 171
    skipping, 171
Fat, deer, 51–53
    guidelines for, 53
    and hanging, 52
    saturated, 52
Flanks
    Grilled Venison Tacos, 218,
        218, 219
    Venison Bulgogi, 220
Flanks, shanks, and ribs,
    204–224
Flatiron steak, 42
Flavor, 13
    male *vs.* female, 14
Food Plot, **166,** 167–168
Food safety, 15–18, 230
    chronic wasting disease
        (CWD), 16–17
    E. coli, 15, 24, 116
    heavy metals, 18
    lead, 17–18
    salmonella, 15
    trichinosis, 15–16
Football roast, 45, 46
Free range, 14
Freezer burn, 48
Freezers, 47
Fridge, and dry aging, 27–28

G

Gambrels, 20
Game bag, 20
German Marrow Dumplings,
    254, 255
Glace de viande, 62, 67
Goulash, 164
Gravlax, **290,** 291
Greek Dolmas, 194
Grilled Deer Heart with
    Peppers, 234, **234,** 235
Grilled Ribs, Korean Style, 224
Grilled Venison Kidneys, 249
Grilled Venison Tacos, 218,
    218, 219
Ground venison
    Chinese Potstickers, 197, **197,**
        198–199
    Corned Venison, 263, **263,**
        264

Greek Dolmas, 194
Italian Venison Meatloaf,
    182, **182,** 183
Kefta Kebabs, **200,** 201
South African Bobotie, **202,**
    203
Venison Bolognese Sauce,
    184, 185
Venison Chili, 178, **178,** 179
Venison Lasagna, 180, **180,**
    181
Gut It, Cut It, Cook It
    (Cambronne), 30
Gutting, 22–26
    bone sour, 25–26
    gut-shot deer, 24–25

H

Ham, 295, **295,** 296
Hanging and aging, 26–28, 52
    dry aging, 27–28
Harissa, 135
Head. *See* Brain
Heart
    butchering, 32
    Grilled Deer Heart with
        Peppers, 234, **234,** 235
    gutting, 23
    Jägerschnitzel, **86,** 87
    Peruvian Anticuchos de
        Corazón, **236,** 237
    prep, 229–230, 232, **232**
    Sichuan Spicy Heart Stir-
        Fry, 238
Hen of the woods mushrooms,
    105
Hungarian Pörkölt, 164, **164,**
    165
Hunt, Gather, Cook (Shaw), 97
Hunter Angler Gardener Cook
    (Shaw), 29, 297

I

Icelandic Food & Cookery
    (Rögnvaldardóttir,
    Nanna), 103
Icelandic Venison "Gravlax,"
    290, 291
Icelandic Venison Stew, 147
Icelandic Venison with
    Blueberry Sauce, **102,**
    103–104

Indian Kofta Meatball Curry,
    192–193, **193**
Intestines, gutting, 24
Iron, 14
Italian Pot Roast, 125
Italian Short Ribs, 221, **221,**
    222
Italian Venison Meatloaf, 182,
    182, 183

J

Jägerschnitzel, **86,** 87
Japanese Teriyaki Meatballs,
    190, 191
Jerky, 266–269
    Chipotle Jerky, 267
    Mexican Machaca, 266
    Pemmican-Style Ground
        Meat Jerky, **268,** 269
    Sriracha Honey Lime Jerky,
        266
    Teriyaki Jerky, 266

K

Kabanosy, The World's
    Greatest Meat Stick, 281–
    282, **282**
Kebabs, 135–136
    Kefta, **200,** 201
Kefta Kebabs, **200,** 201
Kentucky Burgoo, 154, **155**
Kentucky Smoked Venison
    Barbecue, 137–138
Kidneys
    butchering, 32
    Deviled Kidneys, **250,** 251
    Grilled Venison Kidneys,
        249
    prep, 229–231, 233, **233**
Knife, 20, 31–32
    boning, 31
    chef's, 31
    sharpening, 32
Kofta, 192–193

L

Lamb
    cooking time, 14
    as substitute for venison, 14
Lasagna, 180, **180,** 181
Leg
    Barbacoa, **126,** 127

Dzik de Venado (Yucatán Venison: Barbacoa Variation), 128, **128**
Grilled Venison Tacos, 218, **218,** 219
Roast Leg of Venison with Bavarian Dumpling, 75, **76,** 77
skinning, 21
smoke-roasting, 78
Liver, 229–233, **233**
butchering, 32
Cajun Boudin Balls, 243, **243,** 244
Deer Camp Liver and Onions, 239
gutting, 23
Liver Dumplings, 240
Loin, 42
Lovely Tongue Sandwich, A, 246–247, **247**
Lungs, gutting, 24

M
Marinades, 58–59
cuts to use, 59
how to marinate, 59
silverskin and connective tissue, 59
using as sauce, 59
Marinated Venison Kebabs, **134,** 135–136
Marrow
German Marrow Dumplings, **254,** 255
prep, 230–231
Massaman Curry, 156, **156,** 157
Meatballs
Albóndigas al Chipotle, **188,** 189
Faggots (British Meatballs), 241, **241,** 242, **242**
Indian Kofta Meatball Curry, 192–193, **193**
Japanese Teriyaki, **190,** 191
Swedish, 186–187, **187**
Meatballs, burgers, and ground meat dishes, 169–203
Meatloaf, 182, **182,** 183
Meat quality factors, 50
Mettwurst, 261–262
Mexican Machaca, 266

Mexican-Style Chorizo, 279, **279,** 280
Minestra Maritata, **148,** 149
Mold, 285
Moose
age and toughness, 13
backstrap, 12
Morels, 103
Morel Sauce, **96,** 97
Mule deer, diet, 12
Mushroom Burgers, 177

N
Neck
Polish Pot Roast with a Venison Neck, **72,** 73
skinning, 21–22
Venison Pierogis, 139, **140,** 141
Niacin, 14
Nicky USA, 19
Nilgali antelope, flavor, 13
Nitrates, 261
Nokedli Dumplings, 165

O
Offal, 22, 229–255
fat, 22
in the field, 231
gutting, **23**
at home, 231
Omega-3 fatty acids, 52
Organic, 14
Organ meat. *See* Offal
Osso Bucco, 213, **213,** 214

P
Pan sauce, 108
Pastrami, Venison Pastrami, 265
Paunch, skinning, 21
Pee needles, 22
Pellets, 22–23
Pelvis, gutting, 22–23
Pemmican-Style Ground Meat Jerky, **268,** 269
Peruvian Anticuchos de Corazón, **236,** 237
Pho, 162–163
Phosphorus, 14
Pierogi Love (Barber), 139
Pierogis, 139, **140,** 141

Piquante, 143
Plastic bags, 20–21
Polish Pot Roast with a Venison Neck, **72,** 73
Population
balance, 15
census, 15
Portuguese-Style Shanks, 208
Potstickers, 197, **197,** 198–199
Potted Hough, **292,** 293
Pozole Rojo, **144,** 145
Primal cuts, 69–78
carryover heat, 70

R
Raw venison, eating, 116
Red deer, flavor, 12
Refreezing, 49
Renewable resource, 15
Resting after cooking, 80–81
Riboflavin, 14
Ribs
Grilled Ribs, Korean Style, 224
Italian Short Ribs, 221, **221,** 222
Smoked Ribs with Bourbon BBQ Sauce, 223
Rillettes, 294
Rinella, Steven, 30
Roast Leg of Venison with Bavarian Dumplings, 75, **76,** 77
Roasts, 119–168
Basic Roast Venison, 121–122
Dzik de Venado (Yucatán Venison: Barbacoa Variation), 128, **128**
Italian Pot Roast, 125
Kentucky Smoked Venison Barbecue, 137–138
marinating, 59
Sauerbraten, 123–124
temperatures, 120–121
tips for roasting, 120
Tri-Tip-Style Venison Roast with Chimichurri, **132,** 133
trussing, 122
Rögnvaldardóttir, Nanna, 103
Romanian Venison Sausage, **276,** 277–278
Rut, and odor, 13–14, 50

S
Salami, 261–262
Basic Venison Salami, 283–285, **284**
Salt, measuring, 257
Sandwich, A Lovely Tongue Sandwich, 246–247, **247**
Satay, 90
Saucisson, 261–262
Sauerbraten, 123–124
Sausages, 256–258, **258, 259,** 260–261
advanced tips, 260–261
basics, 257–258, 260
Basic Venison Salami, 283–285, **284**
Boerenmetworst, 286–287, **287**
British Bangers, 272–273, **273**
casings, 257, 260
dry-cured, 261–262
equipment, 256–257
Kabanosy, The World's Greatest Meat Stick, 281–282, **282**
liquid, 260–261
Mexican-Style Chorizo, 279, **279,** 280
Romanian Venison Sausage, **276,** 277–278
and salt, 257
Spanish Chorizo, 288–289, **289**
spices, 260
Venison Sausage with Sage and Juniper, 270, **270,** 271
Wisconsin Red Brats, 274–275
Scotch Broth, 159
Selenium, 14
Sex, and toughness, 13, 50
Shaking beef, 107
Shanks
Austrian Braised, 209, **209,** 210
Austrian Braised Venison Shanks, 209, **209, 210**
Braised Venison Shanks with Garlic, 211, **211,** 212
cross-cut, 12
Osso Bucco, 213, **213,** 214
Portuguese-Style, 208

Shanks (*continued*)
    Portuguese-Style Shanks,
        208
    Tunisian Braised Venison
        Shanks, **206,** 207
    Venison Pierogis, 139, **140,**
        141
Short ribs, 221, **221,** 222
Shot placement, 50. *See also*
    Gutting, gut-shot deer
Shoulder, 42
    Barbacoa, **126,** 127
    Braised Shoulder of Venison,
        71
    Dzik de Venado (Yucatán
        Venison: Barbacoa
        Variation), 128, **128**
    Venison Pierogis, 139, **140,**
        141
Sichuan Spicy Heart Stir-Fry,
    238
Sirloin tip, 44
Skinning, 21–22
Smell, 13–14
Smoked Ribs with Bourbon
    BBQ Sauce, 223
Smoke-Roasting a Leg of
    Venison, 78
Soups and stews, 142–168
    Cajun Sauce Piquante, 143
    Carbonnade, **152,** 153
    Chilindrón, **160,** 161
    Food Plot, **166,** 167–168
    Hungarian Pörkölt, 164, **164,**
        165
    Icelandic Venison Stew, 147
    Kentucky Burgoo, 154, **155**
    Massaman Curry, 156, **156,**
        157
    Minestra Maritata, **148,** 149
    Pozole Rojo, **144,** 145
    Scotch Broth, 159
    Stifado, 146
    Ukranian Borscht, **150,** 151
    Vietnamese Pho, 162–163
    Vindaloo, 158
Sous Vide Sauerbraten, 124
South African Bobotie, **202,**
    203
South Carolina BBQ Sauce, 131
Souvlaki, 109, **110,** 111, **111**
Spanish Chorizo, 288–289,
    289

Spätzle, 118
Speed goat. *See* Pronghorn
    antelope
Spicy Spanish-Style Rillettes,
    294
Spleen, gutting, 24
Spring vegetables, **98,** 99
Sriracha Honey Lime Jerky,
    266
Steak Diane, **84,** 84–85
Stearic acid, 52, 53
Stew, 147
Stifado, 146
Stir-fry, **92,** 93
Stock, 62–63
    primer, 63
Stomach. *See also* Tripe
    gutting, **22,** 23
Storage, 46–53
    canning, 48, 50
    chamber sealers, 47
    freezing, 46–47
    in fridge for aging, 46
    refreezing, 49
    vacuum sealers, 47
Stroganoff, 117–118
Stuffed grape leaves, 194
Substituting venison for other
    meat, 57
Suet, 52, 53
    and boots, 53
    rendering, 53
Supplies for field, 20–21
Sustainable management
    practices for hunting, 15
Swedish Meatballs, 186–187,
    187

T

Tacos
    Grilled Venison Tacos, 218,
        218, 219
    Tacos de Lengua, 248
Tacos de Lengua, 248
Tartare, 115–116
Temperature
    chart, 80
    dry aging, 28
    hanging, 50
    home freezer, 49
    low and slow, 70
    roasts, 120–121

Teriyaki, 191
    Japanese Teriyaki Meatballs,
        190, 191
    Teriyaki Jerky, 266
Teriyaki Jerky, 266
Thai Venison Satay Skewers,
    90
Thawing meat, 48
Tongue
    Braised Venison Tongue, 245
    butchering, 32
    gutting, 23
    Lovely Tongue Sandwich, A,
        246–247, **247**
    prep, 230–231
    Tacos de Lengua, 248
Tripe
    butchering, 33, **33**
    prep, 230
    Venison Tripe Neapolitan
        Style, **252,** 253
Tri-Tip-Style Venison Roast
    with Chimichurri, **132,**
    133
Trussing a roast, 122
Tunisian Braised Venison
    Shanks, **206,** 207
Tzatziki Sauce, 111

U

Ukranian Borscht, **150,** 151
Urine, dealing with, 22

V

Vacuum
    bag, 263
    sealers, 46
Variety meats. *See* Organ meat
Velveting, Chinese style, 91
Venison
    defined, 12
    history of eating, 8–9
    origin of word, 8
    size, 12
Venison Bolognese Sauce,
    184, 185
Venison Bulgogi, 220
Venison Chili, 178, **178,** 179
Venison Confit, **129,** 129, **130,**
    131
Venison Glace de Viande,
    67–68

Venison Lasagna, 180, **180,** 181
Venison Pastrami, 265
Venison Pierogis, 139, **140,** 141
Venison Sausage with Sage
    and Juniper, 270, **270,** 271
Venison Smashburgers, 175
Venison Steak with Cherry
    Tomatoes, **100,** 101
Venison Stroganoff, **117,**
    117–118
Venison Tartare, **114,** 115–116
Venison Tripe Neapolitan
    Style, **252,** 253
Venison with Caramelized
    Onions and Mushrooms,
    105, 105–106
Venison with Cumberland
    Sauce, **82,** 83
Venison with Morel Sauce,
    96, 97
Venison with Spring
    Vegetables, **98,** 99
Vietnamese Pho, 162–163
Vietnamese Shaking Venison,
    107, 107–108
Vindaloo, 158
Vitamin B6, 14
Vitamin B12, 14

W

Water and carcasses, 24
Whole Grilled Backstrap, 74
Wisconsin Red Brats, 274–275
Wrappers for potstickers,
    198–199

Y

Yucatán Venison (Dzik
    de Venado Barbacoa
    variation), **128**

Z

Zinc, 14